Sikhism

GUIDES FOR THE PERPLEXED

Guides for the Perplexed are clear, concise and accessible introductions to thinkers, writers and subjects that students and readers can find especially challenging. Concentrating specifically on what it is that makes the subject difficult to grasp, these books explain and explore key themes and ideas, guiding the reader towards a thorough understanding of demanding material.

The Baháʼí Faith: A Guide for the Perplexed, Robert H. Stockman
Confucius: A Guide for the Perplexed, Yong Huang
Kabbalah: A Guide for the Perplexed, Pinchas Giller
Mysticism: A Guide for the Perplexed, Paul Oliver
New Religious Movements: A Guide for the Perplexed, Paul Oliver
Western Esotericism: A Guide for the Perplexed, Wouter J. Hanegraaff
Zoroastrianism: A Guide for the Perplexed, Jenny Rose

A GUIDE FOR THE PERPLEXED

Sikhism

Arvind-Pal Singh Mandair

BLOOMSBURY
LONDON • NEW DELHI • NEW YORK • SYDNEY

Bloomsbury Academic
An imprint of Bloomsbury Publishing Plc

50 Bedford Square	175 Fifth Avenue
London	New York
WC1B 3DP	NY 10010
UK	USA

www.bloomsbury.com

First published 2013
© Arvind-Pal Singh Mandair, 2013

British Library Cataloguing-in-Publication Data
A catalogue record for this book is available from the British Library.

ISBN: HB: 9781441193414
PB: 9781441102317
PDF: 9781441117083
ePub: 9781441153661

Library of Congress Cataloging-in-Publication Data

Typeset by Newgen Imaging Systems Pvt Ltd, Chennai, India
Printed and bound in India

For my Parents:
Sardar Karnail Singh Mandair and
Sardarni Parkash Kaur Mandair

CONTENTS

FIGURES

ACKNOWLEDGEMENTS

I want to thank the editorial staff at Continuum/Bloomsbury for taking this book from conception through to completion: Kirsty Schaper who originally commissioned the book, Lalle Pursglove, and especially Rachel Eisenhauer for her patience with my extension of deadlines.

I owe a debt of thanks to the anonymous reviewer for helpful comments on the original proposal. I also want to thank colleagues, friends and graduate students at the University of Michigan who have contributed to some of the ideas in this book either through conversations or feedback in various workshops, conferences and classes over the years: Balbinder Singh Bhogal, Navdeep S. Mandair, Gurharpal Singh, Pal Ahluwalia, Giorgio Shani, Prabhsharandeep Singh, Jaspreet Kaur, Tej Purewal, Virinder Kalra, Anne Murphy, Michael Nijhawan, Nikky Singh, Harjeet Grewal, Punnu Jaitla, Randeep Hothi, Prabhjap Singh Jutla, Ranjanpreet Nagra, Ajit Singh Heir, Manoher Singh, Prabhsharanbir Singh, Jasleen Singh, Daljit Singh (Watford), Sean Chauhan, Nirinjan Khalsa, Tavleen Kaur, Harjot Singh Sandhu, Deepinder Kaur, Amendeep Singh, Seth Harris, Satbir Singh, Gurbinder Kalsi, Dav Panesar and Jasdev Singh Rai. I thank Tavleen for last-minute help with the images! A special note of thanks to my nephew Varun Pal S. Mandair (then 13 years old) for undertaking a creative graphic depiction of the Khalsa's creation. Photographs were kindly provided by Pardeep Singh, Nirinjan Khalsa, Dhamanvir Kaur Sidhu, Inderpal Kaur and Jasleen Kaur.

As ever, this book would never have been completed without the love and support of Preet, Aman-vir and Sukhmani particularly during the summer of 2012.

Finally, this book is dedicated to my father Karnail Singh Mandair, and mother Parkash Kaur Mandair. My interest in the

Sikh tradition was originally kindled through a return visit to Punjab with my father when I was 9 years old. Since that time we had been in constant and lively conversation about *Sikhi* until March 2011 when he began to succumb to a neurological disorder, eventually losing most of his bodily functions including, perhaps the most painful loss of all, the faculty of speech. This is a small token of my gratitude to him and to my mother who now cares for him in the final phase of his life.

Introduction

What is Sikhism? Who are the Sikhs? If these questions had been posed 50 years ago to the average person in the United Kingdom or North America, most would probably have shaken their heads and guessed that it was an obscure religious sect, perhaps from India or the Middle East. In the 1960s when Sikhs began to emigrate to the West in large numbers, there were few if any, resources for obtaining knowledge about Sikhs and Sikhism even in well-stocked libraries. Twenty-five years later, by which time there was a visible presence of Sikhs in many large cities, a small but growing number of scholarly monographs on Sikhism and a checkered media presence, the same questions might have garnered a different response: a fundamentalist sect demanding a separate state? A cross between Hinduism and Islam? People who carry swords and wear turbans and beards and fight a lot in their places of worship? During the 1980s and early 1990s, it was common to hear Sikhs complaining (and rightly so) not only about their discomfort with such representations of their community and their tradition in the media and in scholarly publications, but also about the lack of access to the tools for generating a body of knowledge that Sikhs themselves could identify with and feel comfortable about.

Now imagine posing these same questions to non-Sikhs today. Chances are that most people, certainly in the United Kingdom and Canada, will have met a Sikh or read about Sikhism. And even if one hasn't it is not difficult to imagine that he or she could simply google the terms and almost instantaneously immerse oneself in a wealth of information about Sikhs and Sikhism. Unlike 25 or 50 years ago, today, there is a respectable body of scholarly publications in the form of books and journals on this subject, an ever-increasing number of textbooks on world religions that routinely include Sikhism, excellent film documentaries and a vast store of movie clips on YouTube. Indeed, in this information age, there seems to be no reason why a non-Sikh would continue to be perplexed about Sikhism or why Sikhs themselves would have any reason for further complaint. Surely the available body of information helps non-Sikhs to easily identify who Sikhs are and what Sikhism is? Or for Sikhs to easily identify themselves in the mirror of these representations? Indeed many Sikhs would not see a problem with the available representations as it gives them an easily identifiable location within the kaleidoscope of world cultures and a level of comfort derived from the understanding that they have a meaningful place in the order of things.

Before coming back to some of these questions let us take a quick look at what answers we might expect to the questions 'What is Sikhism? Who are the Sikhs?' in currently available sources such as school and university textbooks, encyclopaedias and film documentaries.

Most accounts of Sikhism begin by acknowledging the popular media image of Sikhs as turban-wearing males. But while many do wear turbans to cover their long uncut hair and sport full beards, there are many Sikhs who do not conform to this image. It is also common to present Sikhism as the fifth largest and youngest of the so-called world religions. Current census figures suggest that there are 23 million Sikhs in the world. Of these 21 million reside in India (17 million in the state of Punjab and 4 million settled in other parts of India). The remaining 2 million live in what is known as the Sikh diaspora, with main places of settlement being the United Kingdom (0.6 million), North America (0.6 million) and smaller numbers in Europe, Malaysia, Singapore, East Africa, Australia and New Zealand. Sikhs are regarded as energetic, hardworking and hospitable to outsiders almost to a fault. Although they make up only 1.5 per cent of India's population, Sikhs constitute the most successful minority and have made significant contributions to sectors such as the armed forces, business and agriculture. Sikhs have routinely held posts as cabinet ministers in various governments and as the President of India. A Sikh currently serves as the Prime Minister of India. Wherever they have settled abroad Sikhs have established a vast network of more than 700 gurdwaras (places of worship and community centres). Diaspora Sikhs also have a strong record of personal achievement becoming mayors, MPs, government ministers, successful scientists and businessmen. Sikhs have a strong sense of community with a history of struggle and a continuously evolving sense of identity, particularly in relation to Muslims and Hindus.

The origins of Sikhism can be traced to the Punjab region of North India (lit. land of the five rivers) five centuries ago. However, the term Sikhism is a Western word coined not by Sikhs but by Europeans, specifically the British in the nineteenth century. In this sense it is like the words Hinduism, Buddhism, Jainism which also are not indigenous to the Indian lexicon. Sikhs themselves use the term *Sikhi* which, like the word Sikh, is derived from the Punjabi verb *sikhna*: to learn. Unlike Sikhism, the word *Sikhi* does not denote an object or thing. Rather it has a temporal connotation and refers to a path of learning as a lived experience. This of course raises an important question about the very legitimacy of the term 'Sikhism' and why it even continues to be used, a point which will be discussed in detail below.

Sikhs are therefore those who have undertaken a path of self-perfection under the guidance of a spiritual master called Guru (to be distinguished from the lower case 'guru' which is traditionally used in India to refer to any respected teacher). For Sikhs the Guru (upper case) refers to a succession of ten spiritual masters, each of whom played a role in evolving the path of *Sikhi* and a teaching or philosophy known as *gurmat*. But the term Guru as the Sikhs use it, has wider meanings that include the poetic compositions of the Gurus as embodied in Sikh scripture (*shabad-guru* as Guru Granth Sahib), to the teaching or philosophy of the Gurus (*gurmat*) and to the 'divine' inspiration behind all of these (the *satguru*). The community as a whole is known as the Panth (also derived from the Sanskrit *pth* meaning path).

The founding figure behind the entire Sikh movement was Guru Nanak whose teachings and life-experience became the inspiration and model for the nine Gurus who followed him. The Sikh Gurus passed on their teachings to the community that grew around them, in the form of several thousand poems and hymns of surpassing beauty and directness, that were enshrined in the two key scriptures of the Sikh Panth: the Adi Granth and Dasam Granth, both recognized masterpieces of Indian devotional literature. The Adi Granth is so important in Sikh tradition that it occupies centre stage in the physical layout of all gurdwaras and in ceremonies of worship. It possesses a unique status marked by its honorific title of Guru Granth Sahib. Because of its remarkable influence, Sikhism is often described as a 'religion of the Book'.

No account of Sikhism is ever complete without acknowledging the transition of the Panth from the path of disciplined devotion in the fifteenth and sixteenth centuries to the path of the warrior-saint in the seventeenth century. This transition is normally attributed to the martyrdom of the fifth and ninth Gurus, from which point on spiritual devotion and militant resistance against all manner of oppression went hand in hand. The tenth Guru, Gobind Singh, introduced radical new measures (including a new form of initiation, discipline and external form, as well as bequeathing ultimate authority to the scripture) which combined to give the Sikh Panth its sense of distinctness from others. The spirit of resistance against tyranny inculcated by the Sikh Gurus inevitably brought the evolving community into conflict with the Mughal empire. Although Sikhs were hunted almost to the point of extinction in the early decades of the eighteenth century, they not only survived, but by the early nineteenth century had risen to establish a sovereign Sikh kingdom that extended from Afghanistan to Delhi, but which lasted less than half a century until the arrival of the British. Following two bitterly fought wars the Sikh kingdom was annexed by the British who absorbed the Sikhs into the British Empire. The Sikhs had lost their sovereign kingdom but far from languishing under colonial rule their encounter with modernity and their interaction with the British proved to be advantageous, enabling a reconstruction of the community's cultural framework through the agency of a lay reformist movement called the Singh Sabha. By the early twentieth century, leading Sikh scholars helped to construct a modern self-representation of the Sikh tradition as a 'world-religion' and as a nation (*qaum*) by allowing indigenous terms such as *Sikhi*, Sikh *dharam*, *gurmat* or Panth to be translated as Sikh*ism*.

It is this peculiarly modern self-representation that tends to be reproduced in most contemporary accounts as Sikhism which is presented as a neat package that includes: (i) a distinct theology or doctrine whose core is ethical monotheism; (ii) a distinct set of beliefs and practices; (iii) a historical founder (Nanak); (iv) historical places of worship and pilgrimage (gurdwaras); (v) a community with well-defined boundaries (the Khalsa); (vi) a distinctly Sikh world-view. As indicated above, this neat repackaging of what continues to be an internally fluid path (*Sikhi*) into a seemingly fixed and immutable entity (Sikh*ism* as a 'religion' among the other religions of the world) which is reproduced seamlessly in world-religions textbooks, film documentaries and whenever Sikhism is googled on the internet, has certain advantages. For one thing it enables Sikhs and Sikhism to be easily identifiable, although the mechanism of this identification depends on the creation of a superficial relation to Christianity which provides the essential type for 'religion' in general, and for other 'religions' of the world. Once it is packaged as a 'religion' or an essentially 'religious' community, Sikhs and Sikhism are made familiar to our modern sensibilities. They no longer appear to be perplexing particularly to outsiders, for the simple reason that everyone is familiar with what religion is. This becomes patently obvious if we consider standard definitions of 'Sikh' and 'Sikhism'. For example, the *Oxford English Dictionary* provides the following definition:

> *Sikh:* Member of an Indian monotheistic sect founded in the fifteenth century.
>
> *Sikhism:* The religious tenets of the Sikhs.

Right away we're given the impression that Sikh/Sikhism are reducible to a religious type (monotheism), an ethnic type (Indian), a geographical location (India) and a historical period (fifteenth century). A clear indication that Sikhs and Sikhism have settled into a comfortable position within the Anglophone consciousness, and through that into the seemingly natural and neutral environment of our everyday language as found in the English dictionary.

At a certain level this kind of representation is by no means unhelpful, especially if all one requires are quick and uncomplicated answers to the questions 'What is Sikhism?' or 'Who is a Sikh?' This is why it works well in encyclopedias, world-religions textbooks and even the internet. But if one wishes to probe beyond that, it can become a hindrance and source of confusion for several reasons. First, it characterizes Sikhs and Sikhism as defined objects with a truth-value that corresponds unproblematically to the lived experience of Sikhs. The apparent truth-value of such definitions renders them difficult to contest and be redefined within the Sikh community, partly because Sikhs themselves have internalized them as truth statements that appear to correspond to the way they live. As seeming truth statements they elide the fact that 'Sikhism' is not an indigenous term but a colonial construct. The indigenous

terms *sikhi, gursikhi, gurmat* or *dharam* are extensively used by
Sikhs who speak Punjabi. But in English or other European languages, it is Sikhism that takes precedence thereby forcing the identification with the category 'religion'. There is now overwhelming
evidence to show that this process of 'religion-making', that is
the transformation of an action-oriented *Sikhi* into a rigid object
Sikh*ism*, occurred during the colonial period through a process of
inter-cultural mimesis between Sikh and European scholars dis-
guised as natural translation.[1]

Secondly, the notion that 'religion' is a convenient and benign
category for representing and translating non-Western cultural
concepts, has been thoroughly discredited in scholarly circles,
no more so than in the discipline of Religious Studies.[2] It is now
widely accepted that the discipline of religious studies has been historically constructed around 'religion' – a category that has always
been highly unstable and strongly contested. Yet especially during
the last century scholars have researched and described 'religion' as
if it had always been a transparent notion, based on common sense
observable reality, universally applicable, a word or an idea that
can be translated unproblematically into any language, of any culture, at any time in human history.[3] In reality, though, as the work
of many different scholars has shown, 'religion' is a modern invention which authorizes and naturalizes a form of Euro-American
secular rationality. In turn, secular rationality constructs and
authorizes its other: 'religion and religions'.[4] Consequently, the way
that we normally talk about religions and spiritualities is perme-
ated with notions about the universal availability of some supposedly distinctive kind of experience, practice or institution, which
in its essential nature, is private, otherworldly and non-political.[5]
All too often, though, this originally 'religious' experience is com-
promised in actual practice because practitioners cannot avoid
an (illegitimate) attachment to 'political' power. In turn, secular
politics – itself a modern invention arguably parasitic on the modern invention of 'religion' – has been disseminated as the universal arena of rational, non-religious practice validated by common
sense. These Anglophone constructions, which present 'religion'
and 'politics' as essentially opposed, have embedded themselves
into our everyday language about the world we live in. As with
the *OED* entries on 'Sikh' and 'Sikhism', we tend not to question
the framework behind these definitions, because we feel that our

everyday language reflects natural rationality, a reasonable proposition that any normal person would agree with.

This is precisely what is happening when indigenous terms such as *sikhi* or *gurmat* are represented as 'Sikhism' or 'Sikh religion', which are in turn presented as essentially different from 'Sikh politics'. Such constructions effectively repress what is most interesting about Sikh tradition, namely its complete involvement from the outset in the material world, in worldly politics, the close connection between its devotional mysticism and its intimate connection to the question of violence. We see this repeated far too often in the discourse of Sikh studies particularly in textbooks that serve as an 'Introduction to Sikhism'. While the majority of such texts do an excellent job of laying out the empirical facts and familiarizing readers with a potentially tricky subject matter, it is also the case that they tend to portray Sikhs as essentially religious subjects, without realizing that they are simply reading the religion-secular binary back into the narrative of Sikh history. Thus from the very beginnings of their history the Sikhs are presented as an essentially religious type whose lived experience has to be placed within the private sphere of devotional experience. As such they have to be kept distanced from the exercise of public power which belongs to the 'political' types (emperors, administrators, politicians, colonial rulers, etc.). But even a casual glance at Sikh history shows that this was never the case as it did not reflect the way Sikhs have understood the relevance of their lived experiences in relation to the wider world.

Sikhism: A guide for the perplexed

One of the main challenges in writing this book was to find a way to negotiate between two seemingly opposed ideals. On the one hand, a desire to do justice to the Sikh life-world and the key principles that animate *Sikhi* as a living tradition. On the other hand, the need to remain faithful to scholarly principles of objectivity and avoid a lapse into the insider's standpoint. Since the nineteenth century these two seemingly opposed ideals have been concretized in two distinct and divergent disciplines within the Western humanities: (i) philosophy of religion (also called philosophical theology) whose task is to theoretically, and therefore subjectively, probe the inner principles of the study of religion (nature of religious experience, belief, God, self, etc.); (ii) history of religions whose task it is to present objective data pertaining to concrete religious phenomena. Scholars in religious studies normally choose to work within one or the other of these disciplines, but almost never bring them together. Those who chose to study non-Western cultures (Sikhism being a good example) normally chose historicism as their central methodology which carried a certain legitimacy in the modern academy as a 'critical' standpoint, with the idea of the 'critical' itself being premised on a break or distancing from the 'insider' standpoint of traditionalist Sikh theology. It is this historicist methodology that enables distinctions such as private/public, religion/secular to be imported into the heart of Sikh studies and from there into the practice of teaching.

My approach in this book is based on a strongly interdisciplinary training that doesn't simply combine historical and philosophical approaches, but allows them to actively inform each other. By doing this I have been able to develop a form of pedagogy that goes beyond the simplistic 'insider/outsider' opposition. To do this it is necessary to adopt a scholarly position that is more reflexive than the conventional 'critical' position which is actually just another name for the principle of secularity.[6] The conventional critical standpoint adopted by historians has been based on being able to firmly define the inner experience of Nanak/*Sikhi* as 'theological', as a dialogical covenant between God and man. This may be fine for comprehending the Christian experience, but as I have argued elsewhere, it commits a conceptual violence towards the Sikh experience as we find it articulated in all manner of Sikh scripture and literature. In contradistinction, the move that I am advocating in this book works by dislodging belief in the religion-secular binary, and therefore the idea of an absolute opposition between religion and the secular, which has been so central to the discipline of religious studies and Sikh studies. Such a move allows us to reconceptualize the nature of experience. It is no longer *religious* experience, if by religious we mean an experience that is other-worldly, non-temporal or metaphysical. In fact the experience, is no more religious than it is secular. It must either combine these spheres absolutely or look beyond them. In other words experience has to be rethought by a return to the body (specifically affect: feelings, emotions, drives) as the locus of experience, thereby balancing the relationship between body and consciousness. In this way, experience is shown to be intrinsically connected to the world and therefore to temporal processes. It is *lived* experience, grounded in life itself.

By rethinking the notion of experience in a manner that retains philosophical rigor *and* historical specificity, it is possible to adduce several important consequences as far as this book is concerned. First, it leads readers away from the impasse between academic ('secular') historians and traditionalist ('religious') historians which has tended to overshadow many debates in Sikh studies. It does this by reading the narrative of history without the artificial public/private distinction. History is no longer in thrall to either religion or the secular. Because history is no longer defined in relation to a metaphysical being, or otherworldly entity, the narrative of history does not have to privatize 'experience'. Having said that, history is also opened up to 'experience' – it has to acknowledge the effect of 'experience', in which case history becomes part of a cultural memory, in this case a Sikh memory. Thus, history becomes what it should have been all along: a way of narrating/writing time and thereby weaving new forms of consciousness that can be read by all. History is not therefore a neutral medium for representing Sikhs, rather Sikhs *make* history which becomes cultural memory. This notion of history as cultural memory is much closer to the lived experience of *Sikhi* and to the structure of time and consciousness as articulated by the Sikh Gurus in their writings (see Chapter Five).

Secondly, the concept of 'experience' as outlined above, actually helps rather than hinders the practice of teaching. Like many others who regularly teach courses in religious studies or Sikh studies, I have often been frustrated by the stark conceptual dualities that we have to struggle with and then (often reluctantly) transmit to our students, who struggle even more. The easy way out of this was simply to distance oneself from the Sikh life-world by accepting the secular imperative and privatizing experience as 'religious', as something that 'they' (the Sikhs) believe in, but which 'we', the more enlightened modern scholars and students, don't have to dirty our hands with. Ultimately what this practice does is to designate Sikh experience as a kind of 'dream time', an illusory experience that 'we' tolerate and allow 'them' to enjoy as long as it doesn't interfere with the real task of teaching and learning. In

fact all we're doing is imposing a secular ideology and expecting
our students not to question it. The downside of such pedagogi-
cal practices is that they prohibit students from thinking critically
through the more perplexing aspects of the study of Sikhs and Sikh
cultural memory in the present. These perplexing issues include the
role of violence/non-violence, the notion of authority and the possibility of something called Sikh thought. It is topics such as these
that make the study of Sikhism difficult to grasp.

In this book each of these topics – violence/non-violence, authority and Sikh thought – are treated as central rather than peripheral
to the narrative of Sikh history. They are issues that animate Sikh
activity from its very beginnings to the present day. In order to
explain and explore these themes as they emerge repeatedly over
the five centuries of Sikh history and especially today, I have provided guidance for the reader by inserting two 'Excursus' sections
into the first two chapters that deal with the evolution of the Sikh
tradition from the fifteenth to the early nineteenth centuries. The
first 'excursus' appears in Chapter One immediately after the life of
Guru Nanak. Its purpose is to explain the teaching of Guru Nanak
and to discuss the notion of experience out of which that teaching
emerges. My interpretation of Guru Nanak's experience avoids any
resort to 'theology', natural or otherwise. Instead it relies on the
testimony of his own poetic verses which provide a more interesting
model of experience. This model of experience becomes central to
explaining how authority is transmitted from one Guru to the next
until it is finally vested in a text, the Adi Granth which becomes
designated as Guru Granth Sahib. To better explain the continuity
between the ten living Gurus, the text of the Guru Granth Sahib
and the community (the Panth), I resort to a set of terms which
might, at first sight, seem problematic, namely, the terms 'sovereign', 'sovereign principle' and 'sovereignty'. However, the term
'sovereign' as I use it has nothing to do with the secular notion of
State sovereignty which has become the dominant understanding
of this term. Instead, 'sovereignty' as I use it in this book refers
to and derives from the principle that undergirds not only Guru
Nanak's experience and therefore the whole of Sikh thought, but
to the mystical process as such. 'Sovereignty' as I have redefined
and deployed it in the following chapters, refers to the power that
gives itself its own law. In the Western theological tradition such
a power is normally derived from a transcendental source such as

'God', but in the teachings of the Sikh Gurus such power is more usefully conceived in terms of the liberative process of ego-loss, the struggle of the self to overcome itself in order to perfect its mode of consciousness. In other words, Sikh Gurus locate this power to the force of life itself and this is spelled out over and over again in their writings.[7] Such a definition of 'sovereignty' can be traced to the writings of Guru Nanak himself and becomes central to the continuity of the Sikh historical narrative, to its cultural memory and therefore to the way that mainstream Sikh tradition has understood itself. This notion of 'sovereignty' becomes the very jewel that Sikhs have sought to protect and keep alive often at the cost of their own lives.

The second 'excursus' which appears in Chapter Two, provides an interpretation of the role of violence in the Sikh tradition. Once again, this is a hugely misunderstood concept. Rather than apologizing for its presence by treating it as a deviation from an originally pacifist movement, I seek to establish its centrality for understanding notions of continuity, authority and experience in *Sikhi*. This becomes important because Chapter Three examines the Sikh encounter with Western modernity and colonialism, an encounter that gave rise to a different form of sovereignty more in line with modern Western (and therefore secular) understandings of sovereignty that in turn led to the emergence of modern Sikhism. Both excurses bring current discussions in philosophy of religion into contact with historical narratives of the Sikh tradition, thereby helping the student get to grips with difficult concepts and providing them with more nuanced ways to comprehend the complexities of historical and contemporary issues treated in later chapters.

The chapters of this book are organized around three main themes: (i) history, (ii) teachings and practices and (iii) the challenges of contemporary global pluralism. The first section, 'Evolution of the Sikh Tradition', provides an overview of the lives of the ten Sikh Gurus and the emergence of Sikh tradition between 1469 (the birth of Guru Nanak) and 1708 (the death of Guru Gobind Singh). The central emphasis in the first two chapters is on the development of institutions, practices and concepts that become concretized over time into a distinctive tradition and a cultural memory called *Sikhi* by its adherents. The third chapter looks at the far-reaching encounter between Sikhs and the West which gave rise to modern Sikhism. Section 2 'Teachings and Practices' looks at some of the main institutions that organize the contemporary Sikh way of life: role of scripture, the gurdwara, ceremonies and festivals. The chapter on Sikh Philosophy provides highlights and discusses some of the main concepts in the writings of the Sikh Gurus that underpin the lived experience of Sikhs, their way of life.

Section 3 is organized under the broad theme of pluralism and its challenges. Pluralism describes a condition in which numerous ethnic, religious or cultural groups co-exist within a society. It also refers to a belief that such a condition is desirable or socially beneficial. While Sikh tradition espouses an important perspective on pluralism, the dominant understanding of pluralism and the response to it by Sikhs, is governed primarily by the nature of the world we live in – a world that has resulted from three centuries of unprecedented Western expansion across the globe. Thus the issue of pluralism cannot be separated from questions about the nature of the Western framework which manages diversity through the binary opposition between public sphere and private sphere. This opposition in turn derives from the model of liberal secular democracy and its historical relationship to religion.

Two ways in which Sikhs are increasingly being forced to respond to this world order, are through ethical dilemmas posed by modern technology and social conditions to traditional Sikh thought and practice (Chapter Six), and the role of Sikhs in today's public sphere (Chapter Seven) which itself is being transformed through new forms of technology. Although Chapters Six and Seven ('Sikh Ethics' and 'Sikhs and the Public Sphere' respectively) highlight some of the challenges of today's globalized environment, it needs to be noted that they are continuous with earlier chapters. Thus, themes that are developed in Chapters One and Two, such as 'experience', 'violence and non-violence', authority and encapsulated under a redefined notion of sovereignty, all come to be tested in Chapters Six and Seven. The aim of the third section is therefore to help students to analyse the ramifications of the encounter between Sikhs and modernity and to explore ways in which the transformations of the social imaginary can be used to redefine the role of Sikhs and *Sikhi*sm in public life today and in the future.

It remains for me to say a few words about the deployment of the terms Sikhism and *Sikhi*sm. The term 'Sikhism' corresponds to what the modern Anglophone consciousness understands as the 'religion of the Sikhs', an entity that can be privatized. It is the result of a strictly modernizing process and carries the implication that this -*ism* has always existed since it was founded in the fifteenth century. However, throughout the book I shall use the alternative term: *Sikhi*sm. This alternative term refers to the same phenomenon but has the advantage that it carries intact the indigenous verb *Sikhi*. As argued above, *Sikhi* is indicative of an internal fluidity and an internal difference, which cannot be reduced to simple quantitative pluralism (where one simply counts the number of sects and subsects within one overarching religion). Rather *Sikhi* carries the sense of a qualitative difference that an entity has with itself, its potential for self-transformation even as it retains a certain identity. The way I use *Sikhi*sm is meant to highlight the intertwining of the premodern and the modern, suggesting that the indigenous meaning(s) are still alive and well particularly in the Punjabi language, that it has not been completely repressed and concretized by the modernizing encounter with the West.

Let me be quite clear, though. I am not suggesting that Sikhs should romanticize pre-modern formations and try to ditch the modern version. As the community has become more cognizant of the vestiges of its colonial past, many have begun to use *Sikhi* to designate pre-modern authenticity which can be retrieved at will. As I see it, however, *Sikhi* by its very definition cannot entertain any such pretensions to authenticity by simply forgetting the implications of its encounter with the West – which is why I prefer the more complex term *Sikhi*sm (with *Sikhi* italicized but not entirely removed from the -ism). Rather the term *Sikhi*sm suggests that the different formations, premodern/modern, indigenous/foreign, Punjab/non-Punjabi, authentic/inauthentic, now co-exist in a single body, implying that the consciousness of every Sikh is singular–plural. Hence what I am suggesting is that the living force called *Sikhi* possesses a natural tendency to adapt to, and transform, whatever environment it migrates to, but without dissolving or assimilating into another culture. As I have argued elsewhere, while Sikhs have translated their tradition relatively easily into the modern world as Sikhism, the living force corresponding to *Sikhi* not only resists such translation but has the potential for affecting the categories and concepts of any host culture. In short the term *Sikhi*sm serves two purposes: (i) to unsettle the complacency of modern Anglophone consciousness by pointing to the living force, the sovereign principle, behind a reified meaning; (ii) to encourage Sikhs to be vigilant about the terms they use for self-representation, while recognizing that they have the potential for changing the categories of the host language and culture, but, ironically, only by accepting the host culture as their own.

PART ONE

Evolution of the Sikh Tradition

CHAPTER ONE

Guru Nanak and His Early Successors

Sikhi(sm) originated in the Punjab region of northwestern India with the teaching and life experience of one man, Guru Nanak. Owing to its geographical location Punjab was known as an important gateway to the Indian subcontinent and as a veritable melting pot for people of diverse cultural and ethnic backgrounds who settled in the region. The Indus Valley sites of Harrapa and Mohenjodaro, and the Ghandaran settlement of Taxila are reminders of ancient civilizations that once flourished in the Punjab region. For several millennia, Jains, Buddhists and the entire panoply of Hindu traditions (including orthodox Brahminism, the worshippers of the Hindu deities Shiva, Vishnu and the mother goddess) had flourished in Punjab. By the tenth century CE, the Buddhists had disappeared, but their place was taken by Muslims who became the new rulers of northern India. By the fifteenth-century Punjab was dominated by two traditions: Islam and the variety of Hindu traditions which were highly stratified due to caste divisions. It was during this time that a loosely aligned movement of holy men or spiritual adepts known as the *bhagats* (also called 'Sants') emerged throughout India. Influential figures among the *bhagats* – such as Kabir, Namdev and Raidas – sought to reconcile the two opposing dominant faiths of Muslims and Hindus by emphasizing a path of devotion based on the meditative repetition of the divine Name. Rejecting social distinctions and formal ritual, the *bhagats* expressed their teachings in vernacular poetry based on inner

experience. Although the teachings of Guru Nanak were broadly
in line with those of the *bhagats*, his own mission emerged out
of his direct inner experience and signalled a third way that was
to become the path of Nanak (Nanak Panth) or what came to be
called *Sikhi* by his immediate followers.

The life of Guru Nanak

Guru Nanak was born on 15 April 1469 in the village of Rai Bhoe
Talwandi, known today as Nankana Sahib and located some 40
miles west of Lahore. His father was Mehta Kalu, a member of
the Khatri caste lineage and a *patwari* or village accountant by
profession. Nanak's mother was Tripta and he had an elder sister, Nanaki, who was four years his senior. Although many of the
janamsakhis[1] state that Nanak was born in his father's village, it
is more likely that both he and his sister were born in their maternal home, Nanake, as also suggested by the choice of their names,
Nanaki and Nanak.

Like other hagiographic literature the *janamsakhis* contain
much that is considered anecdotal.[2] Nevertheless they provide a
clear and vibrant account of Guru Nanak's life. Some of these
anecdotes speak about the early signs of Nanak's extraordinari-
ness, such as his being greeted at birth by heavenly beings, or the
amazement of the Muslim midwife, Daultan, when she heard the
baby Nanak laugh like a grown man, or the astrologers who foretold the child's future greatness.

When Nanak reached the age of five, like other children in
his village he was sent to an elementary school run by a pandit
named Gopal. Within a short space of time Nanak had learned
as much as he could and exposed his teacher's inability to give
him any meaningful knowledge. Thereafter, at around the age of
seven, he was sent to another pandit, Brij Nath, who initiated him
into the Vedas and the six systems of orthodox Hindu philosophy.
But Nanak found even this to be unsatisfactory. At the suggestion
of the village chief, Rai Bular, his father sent him to a Muslim
teacher to learn Arabic and Persian. With such an education Mehta
Kalu hoped that his son would follow in his footsteps and pick up
accounting skills or perhaps a mercantile trade. Nanak, however,
took little interest in his studies and spent more time discoursing

with *sadhus* (ascetics or holy men), or simply wandering in nearby forests. By the age of nine he had imbibed much of the oral poetry of the spiritual adepts such as the *bhagats* and Sufis and had begun to compose his own poetry.

At around this time, Nanak's elder sister Nanaki, was married at age 13 and left home to join her husband Jairam at the town of Sultanpur Lodi. The departure of his beloved sister caused Nanak much sadness. Within two years another significant event took place. As with all Hindu boys Nanak was expected to undergo initiation as *dvija* or twice born, by having his head shaved and being conferred with a cotton thread called *janaeu* to be worn across his body. With the family's relations and neighbours all assembled for the solemn occasion, the village priest Hardyal, proceeded to invest the sacred thread on Nanak's body. There was much surprise, however, when the young boy boldly refused to undergo the initiation ceremony, stating that he would rather be invested with a thread that would neither break nor get soiled, nor be burned or lost.[3] Nanak's refusal to be initiated caused quite a stir in his village. It was seen as an act of revolt against one of the foundational pillars of Vedic orthodoxy, and the first sign of his eventual split with the Hindu tradition of his ancestors.

The *janamsakhis* tell us that shortly after this event Nanak become more absorbed in spiritual pursuits. Mehta Kalu became increasingly anxious about his son's indifference towards mundane affairs and resolved to try Nanak's hand at various professions. He was sent to herd buffaloes, but instead tended to his own inner struggles. Next he tried to get him to till the land but there too Nanak did not apply himself. Not giving up so easily, Kalu put him to work in a trade. He was dispatched to a neighbouring town with a sum of 22 rupees to buy goods in order to sell them at a profit. On his way Nanak came across a group of ascetics who had not eaten for several days and spent the money on feeding them. To Nanak this was a profitable business (*sacha saudha*), but when he tried to explain this to his father, Mehta Kalu flew into a rage and slapped him.

Over the next few years, as Nanak went through adolescence, further signs of an existential malaise – periods of depressive melancholia punctuated by bouts of sadness and joy – began to manifest themselves in Nanak's personality. He began to withdraw more and more from society and worldly activity. Not understanding his state of mind, his parents would often reproach him for not earning a livelihood and for the unpractical discourses that he continued to weave. People in the village believed that Nanak had become a 'crazed fool' slowly losing his senses.[4] As time went on Nanak would increasingly fall into periods of quiet inactivity, often sitting transfixed for days. His mother and other relatives exhorted him to forget his devotions even for a while and to take employment with the governor of Sultanpur where his brother-in-law was employed. It was hoped that this might induce him back into worldly life. Nanak replied only with poetic utterances, then became silent, lay down and refused to take food. At this point the whole family was saddened and said it was a pity that Mehta Kalu's son had become possessed. Fearing for Nanak's state of mind the family approached Kalu to call for the village physician or *vaid* who might prescribe some remedy for his ailment.[5] With his family's reputation now at stake Kalu called the *vaid* who arrived and began to take Nanak's pulse. But Nanak withdrew his arm, asking the *vaid* what he was doing. 'I am diagnosing the illness that has disturbed your health', the *vaid* replied. Nanak laughed and responded with the following words which later came to be recorded in the Adi Granth under the musical register of *Raga Malar*:

> They called a *vaid* to prescribe a remedy; he takes my arm to feel its pulse
> But the ignorant fool knows not that the pain is in my mind.
> O *vaid*, go home and take not my curse with you.
> What use is this medicine when this sickness is my state of love.
> The *vaid* stands ready to cure me with store of his pills.
> Yet my body weeps, the soul cries out: 'Give me not this medicine!'
> Go home, *vaid*, few understand the source of my pain
> The One who gave the pain will remove it.[6]

Shortly after this episode Nanak left his ancestral village to find work at Sultanpur where his brother-in-law was able to procure for him a post as an accountant in a nearby village. As Nanak began to earn a proper living, he was able to send for his wife to join him. He was 19 at the time. His life settled into a more regulated pattern as the earlier cycles of melancholic silence were more productively channelled into spiritual activity. During the day Nanak would dil-igently take care of the accounts. Much of the night until the early hours of the morning was spent on meditations centred around the performance of *kirtan* (devotional singing). At dawn Nanak would bathe in the nearby river Bein, then take some sleep before going back to work. While at Sultanpur Nanak was also reunited with his childhood friend, Mardana, a Muslim *rabab* player from his home village of Talwandi. A gifted musician, Mardana would provide faithful accompaniment to the singing of Nanak's poetic compositions.

Twelve years passed in this way. During this time Nanak and his wife Sulakhani had settled into the relatively comfortable life of the trading castes. Two sons were born to them, Sri Chand and Lakhmi Das. However this settled pattern of life was interrupted when Nanak reached the age of 33. On one occasion he failed to return from his usual morning dip in the river. After an exhaustive search by the villagers he was feared to have drowned. For three days no trace of Nanak could be found. Then on the fourth day Nanak appeared as suddenly as he had disappeared, but he had once again become silent and reclusive. His only response to questions was a spontaneous outpouring of verses (*bani*), or the perplexing statement: 'There is no Hindu, there is no Muslim', leading people to believe that he was either mad or possessed.[7]

This particular event at Sultanpur is generally recognized as the culminating experience in Nanak's search for his true calling. The *janamsakhis* describe the experience as one in which God gave Nanak a 'cup containing the nectar of life-death (*amrit*) and a robe of honor'. A mysterious voice blessed Nanak charging him with a mission to go out and bring his fellow man towards a new path whose fundamental precepts included mindful remembrance of the divine Name (*nam simaran*), sharing one's wealth with the needy (*dan*), performance of ablutions (*isnan*) and living a life of service to others (*seva*).

What the *janamsakhis* tell us in no uncertain terms is that this event marked Nanak's achievement of perfection and signals therefore his nomination as Guru. The importance of this scene of nomination is exemplified by prevalent markers such as grammatical immediacy (the Voice) which also sets it up as a sacred origin. This sacred origin, in turn, constitutes the meaning for all Sikh experience, but particularly for the way that Sikhs in the future might understand not only the repetition of this experience, but the nature of future events in the development of Sikh history. For the nature of the Sikh Panth, and its self-understanding will depend on maintaining a certain proximity to, and memory of, this experience rather than its repetition in time. It is surely of importance, however, that although Nanak himself says nothing about *this* pivotal experience at Sultanpur, he does say a great deal about how such experience may be repeated invariably at will. We shall return to this important topic later in this chapter.

Soon after the Sultanpur experience, the fully enlightened master, now called Guru Nanak, began to attract his first Sikhs (lit. learners travelling on a path to perfection). Putting on a form of dress that led him to be associated both with Muslims and Hindus, he set out to teach his message to the world, leaving behind his family. The *janamsakhis* generally agree that Guru Nanak travelled extensively throughout the Indian subcontinent and as far west as Baghdad. On his first extensive tour he travelled eastwards, visiting the key Hindu places of pilgrimage such as Mathura, Varanasi, Bodh Gaya and reaching Bengal and Assam, returning via Jagganath Puri. In his frequent travels throughout Punjab he stopped at major Sufi centres such as Pak Pattan. In his next major tour he went south to Tamil Nadu and Sri Lanka, coming back through the western cities of Malabar and Mumbai, returning via Rajasthan. The third tour was northwards, as far as Ladakh. The Guru's last and most extensive journey was west towards Mecca, Medina and Baghdad. On the return journey he passed through Saidpur which had been recently sacked by Babur, the founder of the powerful Mughal dynasty. These tours or *udasis* as they are known in the *janamsakhis*, cover a period spanning almost two decades of Guru Nanak's life, from ages 33 to 50.

Although scholars continue to debate the details of these itineraries, it is generally agreed that wherever he travelled, Guru Nanak was often mistaken either for a Muslim or a Hindu. This was probably due to his dress which combined styles worn by Muslim *fakirs* and Hindu *sadhus*. During his travels he was accompanied either by Mardana (on the eastern and western *udasis*) or by Hindus of lower caste (to the northern and southern *udasis*). He regularly discoursed with leaders of Hindu and Sufi sects. The Guru did not keep a formal record of these encounters but snippets of the conversations found their way into some of his compositions.

The *janamsakhi* accounts of Guru Nanak's travels constitute a particularly important strand of popular Sikh devotion and the anecdotes related therein continue to hold great appeal for children and adults alike. One story narrates how, on his approach to a Sufi centre at Multan, Guru Nanak was greeted by an overflowing cup of milk – a polite but very clear gesture from the Sufis that Multan already had more than enough religious teachers, and that Nanak's presence was not required. In response Nanak placed a jasmine petal on the milk and sent it back unspilled, indicating that he had no desire to simply add to the number of religious messages, but only to enhance their quality, for which there was always more room.

Another account tells the story of Lalo and Malik Bhago. On his way to Eminabad Guru Nanak chose to stay at the house of a poor carpenter named Lalo. As word spread of Nanak's presence a wealthy merchant Malik Bhago visited him and remonstrated with the Guru, asking him why he would degrade himself by residing with a low caste person, whereas he (Bhago) could offer him better food and accommodation. In reply Nanak asked Malik to send him his food. Taking Bhago's refined bread in one hand and Lalo's in the other, he squeezed both. Malik Bhago's bread oozed blood and Lalo's oozed milk. Again the message was clear. The Guru preferred to eat with those who earned their food through honest labour rather than through exploitation.

On the occasion of his visit to the Hindu holy city of Haridwar, the Guru joined a large group of pilgrims bathing in the Ganges and praying by offering water to the sun. Seeing this the Guru entered the river and started throwing water in the opposite direction. When the bewildered pilgrims asked him what he was doing, he replied that he was sending water to his fields in Punjab. When the pilgrims ridiculed him asking how his water could reach Punjab, Guru Nanak replied by saying his fields were much closer than the sun. The lesson? True devotion is not outside but inside.

In another well-known incident, the Guru on his way to Mecca stayed at a mosque and fell asleep with his feet pointing towards the Kaaba – a sacreligious act in the eyes of Muslims. When the local mullah arrived to start the evening prayer, he rudely reprimanded Nanak for his disrespectful action. Nanak replied: 'Then turn my feet in a direction where the Kaaba cannot be found'. The mullah took hold of Nanak's feet but wherever he turned his legs, the Kaaba would follow. The Mullah realized his folly and left Nanak alone.

By the time he was 50, Guru Nanak's fame as a teacher had spread widely and he began to attract a considerable following. During the itinerant phase Nanak and his companions would normally return to Sultanpur after their travels. According to the *Meharban janamsakhi*, on one such return journey he came across a suitable spot on the bank of the river Ravi where he decided to set up a new abode for himself and his growing retinue of followers. Casting off the *udasi*'s garb Nanak put on the dress of a house-holder and for the last period of his life he returned to a settled life at his newly founded ashram which came to be called Kartarpur. The land upon which the future Kartarpur came to be built was donated by one of his followers. Various *sakhis*, including the writings of Bhai Gurdas, suggest that this last period of the Guru's life was very important in so far as he gave practical expression to his inner experience in the context of his worldly life.

As devotees continued to flock to Kartarpur, Guru Nanak concretized a way of life and a form of discipline to be followed by his Sikhs. The first members of the Kartarpur community, or what came to be called the Nanak Panth, probably consisted of his relatives, friends and members of the *Khatri* (or mercantile) caste. Soon thereafter the ranks of community or *sangat* were swelled by *Jatts*, an originally nomadic agrarian people who had long maintained a dismissive attitude towards the Brahmanic caste system and happened to comprise a majority of the population in Punjab. The daily routine followed by the early community was centred around disciplined devotion, regular instruction from the Guru and an emphasis on honest labour. A Sikh had to rise before dawn, bathe and gather at the Guru's ashram where they joined other members of the *sangat* to practice *nam simaran* – a form of mindful meditation based on repeating the names of the divine – and *kirtan* (or singing of devotional hymns). In time the practice of *nam simaran* was formalized through recitation of Guru Nanak's own compositions such as Japji, which he had been perfecting since the Sultanpur experience. After the morning service people were free to go about their daily work. Asceticism was explicitly rejected by Guru Nanak. Every Sikh was required to lead a life of disciplined worldliness. To set the tone for this, the Guru worked in his fields and did jobs that any peasant would do. In the evening people would again gather for an evening service centred around *kirtan*. The same routine was followed in other towns and villages where the Guru had created groups of followers. Hymns composed by Nanak, such as Japji,

Kirtan Sohilla and Rahiras, were memorized, copied and distributed to these centres which had their own leaders to instruct them.

Several other institutions were developed and fostered by Guru Nanak at Kartarpur. One was the *langar* or common free kitchen. Everyone was expected to work for a living and to donate part of their earning towards the maintenance of the *langar*. Irrespective of caste, class or religious orientation, everyone was expected to sit and eat together (*pangat*). Thus Muslims sat shoulder to shoulder with Hindus, Brahmins sat with lower castes and outcastes, and kings with paupers. The idea of a free common kitchen was not entirely new. Various Sufi orders and the Gorakhnath order in Punjab already operated free kitchens, but for Nanak the *langar* was an intrinsic part of the institutional framework he was developing and served to evolve the community towards a state when it would be free of social and economic prejudices.

Another important institution was the initiation ritual known as *charan pahul* (nectar of the feet) which was adopted by the Guru to differentiate his following from surrounding groups. Aspiring devotees were initiated by drinking water that had been consecrated by the touch of the Guru's toe. Initiates had to drink from the same cup, a practice that served to foster camaraderie and break social taboos that riddled North Indian society.

Arguably the most important institution inaugurated by Guru Nanak, and one that was calculated to allow his work to be consolidated and continued after his death, was the institution of Guruship itself. The issue of Guruship entailed much more than simply nominating a successor. It was intrinsically connected to the question of Nanak's authority as Guru, and thus to the sovereignty of the thought process and practice that he had created. Nanak had experienced the sublime truth of existence at the most profound level, which he was convinced could change the nature of humanity. Yet the complexities of the social, political and cultural milieu in which he lived prevented him from completing his task before the end of his life. Clearly it was necessary to find some person who could continue Nanak's work in accordance with the founder's own intentions. But what was to be the touchstone for choosing a new successor? If the touchstone was proximity to the master himself, then an obvious choice might have been Guru Nanak's own family. Perhaps one of his own two sons, Sri Chand or Lakhmi Das? In fact Guru Nanak rejected both of his sons as possible successors. The older son, Sri

Chand, rejected the householder life espoused by his father and choose the path of aceticism. Sri Chand would later found an order of *sadhus* (wandering ascetics) known as *Udasis*. The younger son, Lakhmi Das was simply not interested in spiritual affairs. As the Sikh poet Bhai Gurdas records, both these sons 'proved intractable and disobedient', and failed a number of tests that were designed by the Guru to probe the depth of his disciples' inner qualities.[8]

The person chosen by Nanak to succeed him was one, Bhai Lehna. The son of a petty trader from the village of Khadur, Lehna was an ardent devotee of the Hindu goddess Durga who was widely worshipped throughout North India. Lehna probably met Guru Nanak when he was in his late twenties. He had heard much about Guru Nanak and decided to visit him at Kartarpur while on his way to a festival honouring the goddess. Lehna's first meeting with Nanak affected him so profoundly that he joined the Kartarpur community as a disciple. Over the years his service, devotion and humility was recognized by Guru Nanak and his inner circle who regarded Lehna as an exemplary and inspirational figure. So when the time came for Nanak to choose a successor his choice fell on Bhai Lehna who proved to be the fittest in every way. The various tests to which Lehna was put displayed his proximity to the cardinal virtues that Nanak desired in his successor: humility, complete devotion, a love for humanity, respect for the householder's life, but perhaps most importantly that the two men drew their spiritual experience from the same well-spring, as evidenced by the proximity between their poetic sensibilities. It is this absolute proximity that the *janamsakhis* speak of as the passing of light from one body to another. Accordingly, to indicate the succession of Guruship, in the last months of his life, Guru Nanak placed a coconut and 5 *paisse* before Lehna and renamed him Angad (lit. part of my own body). Prostrating himself before his successor, Guru Nanak proclaimed to the Kartarpur community that Angad would be their new Guru. As the bards Satta and Balwand recorded in Tikki Ki Var: 'He Lehna had the same light (as Nanak), the same ways. Only the body of the Guru had changed.'[9]

The importance of Guru Angad's nomination to the *gurgadhi* (or seat of the Guru) was a profoundly important event in the early formation of the Sikh community. The fact that Guru Nanak set aside the claims of his sons and chose a successor from among his disciples, was itself nothing new in the North Indian context. It was practiced by many ascetic orders. What made it unique was that Angad was installed by Guru Nanak himself, which sent out several important signals: (i) that Nanak intended for his work to be continued; (ii) that it was possible for any one of his Sikhs to achieve perfection (the status of Guru or *gurmukh* lit. of the guru's own mouth) within one's lifetime, and that the positions of Guru and Sikh were interchangeable – they were not divinely ordained; (iii) that there was no difference, spiritually, poetically, philosophically, between the founder and the successor. Had Guru Nanak not chosen a successor, it is likely that the Kartarpur community would soon have been dispersed or absorbed into other sects.

Guru Nanak passed away on 22 September 1539 in a manner befitting someone whose life and teaching had united Hindu and Muslim communities as never before. According to the *Puratan Janamsakhi*:

> Just before Nanak's death, a quarrel arose between his Hindu and Muslim followers over the disposal of his corpse. The Hindus wished to burn it, the Muslims to bury it. Nanak was asked to decide. He said 'let the Hindus place flowers on my right and Muslims on my left. They whose flowers are found fresh tomorrow morning may have the disposal of the body.' After the flowers had been set on each side of him, the Guru drew his sheet over the flowers as well as himself. When the sheet was removed the following day, both sets of flowers were still fresh but the body had disappeared.[10]

At the time of his death, Guru Nanak had left behind a young but functioning community with its own distinctive practices, a rite of initiation and a successor fully authorized to continue the development of the community. But the important legacy that Nanak left to his successor and to the fledgling community was his authentic teaching and ideas recorded as a body of sublime poetry. Although there was no systematic doctrine within these compositions, nonetheless they contained a force that affected all who were touched by it. It is the sovereign aspect of this teaching that would provide continuity and focus for the community as it would evolve over the next two centuries.

Before resuming our narrative of the Sikh Gurus, it will be helpful to touch briefly on the vital aspects of Guru Nanak's teaching, a topic that will be covered more systematically in Chapters Four and Five.

Excursus 1: The teaching of Guru Nanak

A great deal of what Guru Nanak taught has much in common with the loose lineage of spiritual masters such as Sheikh Farid, Namdev, Ravidas and Kabir who generally hailed from the lowest classes of Indian society and were known as the *bhagats*[11]. Combining the search for perfection with devotional discipline, the poetic compositions of these teachers contained insights in common with Islamic, Hindu and Buddhist mysticism. Not unlike the *bodhisattvas* of Mahayana Buddhism, these were persons who had experienced the highest states of spiritual enlightenment through self-transformation, but then went out into the world to help others to achieve that same experience.

Guru Nanak emphasized that the aim of life was to cut through the shallowness of ordinary social existence in order to achieve a perfection of consciousness through a transformative sovereign experience. The essential marker of this experience is a state of oneness with all existence, whose essential characteristic is the fusion of a person's affective (unconscious) and conscious states of existence. This fusion results in an outpouring of poetic language (devotional poetry). Psychologically this state might be referred to as the emergence of a poetic consciousness characterized by unconditional and infinite love for one's fellow humans and respect for all life. It is a state of being-in-the-world where plurality punctures one's sense of individuality, which is not true oneness at all, and where one's actions are spontaneous. Crucially, this experience is potentially open to anyone at any time and any place. The person who achieves such a sovereign state of mind/consciousness/existence can be considered liberated from the fears and anxieties of social existence. Guru Nanak refers to such a sovereign person, marked by poetic consciousness, as *gurmukh* (lit. one's whose visage or language is that of a Guru). Only one thing stands in the way of achieving such perfection: the self, especially when the self becomes overly attached to itself, as when it says *my*-self or *our*-self, (individuation). Those who remain in the state of individuated self-attachment – believing they are free because they can act voluntarily – are in fact deluded. Guru Nanak refers to such individuals as *manmukh* (lit. whose visage or language is centred around themselves). Thus *manmukhs* are trapped by the very thing that is to be liberated: the self.

But how to achieve this transformation from un-free existence (*manmukh*) to sovereign existence (*gurmukh*)? As we noted earlier, before Guru Nanak achieved the breakthrough that gave him his life's task (the Sultanpur experience), he patiently submitted himself to a certain kind of discipline (*sadhana*). Prior to this, his experiences were intense but sporadic in nature. The discipline that Nanak surrendered himself to might be considered in terms of three practical concepts that were absolutely necessary for perfection: *satguru*, *satnam* and *satsang*. These practical concepts are really part of a single process, but it will be helpful to consider them separately in turn.

Satguru (lit. 'true Guru')

This refers to the authentic source of enlightenment and is key to understanding the nature of spiritual authority for Guru Nanak (as for the *bhagats* before him). The term *satguru* indicates that Nanak's experience did not come from a human preceptor or living guru. As Nanak himself tells us in his writings, it came from a non-human source that is found within all of us as a potentiality. It is an absolutely interior well-spring, a living force that remains hidden from us. But it is a force than can emerge only if we correctly attune our consciousness. Again and again in his hymns Nanak gives clues that to understand what the *satguru* is, we have to understand the intricate relationship between language and consciousness. *Satguru* is quite simply the force immanent within us that creates a change or conversion from ordinary ego-centred consciousness to ego-less consciousness. The clearest manifestation of such change or conversion is in the nature of the language that we utter, where ordinary self-centred language gives way to egoless poetic language. The agent of this change is *anhad shabad*, lit. the silent or unspoken Word. The terms silent or unspoken (*anhad*) refer to the hidden force that moves the actual language of poetic consciousness. One might say that these are words that are produced unconsciously, words over which we, our everyday consciousness, has no control. They emerge from a source other than our self-possessive ego. So the *satguru* consists at the same time, of concrete actual Word(s) (*shabad*) plus the silent, hidden force (*anhad*) behind it, yet these are not two different things. They are one.

But here is the interesting thing. This may sound like a mystical process but Nanak categorically states that it is within anyone's grasp, for the change in consciousness depends on a change in our relationship to language. The idea that *satguru* refers to language or Words that are qualitatively different from the words we normally speak insofar as they come from a different source, effectively displaces the need for human mediation in achieving perfection. A human agent becomes unnecessary. Hence the sovereign experience through which this language is released itself becomes the touchstone of all authority.

Of course, the question here is that if such experience is available to all, why don't we realize it all of the time? And how to achieve it? Now, Guru Nanak provides answers to these questions but not in the form of a systematic rational argument leading from one step to another. His answers do not come in the form of 'knowledge' but rather in the form of 'non-knowledge' – something that can only be felt . . . not known. Thus his preferred means of achieving the enlightened state of non-knowledge, is through forms of devotion based on the practice of repeating the true name or *satnam*.

Satnam

This refers to the practice of imbibing the true name within one's consciousness. It begins with a technique or mnemotechnic which through diligent practice leads to a spontaneous or unconscious repetition. The basic techniques are *nam japna*, the chanting or vocalized repetition of the Name (any divine name such as Madho, Hari, Waheguru) and *nam simaran*, the mindful remembrance of the Name. The technique favoured by Guru Nanak was devotional singing which aims to produce an ecstatic state of mind where the name(s) resonates effortlessly within one's consciousness. *Kirtan* was favoured by Guru Nanak for two reasons. It already incorporates the essential meditative elements of *nam japna* and *nam simaran* as mindful remembrance is enhanced by the nature of music accompanying the poetic verses to be sung. Secondly, *kirtan* is meant to be performed in association with others, that is, within a congregational gathering called *sangat* (or *satsang*)

Satsang

The term *satsang* refers to the community (*sangat*) of like-minded individuals, those who are drawn together by their devotion to a true spiritual master or *satguru*, and by a common method of adoration based on mindful remembrance of the true name, *satnam*. Satsang is therefore the community of those who travel together on the path towards a liberative experience. The path is not a clearly demarcated road or way drawn in space. Rather the path is the journey between life and death, a path that is essentially temporal and temporalizing.

Taken together, the terms *satguru*, *satnam* and *satsang* form the nuclear elements of a life-world that connects such travellers. And this life-world, which is nothing more than the cumulative lived experience of the community, is known in North Indian lexicon as *panth*. The term *panth* is therefore both the temporal life-path for achieving perfection, plus the spatial world that is created and lived in. In this sense, the term *panth* does not correspond to what is designated by the modern western term 'religion'. *Panth* does not recognize any distinction between religion and world, sacred and profane, religion and politics, etc. Nor does it designate a community centred around 'belief'. Rather the common focus of a *panth* is that towards which devotion is targeted, namely, inner experience. This is not the memory of an experience that may or may not have happened, but the actual striving to experience anew, to experience creatively – experience as the creation of newness in the world.

Sovereign Experience

But what is this experience? Scholars have always had trouble trying to locate this experience within a particular sphere of meaning. The name commonly attributed to this experience by Western historians of religion is *nirgun bhakti*. Since the late nineteenth-century historians of religion reinterpreted indigenous understandings of devotional practice in India by arguing that it could be divided into two types: *saguna bhakti* and *nirguna bhakti*. *Saguna bhakti* or devotion to a God who has attributes, qualities or form, refers to a God that exists. This was the path followed by Hindus who devoted themselves to a personal God, for example Vishnu, a god who exists, has tangible form and could be represented through images, icons and idols. According to the theological interpretation of western historians of religion, *saguna bhakti* gave rise to an exterior piety that produced conflicting truth-claims and therefore had the potential to catalyse communal violence. By contrast, *nirguna bhakti* is devotion to a God without attributes, qualities or form, and insofar, a God that is non-existent. According to leading historians of South Asian religion, it was a path followed by the Sants or *bhagats* and by Guru Nanak.[12] Consequently, worship of idols and images representing the divine are forbidden in Sikh tradition. Since the focus of devotion is a formless God, the experience of this non-existent God is ineffable and gives rise to a strictly interiorized piety, one that is amenable to privatization and therefore far less likely to produce conflicting truth claims over the nature of God that in turn might lead to communal violence.

There are two obvious problems with this model. First, the idea of an opposition between *saguna* and *nirguna bhakti* was itself constructed by historians of religion. It does not correspond to the actual nature of piety in Hindu and Sikh devotion. Indeed neither the *bhagats* nor Guru Nanak ever used the term *saguna* or *nirguna bhakti* to name their definitive experience. Second, these scholars tried to fit the Indic forms of experience, that were by no means conceptually opposed to each other, within a Christian theological framework. Devotion was understood in the Christian sense in terms of the central definition of God's nature: that God exists, and cannot *not* exist. And this definition was regarded as the central attribute of religion-in-general, meaning that it could be translated and applied to all cultures. This definition of God is itself framed by a logic of non-contradiction, the so-called law of non-contradiction.

If anything, the experience that Guru Nanak does speak of – and he is prolific in speaking about the experience – makes the opposition between *nirguna* and *saguna bhakti* meaningless. According to Guru Nanak, if we are to speak of this experience propositionally, all one can say is that it is an experience of non-duality, of absolute oneness. We can speak of this one as personal, as a feeling of an infinitely close presence, and we can give this infinitely close presence a variety of names such as Madho, Hari, Ram, thereby suggesting that it is an experience of a personal God. At the same time, however, this very same One is experienced as continually slipping away. We are unable to grasp it. It becomes absent in the very moment that we say something positive about it, like a name or quality for instance. So the One, according to Nanak, is both absent and present at the same time.

But is this not a contradiction? How can anyone show devotion to an experience/One that is both there and not-there? Guru Nanak's answer to this is deceptively simple and is elaborated in many of his hymns especially the Japji. We shall discuss this in more detail in Chapter Five on Sikh Philosophy. For now, a shorter and slightly different explanation must suffice.

For Guru Nanak the problem lies in the fact that our ordinary states of consciousness are unable to accept this contradiction, that our ordinary mind refuses to surrender to the contradiction. Instead we instinctively try to overcome the contradiction by objectivizing and polarizing the two aspects. Our social projects insert 'God' into the experience and objectify it. For example, both Hindus and Muslims say that God is One but they conceptualize this Oneness in opposing ways. While Hindus say that God is infinitely near to us, and try to express his proximity through idols and images, Muslims regard this One as transcendent, infinitely beyond us. But neither *experiences* that One. This is why Guru Nanak said: 'there is no Hindu, there is no Muslim' – implying that both miss the experience which must include the other. As such they stopped *being* Hindu and Muslim. Instead both traditions began to emphasize the social projection of God, and through these social projections, began pitting themselves against each other. For Guru Nanak, this social projection was nothing more than the anxiety of a deluded ego.

Guru Nanak by contrast emphasizes that to attain this experience, the devotee should focus not on 'God' but on that which at the same time *prevents* the experience and is the very *means* of that experience: the ego, mind or self. So Guru Nanak suggests a more workable formula by asking the devotee to keep in mind that God (or the experience of the One) and ego cannot be in the same place at the same time. Listen to what both Nanak and Kabir say on this issue:

Nanak

When I act in ego, You're not present.
When you're present, ego is absent.
O Nanak repeat these words: 'He is me, I'm him'
The One in whom the three worlds are merged.

Kabir

When I am, Hari is not.
Now Hari is, and I am no more.
By saying 'You, You' I have become You
'I am' is in me no longer.

Judging from what both Nanak and Kabir say, the heart of the problem seems to be that we are socially conditioned to live, think and act only on the basis of ego ('when I am, I act in ego'). Yet there is something in the very structure of this ego that prevents us experiencing Oneness (You're not there/Hari is not). To undergo the experience the ego needs to be absent. One has to struggle with it and yet remain within the world. This is no easy task. In fact Nanak likens it to crossing a mighty ocean in a small raft. But he also says that the means for achieving this is within the reach of everyone without exception. Yet it cannot be achieved without a true Guru (*satguru*), and Nanak's *satguru*, the one he recommends to us all, is the word (*shabad*): 'Word is my Guru, the consciousness attuned to it is its devotee' (*shabad-guru surat dhun chela*). The Word or *shabad* is the boat that allows us to cross the ocean of existence, the ups and downs of this world that we inhabit and attain that sovereign experience, indeed to become sovereign, free.

This basic insight – that attainment of a sovereign consciousness, perfection, *gurmukh,* is everyone's birthright – is ingrained into the nature of the self and attainable through transformation of our everyday consciousness (ego mind) into poetic consciousness (egoless mind). It becomes the criterion by which Nanak passed on the title of Guru to his successors. Not simply the attainment of perfection but the desire to bring others to perfection (*gurmukh*). It is this sovereign experience, and the need to protect everyone's access to it, that becomes the central focus of the Panth, the well-spring from which it draws sustenance. It is this sovereign experience that constitutes the bond between Guru and Sikh, that enables Sikh to become Guru and a Guru to become the Sikh of one who has perfected herself.

Let us continue to look at how this bond of sovereign experience functions in the history of the Sikh Gurus and later on in the evolution of the Panth.

Guru Angad (Nanak 2)

Bhai Lehna, who was renamed Guru Angad, was born in 1504 in the village of Harike in Ferozepur district but lived much of his early life at his ancestral village of Khadur near Tarn Taran. Shortly after his installation as the second Guru of the Sikhs, Angad left Kartarpur and moved back to Khadur, taking with him the largest part of Guru Nanak's following and certainly all of his inner circle. The move to Khadur was probably advised by Guru Nanak himself who foresaw the possibility of conflict with Sri Chand and Lakhmi Das as they refused to recognize Angad's succession, being Nanak's legal heirs and claimants to the *gurgaddi.*

At Khadur Guru Angad applied himself to the task of consolidating the Nanak Panth and spreading the teachings of its founder. As the number of disciples increased, the Guru opened more centres and implemented a more regulated system for the collection of offerings. The *langar* or common free kitchen was enlarged to cater for the growing numbers of visitors. The relatively simple cuisine was standardized and rules were established for the volunteers (*sevadars*) who served visitors. *Sevadars* were asked to maintain politeness and hospitality to all who sought refuge.

To preserve the compositions of Guru Nanak, Angad adopted a new script called *gurmukhi* (lit. from the mouth of the guru) by selecting letters that already existed in other scripts current in North India. This was an important step as it allowed the Sikhs to develop their own written language distinct from Persian (the language of the Mughal empire and of Islam) and Sanskrit (the language of orthodox Hindus), thereby fostering the community's sense of distinctness. The new script helped Angad to consolidate the compositions of Nanak and provided a medium for the composition of his own short verses. Specifically, Angad composed his own verses under the name 'Nanak', indicating that there was no qualitative difference between the poetic consciousness or inner experience of the founder and the successor. This practice was followed by Angad's successors.

Along with these organizational steps Guru Angad also promoted the physical well being of his Sikhs, enjoining them to take interest in physical exercise. For this purpose he ordered the construction of wrestling arenas at Khadur and other centres. His followers were encouraged to take part in regular drills and competitive games after morning services. In effect, the Guru sowed the seeds for a competitive martial spirit in his disciples that would make it relatively easy for his successors to raise bands of able-bodied men from among his disciples.[13] This competitive spirit would prove most useful during the turbulent days of the sixth and tenth Gurus.

Guru Angad presided as Guru for 13 years during a crucial time in the community's evolution. He expanded the community's membership, which was still dominated by the mercantile caste, to include ironsmiths, barbers, storekeepers, cooks and of course the *Jats* or peasant farmers.

Angad had two sons Dasu and Dattu, but his choice of succession fell not on a member of his family but on his oldest, though most devoted follower, Amar Das, who had achieved perfection (*gurmukh*) under his guidance. Guru Angad died in 1552 at the age of 48. Shortly before his death he summoned Amar Das, placed a coconut and 5 *paisa* in his lap, prostrated himself before the new

Guru in the presence of the congregation. Amar Das became Guru when he was 72 years old.

Guru Amar Das (Nanak 3)

Guru Amar Das was born in 1479 at the village of Basarke. Long before he met Guru Angad he had been a devout adherent of the Vaisnava Hindu sect and had established a reputation for piety. But despite practicing severe austerities and making regular visits to Hindu pilgrimage centres, the essential liberative experience continued to elude him. On one occasion, however, he heard melodious recitations of Guru Nanak's Japji being recited by Bibi Amro, the daughter of Guru Angad, who was married to his own nephew. Amar Das requested her to acquaint him with her father. On meeting Guru Angad he found the mentor he had long sought and became his ardent devotee at the age of 60. Under the second Guru's guidance he renounced his Vaishnava practice and undertook a different kind of austerity: the selfless service of society (*seva*) while living the life of a householder. In recognition of his humility, devotion and perfection of mind, he was appointed by Guru Angad as the third Guru of the Sikhs, thus overlooking his sons.

To avoid conflict with Dasu and Datu, who again, were the legal heirs of Guru Angad according to the state laws, Guru Amar Das decided to shift from Khadur to Goindval, a town which he had helped to construct under instruction from Guru Angad who had foreseen the problems of succession. During his 22-year-long tenure as Guru which began at the age of 72, he implemented a number of steps that ensured the steady growth of the Nanak Panth. He made the *langar* a central institution, insisting that all who wanted to meet with him must first partake of food from the common kitchen and eat alongside his disciples.[14] The Guru's further emphasis on following egalitarian practices caused some consternation among local *brahmins* and *khatris* who saw the expansion of the Guru's following as a threat to their established class interests. Eventually they complained to the Mughal Emperor Akbar who decided to visit the Goindval community to see for himself. Akbar was so impressed with what he found that he assigned a gift of several village revenues to Bibi Bhani, the Guru's daughter, on the occasion of her marriage to Bhai Jetha, his most devoted follower. Akbar's patronage further enhanced the prestige of the Guru and the image of the Sikh community among the masses.

Apart from the free kitchen, Guru Amar Das also created a new institution known as the *manji* system for the purpose of ministering to the needs of the expanding community. *Manjis* (lit. bedstead) were parishes or centres where an agent of the Guru would be deputized to receive offerings and give guidance to the *sangat* on behalf of the Guru. While at Goindval he created an anthology of the hymns of his predecessors, to which he added 907 of his own hymns, as well as the hymns of the *bhagats* whose writings were in consonance with those of Guru Nanak. Put together, this anthology of writings swelled to a sizeable corpus that came to be known as the Goindval Pothi. This *pothi* or collection became the basis of the future Sikh scripture.

Guru Amar Das also introduced social innovations designed to begin the process of safeguarding the teachings and practice known as *gurmat* (lit. the instruction or message of the Guru). Part of the reason for this was the growing opposition, not only from the sons of the first two Gurus, but of *brahmins* and *khatris* whose interests were threatened by the growth of the Sikh community and its egalitarian practices, particularly towards women and the lower castes. For example, he strictly forbade the practice of *purdah* or the veiling and seclusion of women. Also forbidden were the practices of *sati*, the burning of women on the funeral pyres of their husbands and *kurimar* or female infanticide. He constructed a well or *baoli* alongside the main ashram at Goindwal, thereby giving the Sikhs their own pilgrimage place. As an annual gathering day he fixed the month of Baisakh, the traditional spring festival of North India. To these measures he added new rites of passage to mark births and deaths, centred around the recitation of appropriate hymns by the Sikh Gurus. Together, these measures crystallized the beginnings of a distinctly Sikh way of life and practice. Guru Amar Das lived to the ripe age of 95. As with previous Gurus he considered his own sons unfit to succeed him. In their stead he chose his son-in-law, Bhai Jetha, who was renamed Ram Das.

Guru Ram Das (Nanak 4)

Guru Ram Das was born in Lahore in 1534 into a life of poverty. As a child Ram Das had to supplement the family's income by selling parched grams. When both of his parents died, leaving him an orphan at the tender age of seven, his maternal grandmother took him to her village of Basarke where he lived for five years continuing to sell parched grams to keep body and soul together. While at Basarke he came into contact with Guru Amar Das who developed a deep affection for the boy and took interest in promoting his welfare. At the prompting of Guru Amar Das, Ram Das and his grandmother moved to Goindval when he was 12, close to the time that Guru Amar Das succeeded Guru Angad. While at Goindval, Ram Das' habits and piety impressed Guru Amar Das so much that he arranged his marriage to his own daughter, Bibi Bhani, and deputized him to represent the Guru's affairs at the court of Akbar.

Ram Das became Guru in 1574. Facing hostility from the sons of the third Guru, Mohan and Mohri, he shifted his residence to Guru-ka-Chak, where on the orders of Guru Amar Das, he supervised the excavation of a large tank designed to become the nucleus of a new township called Ramdaspur. Merchants, traders, artisans and craftsmen were invited to set up their businesses in the new town. The revenues obtained from these businesses helped the new township – later renamed Amritsar – to prosper, thus providing the Guru with the means to expand the steadily growing *panth* to distant parts of India.

During his seven year tenure, one of Guru Ramdas's main achievements was to extend and implement the *manji* system. To regulate the collection of offerings he appointed territorial deputies known as *masands*, who were individually selected on the basis of their integrity and familiarity with the Guru's teachings. In the early evolution of the Sikh Panth the *masand* system helped to provide cohesion and discipline in the various *manjis*.

Guru Ramdas composed a number of hymns to be sung at occasions such as marriage or childbirth. He composed a number of verses known as *ghorian* that were meant to be sung on days preceding the marriage ceremony. *Ghorian* replaced the rustic rural folksongs which were deemed unsuitable for Sikhs. For the marriage ceremony itself he composed the *lavan* in Raga Suhi (see Chapter Four), asking his followers to recite these hymns as a way of solemnizing the marriage and as a way for married couples to embody the meaning of equipoise and true love towards each other. These hymns provided the basis for a distinct social code which would become a necessity several centuries later.

Guru Ram Das was renowned for his great humility. One anecdote suggests that his humility was instrumental in creating a rapprochement with the Udasi sect led by Guru Nanak's older son, Baba Sri Chand who had become a wandering ascetic and mystic of great repute. During one of his travels, Sri Chand met Guru Ramdas and jokingly asked why he grew such a long beard. 'To wipe the feet of saints like yourself' replied Ramdas. Acknowledging the Guru's humility, Sri Chand replied, 'It is this humility that made you so great and me so small'. Thereafter Sri Chand extended his cooperation to Guru Ramdas and the Udasi sect became more closely associated with the Sikhs.

Guru Ramdas had three sons: Prithi Chand, Mahadev and Arjan. Of the three he considered Arjan to be most suited to succeed him. Accordingly Arjan was nominated the fifth Guru of the Sikhs in 1581 in a ceremony officiated by Bhai Buddha, who had served Guru Nanak and had been part of the inner circle of the second, third and fourth Gurus.

Guru Arjan (Nanak V)

The fifth Guru, Arjan was born in Goindval where he lived at the home of his maternal uncle Guru Amardas, with his parents Ramdas and Bibi Bhani for 11 years. As a child he received the affections and blessings of his grandfather Guru Amardas, who predicted that Arjan would one day be a well-spring of the poetic Word or *gurbani*. Arjan spent the next seven years at Ramdaspur, again close to his father. When he was 17, the fourth Guru requested Arjan to represent him at the marriage of a close relative in Lahore. The eldest son Prithi Chand had already refused this task as he was in charge of the Guru's treasury and stood to lose an eminent position to someone else. The middle brother Mahadev also pleaded his inability to go to Lahore due to his indifference to worldly affairs. Arjan dutifully accepted the task. When the marriage was over, however, he was asked to remain in Lahore to look after the *sangat* there. During these months of separation Arjan suffered the pangs of separation from his father and spiritual mentor, to whom he wrote three letters. Two of the letters were intercepted by Prithi Chand and withheld from Guru Ramdas. However, a letter marked '3' was safely delivered to the Guru. On his return from

Lahore, Arjan was asked the reason for the figure '3' on his letter. When the truth of the matter came to light, Prithi Chand was forced to produce the letters which contained beautiful compositions by Arjan expressing his suffering.

According to Sikh tradition, this episode was one of several that convinced Guru Ramdas that Arjan alone was fit to hold the office of Guru. It was also the beginning of many pitfalls that were to be placed in Arjan's path as Prithi Chand refused to accept his father's decision and became bitterly opposed towards Arjan, so much so that Guru Ramdas was forced to call him a *mina* (deceitful hypocrite) and instructed his Sikhs not to associate with him. As alluded to by Bhai Gurdas and by Arjan himself in some of his later compositions, in the years following his father's death, Prithi Chand's attitude became even more hostile, often hatching conspiracies and plying Sikhs with false propaganda that the young Guru had usurped their father's property. To counteract this Arjan transferred his legal property to Prithi Chand, saying that he would live on the offerings of his followers.

All of this was going on between 1581 and 1589 when Arjan was busy completing the building of the new Harimandar temple at Chak Ramdas. This was a major construction project that required the young Guru to raise new funds. For this purpose the Sikhs were requested to donate a tenth of their income (*dasvandh*) and the *masands* were instructed to meet at the beginning of each Baisakhi festival, and to bring with them a contingent of Sikhs plus a remittance of the yearly accounts. The temple was completed in 1589. As a gesture of humility and ecumenism, Guru Arjan invited the Sufi saint Mian Mir, with whom he had developed good relations during his stay in Lahore, to lay the foundation stone of the Harimandar. By doing so the Guru made it clear that the Harimandar belonged to all, irrespective of caste or creed. These sentiments combining pluralism and self-effacement were reflected in the architectural design of the Harimandar. The Guru had the temple built on a lower level than the surrounding city so that visitors would have to physically descend before entering the precincts, suggesting a requirement to efface one's ego, arrogance and hatred of others in order to achieve a meeting with the Guru. Similarly, the Harimandar had four doors open on all four sides indicating an opening to all cultures, but with only one access to the inner sanctum via a causeway, suggesting that the end goal for all was the same. After the foundation stone was laid, the tank was filled with water and the town of Ramdaspur renamed Amritsar (lit. the pool of nectar).

The successful completion of this project was a true milestone for Guru Arjan and the Sikh community. It provided a central pilgrimage place for the Sikhs in the midst of a flourishing centre of trade and industry. The temple complex itself became a rallying point for the community as well as a centre of Sikh activity.

Not long after the temple was built, Guru Arjan undertook a tour of the Majha and Doaba regions of Punjab that lasted five years. During this time he founded three new towns: Tarn Taran, Kartarpur and Hargobindpur, which he named after his son Hargobind who was born in 1595. Because of their location in the heartland of Punjab, the towns of Amritsar, Tarn Taran, Kartarpur and Hargobindpur provided a means for influencing the Jat peasantry in this area to join the Sikh fold and for fostering new trades. Thus Guru Arjan was not only able to expand the numbers of his followers in a relatively short space of time, he was also responsible for creating a new level of prosperity which added to his importance and influence in the entire region.[15] The Guru was now at the centre of a major organization and came to be regarded by his followers not only as a spiritual mentor but as a sovereign leader in his own right, a true king (*sacha padshah*).

Arjan completed his tour of Punjab and returned to Amritsar in 1595, but only to find that Prithi Chand had been active in propagating his own claims to Guruship on two different fronts. On the one hand he made an alliance with a district revenue official, Sulhi Khan, and prepared a formal complaint against Arjan to the Mughal emperor Akbar.[16] In his complaint, Prithi Chand repeated his earlier accusation that his younger brother had illegally usurped his claim to Guruship and had thus shown indifference to imperial law. On the other hand, to bolster his own claim, Prithi Chand had begun to compile a *granth* or volume of poetry to rival the one being prepared by Arjan. At the same time his followers were busy circulating accusations that Arjan's compositions contained passages denigrating Islam. A report containing such an accusation was prepared and sent to Akbar. On one of his trips to Lahore the Emperor stopped near Amritsar and asked to see Arjan's volume. The unfinished manuscript was brought to the Emperor's camp by Baba Buddha and Bhai Gurdas. On perusing the contents of the volume Akbar expressed his satisfaction with the nature of the compositions and made an offering of 51 gold *mohars* to the sacred book and sent robes of honour to Guru Arjan who was absolved of any wrong doing.[17] According to traditional accounts, however, Prithi Chand did not cease hostilities towards his brother. It is said that he subsequently tried to have Arjan's infant son assassinated by various means, but was unsuccessful.[18]

Incidents such as these impressed upon Guru Arjan the need to complete the manuscript as soon as possible to ensure that the Sikhs were able to distinguish between the authentic utterances of the Guru (*gurbani*) and the fake compositions of his rivals (*kachi bani*). As noted earlier, previous Gurus had begun the process of compiling a canon, at the heart of which was the poetic experience of each carrying the signature name 'Nanak'. The community needed access to such a source of experience in order to be able to repeat it. Over the next few years the fifth Guru continued to compose his own poetry and to collect the poetry of saints whose message was similar to Guru Nanak's. The actual work of compiling all the hymns into a coherent volume began early in 1603 and was completed in August 1604. In the early morning of 16 August 1604 the Adi Granth (or original volume) as it came to be known was ceremonially installed in the inner sanctum of the Harimandar. Once the installation ceremonies were completed the Granth was wrapped in silk cloths and carried reverentially by Bhai Buddha with Guru Arjan in attendance, to a special chamber where it was placed for the night. As a mark of reverence the Guru slept near the Granth. Early next morning the Granth was carried back to the Harimandar for the morning service. Thus a regular pattern was established with the Granth at the centre of Sikh practice, a pattern that is followed meticulously to this day.

The compilation and installation of the Adi Granth was a landmark event in Sikh history. Apart from putting an authoritative seal on the poetic consciousness and authentic teaching of the Sikh Gurus, the Granth also provided the Sikhs with a sense of distinctness without creating formal 'religious' boundaries. Just as importantly it signalled a change in the outward manifestation of authority. Whereas with Arjan's predecessors the body and voice of the Guru had been the sole locus of sovereign authority, Sikhs now came to recognize the Granth as an equal and legitimate form of sovereign. And this was entirely in consonance with Guru Nanak's teaching for whom the true Guru was *shabad*, the articulated form of poetic consciousness.

While Akbar was still alive, the process of consolidating and expanding the early Sikh community had been a relatively peaceful affair with little interference from the Mughal state. Indeed, as we have seen, the state had on occasion been benignly disposed towards the cause of the Sikh Gurus. Soon after Akbar's death, however, with his son Jahangir at the helm of the Mughal empire, things changed quite dramatically, and the state became more hostile towards the Sikhs and Guru Arjan in particular.[19]

The reasons for the reversal in state policy can, to a large extent, be attributed to the fight for succession of the Mughal throne. Akbar had shown an inclination to overlook the succession of his eldest son Salim (later renamed Jahangir) in favour of Salim's eldest son Khusrau who commanded respect among the influential liberal-minded supporters of Akbar such as Khani Azam Aziz Koka and the Rajput leader, Raja Man Singh. In his quest to claim the throne Salim rebelled against Akbar in 1601 and was able to count on powerful support from the Sunni orthodox circles and conservative Sufi orders such as the Naqshbandis led by Shaikh Ahmed Sirhindi. Towards the end of Akbar's reign both Sunni orthodoxy and Naqshbandi orders had undergone a revival especially in the Punjab, spurred to an extent by the growing presence and popularity of the Sikh movement which had inadvertently pulled Hindu and Muslim followers away from Islam. These conservative elements are likely to have swayed Jahangir's feelings against non-Muslims as is evident from his memoirs.[20] It is known that while Shaikh Ahmed held a strong political antipathy towards Guru Arjan in particular, he was also hostile towards Sufis such as Mian Mir who preached tolerance towards non-Muslims, and ordinary Muslims who adopted Hindu manners and customs such as marriage ceremonies and funeral observances. His antipathy was driven by his theological stance which argued strongly for a return to the Sunni belief in the primacy of prophetic revelation as against 'all types of innovations' – a term that he used for modes of reasoning that allowed syncretism between different faiths. In this way the target of his invective included Shias, Sufis and all non-Muslims.

A compromise was eventually effected between Akbar and Salim such that in 1605 Akbar crowned Jahangir as emperor shortly before his death. Ousted from the succession, Khusrau began a rebellion against Jahangir whose army pursued him from Agra to the Punjab. On his way to Lahore, Khusrau stopped to rest at Goindval meeting with Guru Arjan who had had good relations with Akbar. As was his policy towards all visitors, the Guru may well have provided Khusrau with temporary shelter and food during the latter's short stay at Goindval. Shortly thereafter, Khusrau was captured before reaching the safety of Lahore and imprisoned.

Whatever the nature of Guru Arjan's meeting with Khusrau, it nevertheless provided Shaikh Ahmed Sirhindi with a perfect pretext to file a report to Jahangir that the Sikh Guru had blessed the fugitive Khusrau by placing a saffron mark on his forehead.[21] Within a month, Guru Arjan was summoned to Lahore under the Emperor's orders to stand trial for the treasonable charge of aiding and abetting a fugitive.[22] Prior to his departure for Lahore, Arjan nominated his 11-year-old son Hargobind as his successor. It seems that the Guru had a keen awareness of the change in political atmosphere afoot at the time. He left Lahore probably with the understanding that he might not return. The trial was conducted by Farid Bukhari (later given the title Murtaza Khan) a close associate and devotee of Shaikh Ahmed Sirhindi.[23] The Guru was asked either to pay a fine and admit charges of treasonable conduct, or to convert to Islam. When Guru Arjan refused on both accounts he was sentenced to death by torture.[24] According to traditional Sikh accounts, corroborated by Jahangir's own diary, the Guru was subjected to extreme forms of torture that included being seated on a hot iron plate while burning sand was poured over his body before dipping his blistered body in the cold waters of the river Ravi. The Guru died on 30 May 1606.[25]

By all accounts, the execution of Guru Arjan was a particularly traumatic event for the Sikh community and a major turning point in the history of Punjab. To this day, Sikhs continue to venerate the memory of the fifth Guru as the first martyr of the Sikh tradition.

CHAPTER TWO

Martyrdom and Militancy: Rise of the Khalsa

Guru Hargobind

Shortly after the martyrdom of Guru Arjan, his 11-year-old son Hargobind was formally installed as the sixth Guru of the Sikhs by Bhai Buddha. In accordance with his father's orders and as a response to the altered political climate in which the Sikh community was now living, Guru Hargobind donned a warrior's dress and girded two swords around his waist signifying explicitly what had been implicit in the style of his predecessors, that the Guru was *miri piri ka malik*: one who commanded both spiritual (*piri*) and temporal (*miri*) authority. At the installation he sent out an edict to his followers that from now on they should bring offerings of arms and horses as well as money.

Hargobind began his tenure by raising small bands of armed Sikhs and getting them trained in techniques of self-defence and warfare.[1] This was not a difficult task as the previous Gurus had continued to foster wrestling arenas which provided the necessary initial recruits. He also made two important changes to the Harimandar complex. Opposite the Harimandar itself, he constructed a high platform which came to be known as Akal Takht (Seat of the Timeless One) close to which he built a fortress called Lohgarh. At the Akal Takht the Guru would regularly hold meetings and conduct the political affairs of the community.[2]

It seems that the first few years of his tenure went relatively unnoticed by the Mughal authorities who had left the Sikhs alone after Guru Arjan's death, possibly in the belief that the movement would quietly disintegrate. But as reports about the Guru's activities began to circulate, the Emperor was reminded that the fine imposed on Guru Arjan had not been paid. Jahangir was therefore legally entitled to move against Hargobind. Accordingly Jahangir ordered the arrest and imprisonment of Guru Hargobind in the Gwalior Fort in 1609. Historians are not entirely clear as to how long the Guru spent as a prisoner (possibly between one and two years) but it appears that Jahangir changed his attitude towards the Guru and effected an early release.[3] There may be two reasons for this. First, after 1611, Jahangir more or less reverted to the more tolerant policies of Akbar. As a result the conservative Sunnis and revivalist Naqshbandis fell out of favour with the Emperor, who felt that he had achieved his main purpose which was to secure the throne. Secondly, Jahangir got to know more about the circumstances of Guru Arjan's execution and Hargobind's imprisonment. After his release in 1611, Guru Hargobind travelled back to Punjab and for the next decade and half, until Jahangir's death in 1627, he dedicated himself to rebuilding his army, albeit more discreetly. The relative quiet of Jahangir's last years afforded a window of opportunity for the Guru to reconsolidate the community and turn his attention towards family life. He married three times (the first two wives predeceasing him) and had a number of children including five sons: Gurditta, Ani Rai, Atal Rai, Tegh Bahadur and Suraj Mal. To reconnect with his followers, the Guru undertook various preaching tours that took him to Kashmir, Uttar Pradesh and the *doaba* regions of the Punjab. However, the Guru was not fooled by the lull in Mughal hostilities towards the Sikhs. For he was keenly aware that underneath the calm, troubles were already brewing, partly due to the next battle of succession, spearheaded by Jahangir's eldest son Shah Jahan, and partly due to schismatic elements within the Sikh community such as the *minas*, Prithi Chand and his son Meharban, who claimed to be the sixth and seventh Gurus respectively. The *minas* spared no effort to slander the Guru, suggesting that his character was not in keeping with that of a true Guru, given that he indulged in 'un-saintly' activities. For unlike the previous Gurus, it was said, he hunted, involved himself in warfare with the state and had been imprisoned. That some Sikhs were clearly influenced by this propaganda is attested to by Bhai Gurdas in his *vars*: 'People say the former Gurus used to sit in the temple; the present Guru remains not in place. Former Emperors used to visit former Gurus; the present was imprisoned by the Emperor   he keeps dogs and goes out hunting; he does not compose *bani* nor does he listen to it; he prefers the company of scoundrels over devoted servants . . . .'[4] But Bhai Gurdas argued that Guru Hargobind bore 'an intolerable burden and does not assert himself', and justified the new measures of the Guru with the argument that to grow safely an orchard needs the protective hedge of the thorny *kikar* trees. In other words, the Panth of Guru Nanak needed to assert physical force for its protection.[5]

With the accession of Shah Jahan in 1627 the state, once again influenced by a new phase of Islamic revivalism, began to cause problems for the Sikhs and other non-Muslim groups. In 1628, while Shah Jahan was hunting in the vicinity of Amritsar, some of his troops plundered the property of Guru Hargobind as he was making marriage preparations for his daughter. The offenders were repulsed on this occasion but two years later there was a more serious altercation with a larger Mughal force. The Mughals were defeated, but sensing that Shah Jahan would send reprisals, the Guru left Amritsar and retreated to Kartarpur in the Jalandar doab. According to the Muslim chronicler Mohsin Fani, a battle took place in which two Mughal commanders were killed and the Guru was victorious.[6] Fighting alongside the Guru were his sons Tegh Bahadur and Gurditta. Realizing that it was not possible for the Sikhs to openly contest the Mughal forces in Punjab, the Guru expediently withdrew further into the Shivalik Hills, setting up his base at Kiratpur. The Guru continued to conduct affairs from Kiratpur for the remaining years of his life. His absence from the Punjab allowed his rivals to exert their influence in key towns such as Amritsar and Kartarpur. Meharban set himself up as the seventh Nanak in Amritsar and composed a *janamsakhi* of Guru Nanak to strengthen his claims. Dhir Mal, the eldest son of Gurditta, also did not join the Guru at Kiratpur. Instead he remained at Kartarpur where he took possession of the original copy of the Adi Granth prepared by Bhai Gurdas under Guru Arjan's supervision, and in time received land grants from Shah Jahan who saw an opportunity to influence the line of succession in his favour. As a result Dhir Mal developed a pro-state stance in opposition to his grandfather. With the Kartarpur Bir in his possession he was able to project himself as yet another contender for the *gurgaddi*.

Towards the end of Guru Hargobind's life it seems that the question of succession was becoming a more problematic affair. The oldest son, and the one initially favoured for succession, predeceased him as did two other sons, Ani Rai and Atal Rai. Of the remaining two Suraj Mal was considered overly materialistic, whereas Tegh Bahadur had the required attributes but was not yet ready to take up such office. Thus the Guru nominated Gurditta's second son Har Rai to succeed him as Guru before he died in 1644 at Kiratpur.

Guru Har Rai (Nanak 7) and Guru Har Krishan (Nanak 8)

Guru Har Rai was 14 when he succeeded his grandfather Guru Hargobind as the seventh Nanak. He lived a relatively short life until the age of 31. For the first 16 years of his reign as Guru he resided in the Shivalik Hills well away from the Sikh heartland towns of Amritsar, Kartarpur, Khadur, and Kiratpur where the influence of the schismatic sects was kept in check only by *masands* still faithful to Guru Hargobind and Har Rai.

Although Guru Har Rai continued to maintain the troops that the sixth Guru had raised, he generally sought to avoid open conflict with the Mughals. For the most part his tenure as Guru was a relatively peaceful one. But things changed once again when the war of succession broke out between Shah Jahan's two sons, Dara Shikoh and Aurangzeb. The different personalities and bitter struggle between these two men followed a similar pattern to their predecessors. Dara Shikoh, the older son and heir-apparent, was influenced by the Qadariya school of Sufism which emphasized mystical experience. Like Akbar and Khusrau before him, Dara Shikoh sought common ground between Hindus and Muslims. According to Sikh records, Guru Har Rai developed friendly ties with Dara Shikoh after treating him for an illness.[7] Aurangzeb, by contrast, was a strict Sunni and was supported by conservative Muslim clerics at the imperial court. One of his theological mentors was Masud, the son of Shaikh Ahmed Sirhindi, who turned out to be even more fanatical than his father. Dara Shikoh was eventually defeated by Aurangzeb in two gruelling battles and fled northwards towards Lahore where he was eventually caught and executed on grounds of apostasy.

Upon succession to the throne Aurangzeb adopted an intolerant and aggressive social and political policy towards non-Muslims which continued for the greater part of his reign. This policy was also reflected in his attitude towards the Sikh Gurus. Although the manner of support given by Har Rai to Dara Shikoh is not clear, it provided sufficient pretext for Aurangzeb to summon Har Rai in 1660 to court in order to give account for his alleged ties to Dara Shikoh. Sensing the Emperor's intentions, Har Rai sent his eldest son Ram Rai as his representative. However, Ram Rai proved too weak a personality to stand up to Aurangzeb who decided to keep him in Delhi on the assumption that Ram Rai was the heir apparent of Guru Har Rai and could be manipulated into bringing the Sikhs under his control. With this in mind the Emperor continued to provide patronage to Ram Rai, granting him revenue-free lands in the Himalayan district of Dehra Dun. When news of the manner of Ram Rai's capitulation reached Guru Har Rai, the latter disinherited Ram Rai, instead nominating his son Har Krishan as the eighth Guru. Guru Har Rai died in 1661 at the age of 31. The new Guru Har Krishan was only 5 years old when he was installed Guru.

Somewhat piqued at the investiture of Har Krishan and the disinheritance of Ram Rai, Aurangzeb summoned Guru Har Krishen to his court a few years later, apparently with the intention of re-engineering the Guruship in favour of Ram Rai. Guru Har Krishen was 9 years of age when he arrived in Delhi but before Aurangzeb could meet him he contracted smallpox and died in 1664. On his deathbed, in response to question of his successor, Guru Har Krishen is said to have uttered the words 'Baba Bakale', apparently indicating that the next Guru would be found at the village of Bakala and that succession should not pass either to Ram Rai, Dhir Mal or the *minas*, all of whom were now loudly pressing their claims.

Guru Tegh Bahadur (Nanak 9)

As noted earlier, Tegh Bahadur was the youngest son of Guru Hargobind. Named Tyag Mal at birth he spent much of his early life close to his father, accompanying him on his preaching tours and fighting alongside him in several important battles. His courage in battle prompted Guru Hargobind to rename him Tegh Bahadur (lit. Sword of Courage). The nature and premature deaths of his brothers Baba Gurditta and Atal Rai, both of whom had incurred the displeasure of Guru Hargobind for using occult powers (a practice strictly forbidden in Guru Nanak's lineage), left a deep impression in Tegh Bahadur's mind. For a significant period of his life he became absorbed in meditative contemplation even though he lived the life of a householder. He was married to Gujari. After his father's death Tegh Bahadur moved to Bakala where he lived for 20 years until his nomination as the ninth Nanak.[8]

The very fact that Tegh Bahadur accepted his nomination in 1664 as the ninth successor of Guru Nanak was an affront to Aurangzeb who had tried hard to settle the issue of succession in favour of Ram Rai. Although his tenure as ninth Guru began at Bakala, Tegh Bahadur found it necessary to shift his location three times in the first year, initially to Amritsar, then Kiratpur and then to the village of Makhowal in the Shivalik Hills. At each place he was opposed by rival claimants or by envious relatives. He built his residence on a hillside a short distance from Makhowal and called it Anandpur (or abode of bliss).

In 1665 Guru Tegh Bahadur left Anandpur with his wife Gujari to undertake a lengthy preaching tour of the eastern provinces of India by way of Delhi. Near the outskirts of Delhi, Ram Rai had him arrested on allegations of disturbing the peace. The Guru was soon released following an investigation and proceeded on his tour by way of Agra, Allahabad, Benares and Bodh Gaya, finally reaching Patna in 1666 where he left behind his wife who was heavily pregnant. The Guru travelled on to visit Sikh centres as far as Bengal and Assam. While in Bengal he received news of his son's birth on 26 December 1666. He returned to Patna almost three years later to rejoin his family. In this tour Guru Tegh Bahadur had travelled more extensively than any Guru except Nanak and managed to consolidate Sikh *sangats* in far flung places, restoring a measure of confidence in the community.

Meanwhile, the Emperor had been busy implementing a number of new hard-lined economic and social policies targeting non-Muslims. He destroyed important Hindu temples, stopped land grants to non-Muslims and reimposed *jazia* – a tax on non-Muslims a century after it had been abolished by Akbar.[9] Sikh temples were demolished throughout Punjab and offerings normally collected by *masands* were forwarded to the Mughal treasury. Aurangzeb also imprisoned his father, Shah Jahan and put greater emphasis on the Islamic character of the empire to gain favour with the Caliphate in Mecca.[10]

Guru Tegh Bahadur returned to Punjab in 1671 where the populace was panic struck with fear. To reassure the Sikhs and Hindus, Guru Tegh Bahadur went from village to village in Punjab for a period of two years countering the state's oppression with an emphasis on *dharam* (righteousness). By doing so, the Guru was publicly demonstrating a non-violent resistance to the Emperor's oppressive measures at a time when public opposition to the Mughal state was almost unthinkable. The Guru's overt missionary activities did not escape the notice of the state's intelligence networks which conveyed this to the Emperor. Aurangzeb duly ordered the Guru's arrest. But while these orders were circulating between the correct administrative units, the Guru managed to reach the safety of Anandpur where he continued to reside with his family for another four years.

In 1675 a deputation of Kashmiri Brahmins led by one Kirpa Ram came to see Guru Tegh Bahadur, complaining of systematic persecution and the wholesale conversion to Islam of non-Muslims in the Kashmir Valley. Knowing well the reputation of the house of Nanak for upholding the principle of *dharam* in the face of great odds, Kirpa Ram begged the Guru to somehow intervene. The Guru pondered the situation deeply, knowing only too well that any attempt to intervene on behalf of non-Muslims would constitute an affront to the Emperor's authority, an action punishable by certain death. But his reply to the Brahmins was emphatic. He reassured them, telling them to return to their homes and convey to the authorities that they would have no objection to converting to Islam but on the condition that Guru Tegh Bahadur should first be prevailed upon to embrace Islam. The Guru's stance was a clear and unambiguous challenge, not to the sovereignty of the Mughal state, but to the state's policy of not recognizing the sovereign existence of non-Muslims, their traditions and ways of life. Moreover his stance was supported by his 10-year-old son Gobind Rai, who clearly understood that his father was courting martyrdom as his great-grandfather Guru Arjan had done in 1606. The boy's courage convinced Guru Tegh Bahadur that he would have a worthy successor in the event of his death. Thus on 8 July 1675, the Guru nominated and installed Gobind Rai as successor. On 11 July, accompanied by a select group of Sikhs, Guru Tegh Bahadur left Anandpur to meet the Emperor and either plead the case of non-Muslims in India, or to suffer the consequences.

On his way to Delhi the Guru was arrested near Ropar and detained under orders from the Emperor. After three months the Guru was dispatched to Delhi in an iron cage. In Delhi he was incarcerated for eight days in the city jail under the supervision of Qazi Abdul Wahab Vora, and repeatedly asked to perform a miracle to prove his saintliness. The Guru steadfastly refused saying that it was tantamount to a display of egotism and contrary to Guru Nanak's principles. He was then asked to convert to Islam since he had 'failed' to produce a miracle. The Guru refused to embrace Islam. Having failed to coerce the Guru, his companions Mati Das and Sati Das were sawn alive in front of him, but even this failed to shake the Guru's resolve. Seeing that he was adamant he was ordered to be executed. Guru Tegh Bahadur was beheaded on 11 November 1675 in Chandni Chowk, a market square near the Red Fort. According to Sikh sources, the Guru's body was due to be quartered and exposed to the public as a warning to those who opposed the state. But a dust storm arose that evening and under the cover of darkness the body was recovered by a faithful Sikh, Lakhi Shah, who cremated it using his own house as a funeral pyre.[11] The Guru's severed head was also recovered by one Bhai Jaita and brought back to Anandpur for ceremonial cremation by his son, the tenth Guru, Gobind Rai.

The cruel execution was deeply felt by all those who had been touched by the Guru's life and teaching. But sorrow was underpinned by a strong defiance which was expressed by Guru Gobind Singh in his autobiographical work Bachittar Natak in the following way:

> To protect their right to wear the marks of their tradition
>   He made the ultimate sacrifice in the Age of Darkness.
> To protect the pious he spared no pains
>   Giving his head but uttering not a groan.
> For the protection of *dharam* he suffered martyrdom,
>   He gave his head but not his ideals.[12]

Guru Gobind Singh (Nanak 10)

Guru Gobind Rai, the tenth and last living successor of Guru Nanak, was born in the ancient city of Patna. After seven years in Patna he moved with his family to Anandpur, where at the age of 9 the young Guru was nominated as successor to his father and within months had to receive his severed head. Once Gobind Rai had been installed as the tenth Guru, his maternal uncle Kirpal took overall responsibility for the child's safety and upbringing. To prevent the young Guru becoming yet another target for the Emperor, the entire family was moved to the Himalayan mountain refuge of Paonta where Gobind Rai grew to manhood. He received a comprehensive education including training in languages such as Punjabi, Persian, Sanskrit and Braj, in addition to a full training in martial arts. By his late teens he was able to display many different talents. Apart from being a prolific poet in his own right, he was a patron of arts, a charismatic leader of the Sikh community and a skilled and courageous military commander.

Like the sixth Guru before him, Guru Gobind Rai especially welcomed offerings of arms and horses from his Sikhs. Able-bodied men were encouraged to join the ranks of his growing militia. As annual visits by Sikhs from distant places swelled his following, Paonta had begun to take on the semblance of a small town with a strong armed presence. In time, the growing strength and egalitarian constituency of the young Guru's army began to alarm some of the hill Rajas who governed neighbouring principalities such as Bilaspur, Sirmur and Garhwal.[13] Raja Bhim Chand of Bilaspur initially tried to persuade the Guru to recognize him as his overlord. These attempts proved futile, however, and as border tensions escalated, Bhim Chand persuaded neighbouring hill chiefs to press the Guru to leave the Shivalik Hills altogether. When threats failed they resorted to war. The result was a battle that took place at Bhangani in 1686, some distance from Anandpur. Although the Guru's forces were heavily outnumbered he managed to inflict a defeat on the hill chiefs.[14]

The Guru's victory at Bhangani was a clear signal that the Sikhs were a force to be reckoned with, and it gave the Guru sufficient confidence to return to Anandpur, which he proceeded to fortify and develop as a town. Less than a year later, Bhim Chand had reversed his position and petitioned the Guru for help against the Mughal Governor who had been dispatched to collect revenue owed to the state. Guru Gobind Singh thus fought another battle at Nadaun in 1687, but this time on the side of the hill chiefs and against the Mughal forces.[15] Although Nadaun was a success for the combined forces of the Guru and the hill chiefs, the latter reversed their stand once again and decided to settle terms with the Emperor after all. By now the Guru was well aware that the hill chiefs could not be trusted. He therefore continued to fortify the area by building a chain of fortresses around Anandpur, including Keshgarh, Lohgarh, Fategarh and Anandgarh.

For the next 12 years (1687–99) the Guru was left in relative peace by the hill rajas and the Mughal authorities, allowing him to expand his activities at Anandpur. During this time he turned Anandpur into a thriving cultural and intellectual centre that attracted poets, musicians, scholars and experienced soldiers. The Guru was able to compose some of his key literary works such as *Jaap*, *Akal Ustat* and *Gian Parbodh*. He was also able to marry and had four sons, two from his first wife Mata Jito who bore him two sons, Ajit and Jujhar, before her early death, and two sons from Mata Sundari his second wife, named Fateh and Zorawar. The Guru had a daily routine that consisted of holding court, singing and composing hymns, exercises and administrative duties.

More importantly, these 12 years provided the Guru with a chance to reflect deeply on the present condition of the Panth, its future and his own role as Guru. How was he to deal with the problems of disunity, decadence and dissension within the community? By this time, the *masands* had become increasingly independent, corrupt and unreliable, often entering into alliance with state forces when it suited them and withholding or misusing offerings. Schizmatic groups such as the Minas, Dhirmalyas and Hindalis continued to erode the Guru's support base and to distort Guru Nanak's message. And there was continued interference and persecution by the state which had tried its best to control the destiny of the Sikhs. The main problem, which the Guru clearly recognized, as did his predecessors, was that the house of Nanak (with its sovereign concept of *shabad-guru*) needed a recognizable form of authority, a clear self-understanding and the ability to resist encroachment on the sovereignty of this teaching. Currently, the temporal and spiritual nature of that authority resided in the living persona of the Guru and in the Adi Granth text. With sons to succeed him, if nominated, this state of affairs would continue. But it would not solve the problem. Others would continue to confuse the community's self-understanding by throwing up rival gurus and fake texts. Perhaps, then, the problem resided in the nature of *living* Guruship itself? Indeed, if as Guru Nanak had taught, the source of sovereignty and authority was the impersonal principle of *satguru* = word = *shabad-guru*, then perhaps it was time to abolish the line of personal succession? But to replace it with what? And how would the concept of *miri–piri* be embodied in the absence of a living Guru?

That these questions occupied the Guru's thoughts during these years is evident from a number of sources including his *Bachitar Natak*, and the *hukamnamas* (letters of authority) he sent to various *sangats* across Northern India.[16] In *Bachitar Natak*, the Guru presents himself as fulfilling Guru Nanak's mission to uphold the virtue of *dharam* (or righteous action). In his own time that mission entailed resistance through the use of force, where necessary, against those who threatened the existence of Nanak's teaching and his community. The *hukamnamas* reveal that in the years leading up to 1699 the Guru asked his followers to congregate each year at special occasions and especially on the occasion of Baisakhi. They were asked to make a special effort to gather at Anandpur for the Baisakhi festival of 1699. It would appear that Guru Gobind Rai had formulated a plan for the future organization of the Panth and wished to put his plan into operation on the Baisakhi of 1699.

Creation of the Khalsa[17]

According to traditional Sikh sources[18] Guru Gobind Singh fulfilled Guru Nanak's mission through the creation of the Khalsa on Baisakhi day of 1699, an event that has become central to the Sikh psyche. He did this by staging a dramatic spectacle that was heavily layered with mystical and political resonances. The spectacle itself was staged as a three-part drama which Sikh story tellers and poets have divided into three separate acts (see Figures 2.1 to 2.3), just as if it were a theatre performance. The three scenes of the drama are as follows: *Scene 1:* The willing sacrifice; *Scene 2:* Initiation of the double-edged sword; *Scene 3:* Immolation of the God-King.

FIGURE 2.1 *The willing sacrifice.*

Scene 1: The willing sacrifice

In accordance with the Guru's *hukamnamas*, a large crowd had
gathered at Anandpur on the evening of 30 March 1699. There
was excitement in the air and a mood of expectancy as a tent had
been erected on a dais overlooking the crowd for some unknown
purpose. The Guru himself had been in a pensive mood for some

days prior to the event. When the Guru came out of the tent, sword in hand, he asked if there was one among them who was willing to sacrifice his or her head for the Guru. A strange hush fell on the crowd. No one answered the call. The Guru repeated his call several times until at last, one Daya Ram, a trader from Lahore, stepped forward and offered his head. The Guru grabbed him by the arm, took him into the tent and a loud thud was heard. Shortly the Guru came out of the tent, his sword dripping with blood. To the dismay of the congregation he called for a second willing victim. This process was repeated until five Sikhs had offered their heads. The other four willing victims were Dharam Das, a farmer from near Delhi, Mokham Chand a washerman from Dwarka, Himmat Rai a cook from Jagganathpuri, and Sahib Chand a barber from Bidar. After a short time the Guru came out of the tent with the five willing victims all dressed in blue and saffron robes. They were introduced to the *sangat* as the Guru's five beloved ones (or Panj Piare) and as the nucleus of a new sovereign order called Khalsa.

Scene 2: Initiation of the double-edged sword

FIGURE 2.2 Khande-ka-Pahul *initiation showing Mata sahib Kaur adding sugar crystals to the* amrit.

In the second part of this strange drama the Guru proceeded to initiate the five beloved ones into the new order of the Khalsa by a new rite called *khande-ka-pahul*, replacing the older method of initiation called *charan pahul*. The Guru placed water sweetened with sugar crystals into an iron vessel and stirred it with a double-edged sword while reciting the hymns *Japji*, *Jaap*, *Anand*, *Swayai* and *Chaupai*. The resulting nectar, called *amrit* (lit. the elixir of life–death) was then administered to the five neophytes. As it was sprinkled in their eyes and hair each was asked to repeat:

> *waheguru ji ka khalsa, waheguru ji ki fateh*
> The Khalsa belongs to the true Guru (*waheguru*), to the true Guru belongs the victory.

The Guru took the iron vessel in turn to the initiates asking each to take a drink of the *amrit* from the same vessel, signifying a dissolution of all social boundaries between them, and their rebirth into a new form of association. To seal this part of the ceremony the Guru told them that from then on they were to break with their family names and adopt a new name: Singh for men (meaning lion), and Kaur for women (meaning princess). Finally they were given a new code of conduct. They were to carry on their body five *kakar* or five Ks[19]: (i) *kesh*: or long uncut hair signifying one's connection and affirmation of the law of nature; (ii) *kanga*: a comb to keep the hair clean and intact, also signifying an affirmation of the householder's life and a rejection of asceticism; (iii) *kirpan*: a dagger or short-sword signifying the right to bear arms as well as a strict moral duty to protect life – not only one's own life but even more importantly the lives of others who cannot protect themselves; (iv) *kara*: an iron wrist-ring or bracelet whose circle serves as a reminder of one's mortality, that one is bound to the circle of life and death, that one's actions are ultimately answerable to the true Guru to whom one is constantly bound, and that if one is to exercise force it must be done so with moral restraint; (v) *kacch*: or short breeches signifying the need for sexual restraint whether one is a householder or whether one is in the position to exercise power. These five Ks were to be worn as bodily signifiers marking a Khalsa as different from others, one who could not hide behind others in difficult times, as a householder who lived by a certain discipline. In addition to the five Ks they were given a set of moral injunctions to adhere to.

To all intents and purposes the initiation ceremony seemed to be complete. For through this new ceremony the neophytes had severed all allegiance to previous caste occupations (*krit nas*), to family ties (*kul nas*) and to previous creeds (*dharam nas*), in addition to rituals not sanctioned by the Sikh way of life. But the drama was not over! A strange twist was yet to come.

Scene 3: Immolation of the God-King

FIGURE 2.3 *Immolation of the God-King.*

Immediately after initiating the *Panj Piare* or five beloved ones, Guru Gobind Rai stunned the congregation once more. He dropped to his knees in front of the *Panj Piare* and begged them to initiate him into the Khalsa. At first the Panj Piare were taken aback and refused, saying that he was the Guru and they were his Sikhs. How could a disciple initiate the master? But when the Guru pleaded with them to initiate him, they relented and administered the *amrit* to Gobind Rai in exactly the same way. By receiving *amrit* the Guru also became a *khalsa* and relinquished his caste and kinship name (Rai/Sodhi) and became Guru Gobind Singh. Although this seemed like a revolutionary act on behalf of the Guru, it slowly dawned on the congregation that with this final act the Guru had not really done anything new. The Sikh community had witnessed this act before – nine times as a matter of fact! Guru Nanak himself had performed the same act by becoming the disciple of Guru Angad, who in turn went from being Nanak's disciple to Nanak's Guru. And so on with the other Gurus until this moment. From this moment on the principle was established that the five Khalsa Sikhs could represent the entire community and initiate other Sikhs into the order of the Khalsa.

The inauguartion of the Khalsa caused an immediate stir within the Sikh community. Although many thousands of Sikhs embraced the new order, many others expressed dissent. This was especially the case with many Khatris, some of whom remained aloof from the Khalsa professing that while they had followed Guru Nanak and the other Gurus, the new Khalsa order represented a *destructive violence* that broke with the main signifiers of the ancient Brahmanical social order based on the Veda, Shastras and the *varnashramdharma*. It seems that while they had been willing to pay lip service to the ideal of a casteless society, they could not stomach any physical mixing with lower caste peasants. For Khatris such mixing violated the divine foundations underpinning their social status and sense of self. Nor could they accept Guru Gobind Singh's injunction for the Khalsa to bear arms.

From the standpoint of the downtrodden castes, however, the Guru's inauguration of the Khalsa represented a *creative violence* – like a lightning storm that fertilizes the dead soil of the social order, enabling them to flourish in the same soil as the upper castes. To many others, including official functionaries of the Mughal state, since entry into the Khalsa made it obligatory for Sikhs to bear arms, it suggested that the Guru intended to raise an army modelled on the figure of the warrior-saint (*sant-sipahi*) combining devotional self-surrender (*bhakti*) with the ability to use force and wield power (*shakti*), thereby further embedding the ethos of *miri–piri* that had become explicit with Guru Hargobind. From 1699 until the present day, although the concept of the warrior-saint has become more or less associated with the order of the Khalsa, the actual relationship between violence and spirituality, *bhakti* and *shakti*, *miri* and *piri*, violence and sovereignty, has been deeply misunderstood. Indeed the role of violence itself has been largely stereotyped as the mere negation of saintliness or mysticism. Before returning to our historical narrative, it will therefore be helpful for us to reassess the role of violence in the creation of the Khalsa and to understand its significance in earlier and later Sikh history.

Excursus 2: The interplay of violence and the sacred in the Khalsa narrative

How do we assess this three-part drama which gives birth to the order of the Khalsa? Does it simply fulfil the need for a more concrete identity, one that had been merely implicit in early Sikh tradition? By externalizing itself with a concrete form, with its emphasis on the bearing of arms, and its penchant for political resistance, does the creation of the Khalsa not represent a deviation or violation of the sacred, that is, a deviation from the seemingly more peaceful path of the earlier Gurus? Does the Khalsa's claim to sovereignty not interfere with the sovereignty of the State (Mughal or otherwise)?

Whichever way we look at it, the creation and meaning of the Khalsa cannot be conceptualized without understanding the relationship between violence and the sacred, thereby complicating the above questions. To do this, let me return to the central theme(s) of the drama which is, in effect, sacrifice.

In Scenes 1 and 2 the Guru demands a sacrifice and therefore a willing victim: 'I want a head'. In this demand-imperative-command there is an implicit violence as a thirst for life. We can represent this as Violence-1. The demand for sacrifice is followed by a decision by the Sikh to *risk* what is most precious to him or her, namely, one's life. This decision is the source of ethical responsibility, where responsibility means to respond to the call of death willingly, to give up what is seemingly one's own-most. But the sacrificial demand also happens at another level, namely, where the Sikh is asked to sacrifice his/her social identity (ego). In any case, it is all a risk. There is madness here, a suspension of customary laws, a suspension of the safety of the traditional caste framework. We can designate this *violence towards the self* as Violence-2. But here the Guru also returns their lives by: (i) presenting their bodies to the *sangat* and (ii) giving them a new, unfettered identity – a new community.

Now this sacrificial scene can be usefully compared to other sacrificial scenes, notably the Akedah (Genesis: 22), the binding of Isaac by Abraham, which is the Biblical lesson on the meaning of sacrifice. But the real difference is in the Khalsa scene 3 where the Guru (God's representative), the giver of *amrit*, now reverses the scene of sacrifice and the usual meaning of sacrifice as the gift to the sacred divine.

If we agree that the Guru was carrying out a performative, then the reversal of the *amrit* ceremony can be seen as an exercise in political theology. On the one hand it can be seen as a move that is analogous to the immolation of the God-King in solar mythology. Thus the fact that the Guru became a disciple (*chela*) and begged to be initiated as an ordinary member of the Khalsa, his merger with the rank of the ordinary person, is an exercise not simply in humility, but the enactment of a certain kind of democracy. That is, the Guru's giving power (*kratos*) to the common people (*demos*) by emptying his divinity/kingship, by negating his transcendental status, or transcendence in general. This donation of power to the common people through willing sacrifice of the divine (death of God) can be seen as a violence committed *by the sacred to its own sacredness* (its divinity), such that it *chooses not to be sacred*; it actively *chooses to lose its divinity*. This would be a third violence, Violence-3, where the sacred is in effect manifested as **self-loss**. One could say that the sacred manifests its essence only in emptying itself as the sacred is enacted in the world. Where, then, does authority now lie? Clearly what the Guru has done is to authorize the Khalsa through his own immolation and subsequent rebirth through initiation by the Khalsa. The Khalsa now becomes the author of the Amrit ceremony. It is sovereign and empowered as a political force. It needs no higher authority since that highest authority has bequeathed to it, its own essence; and that essence is not an ontological fullness but *self-loss*, or, to adopt the term that was introduced in Chapter One, *ego-loss*.

If we look at this scenario more closely, it is clear that there are three levels of violence operating in this democratization of the *Sikh Panth*. The first violence comes into play during scene 1. It is the Guru's demand for his Sikh to freely give up what one owns most of all, that is one's own life. The second violence, enacted in Scenes 2 and 3, comprises the Guru's demand that the Sikhs now give up their (social) ego, that is attachments to tradition, family etc. through caste and *biradari*. But Violence-1 and Violence-2 are countered or equalled by the Guru's giving back the Sikhs' physical bodies and his gift of a new identity (Khalsa). The first two forms of violence balance themselves out and maintain an economy of violence. The third form of violence [Violence-3], however, constitutes an excessive violence where the Guru sacrifices his transcendence/authority and therefore does violence to the very order of sacredness, and empowers the Khalsa. Thus Violence-3 (the violence of sacred death = renunciation or ego-loss) exceeds the first two forms of violence and shatters any possible economy by making the creation of the Khalsa a non-economic transaction. This non-economy that comes from the excessiveness of the divine (as becoming Other than itself, becoming secular/worldly of the divine) is what founds the democratic nature of the Khalsa, that is, its ability to govern itself. Guru Gobind Singh's creation of Khalsa is grounded in the giving of a gift without return which is the only economy of sacrifice (of self loss).

We can now return to what is perhaps the central question concerning the Khalsa: was it really a transformation of the earlier Panth of Guru Nanak? The answer has to be both yes and no! Clearly the actors and the circumstances are different from the time of Guru Nanak. The Panth is certainly given a different form which it did not possess at the time of the early Sikh Gurus. But the underlying philosophy and central emphasis remains pretty much the same. The sacrificial economy that gives rise to the Khalsa is qualitatively the same sacrificial economy that Guru Nanak enacted on the one hand through his sovereign experience of absolute self-surrender or ego-loss while remaining in the world, and on the other hand, in transferring Guruship to Angad. That is, inorder to transfer Guruship to Angad, Nanak had to become Angad's disciple, and in order to become his disciple he had to become a Sikh and absolutely surrender his 'divinity' to the *satguru*. This involved qualitatively the same economy of violence to the self (ego-loss) that created the Khalsa. So the question of 'transformation' is actually a misleading one. Rather, if the meaning of violence itself is centred around ego-loss, self-sacrifice, we should ask whether Guru Nanak was in any way less 'violent' than Guru Gobind Singh? If the true meaning of violence is first and foremost a struggle with one-self, a struggle with one's ego, then violence is inseparable from mysticism or spirituality.

So what exactly is violence? Is it a violation of the public realm, a violation of the sphere of politics, due to the return of the sacred or religious, as we are led to believe by the modern secular state?[20] Or is there a more primary meaning of violence, in the sense of an act committed by the sacred against the (self of) the sacred? Is such violence not the essence of mysticism as self-loss? Is violence not therefore written into the very nature of the sacred as democratic change – the ability of the common people to make change happen by making and remaking their own laws? The Khalsa is precisely such an entity: an entity capable of making and remaking its own laws? An entity that derives its right to wield power and govern itself from Guru Nanak's sovereign experience. But here is the catch: the Khalsa's access to power remains legitimate only if it remains true to Guru Nanak's and Guru Gobind Singh's sovereign principle: the constant need to undermine the self (ego), the remembrance of absolute self-surrender. Once it forgets this paradoxical principle it self-destructs. As we shall see, this happened time and again in the history of the Panth after the death of Guru Gobind Singh.

Guru Gobind Singh's last years[21]

After 1699 greater numbers of Sikhs began to come to Anandpur and many more took Khalsa initiation. The increasing size of the Guru's army did not escape the notice of the hill chiefs and the Guru was soon thrust into a prolonged war. Battles were fought at Nirmoh (1701) and Basoli (1702).[22] Anandpur was besieged several times. Initially the Guru's army managed to repulse the invaders but the hill rajas did not give up, ultimately petitioning the Emperor Aurangzeb for assistance. The combined forces of the Mughal army and the hill rajas were mobilized against the Guru and Anandpur was again besieged in 1703. The siege lasted until 1704 during which time the Sikhs had to endure considerable hardship, almost reaching the point of starvation. In the end the Guru was forced to make a formal truce which required him to leave Anandpur under promises of safe conduct. The truce carried the seal of the Emperor himself.

Guru Gobind Singh left Anandpur towards the end of 1704 with his family and some of his trusted soldiers. However, while crossing the flooded river Sirsa near the town of Ropar he was attacked by imperial troops. In the commotion that followed he was separated from his wife, mother and two youngest children. After crossing the river the Guru was again surrounded and attacked near the village of Chamkaur leaving him no choice but to face his attackers with his few remaining soldiers.[23] All of his soldiers and his two eldest sons Ajit Singh and Jujhar Singh were killed while making a diversion for the Guru to escape. The Guru barely managed to escape under cover of darkness. After wandering in jungle territory for days barefoot and with nothing to eat, he reached Bhatinda where he was able to regroup with the remnants of the Khalsa army. It was here that the Guru came to learn the fate of his mother, wife and two youngest sons, Fateh Singh and Zorawar Singh who had fallen into Wazir Khan's hands during the Sirsa crossing. The two boys, then aged 7 and 9 were both executed by being bricked alive and the Guru's mother Mata Gujari herself died in custody. Though he remained calm and stoic in the face of such personal tragedies, the news motivated Guru Gobind Singh to write a spirited letter of defiance (*Zafarnama*, the Epistle of Victory) to Aurangzeb, indicting the Emperor and his officials with moral corruption and justifying his own resistive stance.

The Guru's stay in Bhatinda was cut short as he was again attacked by a large Mughal force led by Wazir Khan forcing a battle that took place near the village of Khidrana. The brunt of the Mughal attack was borne by 40 men of the Majha district who had earlier deserted the Guru during the siege of Anandpur. The village of Khidrana was later renamed Muktsar to honour the 40 men who had given their lives. From Muktsar the Guru moved *incognito* from placed to place, until he reached Talwandi Sabo in the Punjabi heartland where the surrounding jungles provided some relative safety for the Guru. The nine months that the Guru resided here provided him with a much needed respite, and because of this Talwandi was later renamed Damdama Sahib (lit. the place of respite). The people from the surrounding areas were loyal to the Guru's cause allowing him to re-establish some semblance of a court and reorganize his forces with new recruits. It was at Damdama that the Guru produced from memory a new version of the Adi Granth complete with his father's hymns and two short couplets of his own.[24]

Meanwhile the Guru's letter had reached Aurangzeb and produced the required effect. Realizing his mistakes and the treachery of his officials in their treatment of the Guru, Aurangzeb sent orders to the Lahore governor Munim Khan to conciliate with the Guru and set up a meeting in Deccan where he was busy trying to subdue the Mahrattas. The Guru set out to meet Aurangzeb with the idea of seeking redress against Wazir Khan's excesses, but on his way to Deccan he learned that Aurangzeb had died in February 1707 and was succeeded by his son Prince Muazzam, who took the title Bahadur Shah. The Guru met Bahadur Shah in August 1707. The meeting was a cordial one, raising hopes that the issue of Wazir Khan could be settled. But for almost a year the Emperor dithered and gave no firm reply one way or another partly because of the weakened political position of the Mughal empire. So when Bahadur Shah left Agra for Deccan, the Guru and his army remained close to the imperial camp in the hope of getting a decision.

By the early summer of 1708, as the Guru had still not received any firm reply from the Emperor, he decided to take a different course and parted company with Bahadur Shah and proceeded towards the city of Nander. The Guru set up his camp at Nander which at the time was bustling with prominent Hindu sects and he began to preach the message of Guru Nanak. On one occasion there was an armed conflict between the followers of a prominent Bairagi ascetic named Madho Das (who was rumoured to possess occult powers) and members of the Guru's own Khalsa militia. The Bairagi's disciples were worsted in this altercation and his own encounter with the Guru resulted in his submission to Guru Gobind Singh's authority, an act which endeared him to the Guru and resulted in his being renamed as Banda.[25]

During these months in Nander, the Guru's regular sermons began to attract many people. Among these was an Afghan named Jamshed Khan who had been hired by Wazir Khan to assassinate the Guru. In early October 1708, the assassin found the right opportunity when Guru Gobind Singh had retired to his apartment after conducting an evening service. Jamshed Khan attacked and badly wounded the Guru. The stab wounds were dressed but the Guru realized that he had been mortally wounded. Summoning his closest Sikhs around him he declared the line of living Gurus to be closed. Then, taking a coconut and 5 *paisa* he prostrated himself before the Adi Granth declared that it was now to be regarded as the Guru of the Sikhs – the Guru Granth Sahib. Final authority was now jointly conferred on the text (Guru Granth) and the institution of the Khalsa (Guru Panth). These twin institutions – Guru Granth and Guru Panth – were invested with sovereign authority. This was not so much a break with convention as a logical development from Guru Nanak's decision to nominate a disciple as Guru during his lifetime. In the last days of his life the Guru gave some final instructions to his Sikhs. These included the deputization of Banda Bahadur to travel to Punjab and raise an army to bring Wazir Khan to justice. On 18 October 1708 Guru Gobind Singh breathed his last and died at the age of 42.

The post-Guru period

Banda Bahadur

Shortly after Guru Gobind Singh's death in 1708 Banda left for Punjab accompanied by some of the Guru's old followers. He carried with him *hukamnamas* issued by the Guru exhorting the Sikhs to support him. For almost a year Banda moved slowly from town to town collecting soldiers and materials for a military campaign.[26] In November 1709 he began attacking the towns of Samana, Sirhind, Hissar and Saharanpur, all of which were in some way connected to the deaths of the Sikh Gurus or the sons of Guru Gobind Singh. Wazir Khan was caught and put to death along with many others. By 1710 Banda had conquered large parts of the Punjab. These uprisings were considered serious enough to warrant Bahadur Shah's personal involvement in subduing them. In 1711 Banda occupied the imperial fort of Mukhlispur and renamed it Lohgarh. It is here that he struck a new coin in the name of Guru Gobind Singh and Guru Nanak to formally declare the beginning of sovereign Sikh rule. One of the coins struck by Banda bears the following Persian inscription:

Sikka zadd bar har do alam, tegh-i Nanak wahib ast,
Fateh-i Gobind, sha-i shahan, fazl-i sachcha sahib ast.[27]

The coin's inscription refers to the 'sword of Nanak' as the bestower and source of all power. Another seal used by Banda in a *hukam-nama* of 1710 carries the inscription:

> *Deg-o-tegh-o fateh-o nusrat bidirang,*
> *Yaft az Nanak Guru Gobind Singh.*[28]

Again Nanak (through the mediation of Gobind Singh) is the source and bestower of *degh* (the cooking pot that feeds the people), *tegh* (the sword that protects them) and *fateh* (the victory). In effect Banda was exercising political power on behalf of the Guru and the Khalsa.

For another four years Banda continued to evade the Mughals until Farrukh Siyar succeeded Bahadur Shah as Emperor in February 1713. Farrukh Siyyar ordered the wholesale extermination of the Sikhs, appointing Abdus Samad Khan as governor of Lahore. Abdus Samad Khan made life much more difficult for Banda Bahadur who nevertheless continued to evade capture. But by 1714 serious differences had arisen within the Sikh camp, owing partly to excesses committed by Banda's troops during their campaign of retribution against the Mughals, and partly to Banda's deviation from key principles of the Khalsa code of conduct. This in turn led to the formation of two different Khalsa factions – the Bandai Khalsa, who were loyal to Banda, versus the Tat Khalsa led by close associates of the tenth Guru and his wife Mata Sundari who remained loyal to the original Khalsa principles. The split within the Khalsa ranks seriously impeded Banda's ability to counter the Mughal armies and he was eventually besieged, captured and taken to Delhi where he was executed along with his son and followers.

The Misl period and the rise and fall of the Sikh kingdom

The three decades following the execution of Banda Bahadur are often regarded as the grimmest in Sikh history as the Mughal authorities redoubled their efforts to exterminate the Khalsa. Abdus Samad Khan was succeeded in 1726 by his son Zakaria Khan, who in turn was succeeded by his son Yahya Khan in 1745, which itself was an indicator that the Mughal empire was loosening

its grip and that the provinces were becoming politically autonomous. Despite being hunted as outlaws and living in the jungle
areas, the Khalsa forces also sensed the shifting balance of power
and continued to live a guerilla existence, roving the countryside
in small bands, plundering and harassing the authorities and their
supporters whenever they got the chance. In this period Amritsar
emerged as a rallying centre for the Tat Khalsa especially during the
Baisakhi and Diwali festivals. Although they suffered some major
losses,[29] particularly to the invading armies of Afghan invaders such
as Nadir Shah and Ahmed Shah Abdali, they were able to survive
and actually grow in numbers towards the middle of the eighteenth
century. By 1765 the leaders of the Khalsa bands such as Jassa Singh
Ahluwalia were confident enough to declare sovereignty by striking
a coin in Lahore after occupying it.[30] The small bands of the Tat
Khalsa had given way to new institutions that helped them occupy
territories and establish a firmer footing in Punjab. These institutions were political and administrative in nature. They included
the *rakhi*, the *misl*, the *Dal Khalsa* and the *gurumata*.[31] Thus the
Tat Khalsa provided protection (*rakhi*) for peasant farmers against
invaders, often for a small cut of their produce. The *misls* were
independent confederacies or small armies led by a particular chief,
with ties of kinship as the basis for allegiance. *Misls* often combined
forces to fight a more powerful enemy. At other times they fought
each other. Combinations of larger *misls* came to be known as *Dal
Khalsa* which unified under the command of a chosen leader for a
particular purpose. At certain times it was necessary for all *misls* to
come together in order to discuss matters of common interest and
form a general consensus. Such meetings were open to all Khalsa
Sikhs and often resulted in a unanimous democratic resolution
called *gurumata* (lit. the Guru's resolution). The *gurumata* was usually organized on the occasion of Baisakhi or Diwali at Amritsar
and was considered to be morally binding on all Sikhs since it was
seen as an application of the Guru Granth-Guru Panth or *miri–piri*
doctrine. There were 12 *misls* in all of which the main ones were
the Ahluwalia *misl* (led by Jassa Singh Ahluwalia), the Sukerchakia
misl (led by Charat Singh and later by his son Ranjit Singh), the
Bhangi *misl* (led by Hari Singh Bhangi), the Kanyhia *misl* and the
Ramgarhia *misl* (led by Jassa Singh Ramgarhia).[32]

In the last decades of the eighteenth century the numbers of
Khalsa had increased considerably but they did not constitute the

entire Sikh Panth. Many had not taken *khande-ka-pahul* but still regarded themselves as Sikh. Even so the Khalsa exerted dominance not merely in terms of numbers, but because of their robust central doctrines: unity of Guruship from Nanak to Gobind Singh, the end of personal Guruship after Guru Gobind Singh and the sovereign principle of Guru Granth–Guru Panth. Central to this doctrine was the idea that ultimate authority and sovereignty lay in *shabad-guru* (the Word as Guru) and that this was the means for achieving perfection of consciousness (*gurmukh*) and just as importantly, that this path was open and available to all irrespective of one's social status.

Nevertheless, despite the fact that the *misls* operated a relatively open system of governance, they could not avoid a level of social stratification derived from the wider North Indian social framework of which they were still a part. The majority of Sikhs who resisted taking *khande-ka-pahul* were descendents of the Gurus and their early disciples who were mainly from the Khatri caste, or Udasi Sikhs descended from the followers of Sri Chand and continued their ascetic traditions. By the mid-to-late eighteenth century, these Sikhs came to be regarded in high esteem by leaders of the *misls* who extended patronage to them. This patronage combined with the fact that they were mainly from the Khatri caste, served to increase their prestige in the Sikh social order. Many were given jobs as custodians of the historical and other Gurdwaras and they were able to hire *granthis*, *ragis* and *bhais* to take care of the day-to-day running of the Gurdwaras. Needless to say, the people they hired were expected to pay due diligence to their social standing.

The legendary unity of the Khalsa survived only as long as they were confronted with a tangible enemy. With the Afghan invaders gone and the Mughal power all but destroyed, the *misls* began to fight each other for control of territory. The eventual winner of this internecine conflict was the Sukerchakia *misl* led by its young and ambitious leader Ranjit Singh. Within a short period of time Ranjit Singh had absorbed all the main *misls* into a new Sikh kingdom with Lahore as his capital. To this remarkable achievement he later added the territories of Multan, Kashmir and Peshawar, earning him the title of supreme ruler, or Maharaja of Punjab.[33]

Ranjit Singh ruled for four decades (1799–1839). During this time Punjab entered a period of stability and prosperity. Many Sikhs remember this as a glorious era of Sikh history when they finally achieved a kingdom they could call their own. Even though they were vastly outnumbered by Muslims and Hindus, Sikhs of the Khalsa were able to leave their mark on the history of North India. Others, however, point to the fact that apart from personal conquest Ranjit Singh did little to further the cause of the Khalsa or make any lasting innovations in regard to Sikh polity. Indeed, although he referred to his system of governance as Sarkar Khalsa, it could be said that his rule was ultimately detrimental to the actual spirit of the Khalsa in so far as he abolished the *gurumata* system, replacing it with an autocratic rule based around himself as the monarch, thereby hastening a reversion to social practices that the Sikh Gurus had long since abolished. Ranjit Singh had acquired for the Sikhs a territorial sovereignty with its attendant material benefits for some, but at the cost of the concept of sovereignty evolved by the Sikh Gurus.

These shortcomings surfaced soon after his death in 1839 as his court descended into chaos and confusion sparked partly by struggles for succession between his heirs, and partly by the encroachment of the British with whom the Sikhs fought two wars (1845–6 and 1848–9). Within a decade of Ranjit Singh's death his kingdom was annexed by the British who had already established their political control over the rest of the Indian subcontinent. The glory of Ranjit Singh's occupation of Lahore in 1799 was replaced by the inglorious surrender of the Khalsa army to the British in 1849. With this surrender the Sikhs had entered painfully and reluctantly into a new era, the era of modernity and European colonialism.

CHAPTER THREE

Modernity and Colonialism

From the time of Guru Nanak until the early decades of the nineteenth century, the Sikh life-world had developed within a broadly North Indian context. While the Sikh Gurus had fostered an aura of sovereignty for their life-world, its mode of self-reference and self-understanding was nevertheless continuous with the interpretative framework common to North Indian culture. But a mere half century under British rule, beginning in the mid-nineteenth century, transformed the very complexion of the Sikh Panth more quickly and more radically than at any time in its history. Between the 1880s and the 1920s it is possible to witness the birth of new modes of identification such as 'Sikh religion', Sikh*ism*, Sikh *quam* or nation. How did these new forms of association differ from previous ones? What is it about the encounter with the West, specifically in the form of British imperialism, that induced such a transformation and continues to affect the way Sikhs think about themselves and others?

In this chapter, we shall look at some of the major factors in the transformation of *Sikhi* into modern Sikh consciousness, the important movement of social and intellectual reform that resulted from this encounter and chart some of the key historical events that not only impacted the Sikh community in the twentieth century but also characterized the very nature of *Sikhi's* emergence into the modern world. These events include, for example, the construction of Sikhs as a 'religion' in European colonial accounts, the emergence of a modernizing reform movement (the Singh Sabha), the creation of a Sikh political party (the Akali Dal), Sikh flirtations with secularism, the Gurdwara reform movement, partition of India, the migration of Sikhs outside India and the bid for a separate Sikh state resulting in conflict with the Indian state in the late twentieth century. Undergirding these events is a peculiarly modern interpretative framework whereby Sikhs came to see themselves and their life-world as essentially religious. This new framework is nothing more than a central component of modern Western ideology that presupposes an opposition between religion and the secular. As scholars of South Asia have begun to recognize, one of the main reasons why Sikhs and other South Asians began to identify themselves with the signifier 'religion' can be attributed to the fact that they had internalized Anglophone concepts in the process of colonization. Sikhs, as with other Indians, began to 'make religion' where this entity had not existed before in the native lexicons.[1]

Early colonial encounters

The early European accounts of the Sikhs can be divided into two distinct strands, Orientalist and Anglicist.[2] These two strands paint somewhat opposing portraits of the Sikhs and their system in relation to the 'Hindoos', the term given to other non-Muslims in India, who were regarded by Europeans as polytheists, pantheists or simply heathens. The earlier strand can be regarded as 'Orientalist' and depicts Sikhs as deists, a term which served to differentiate them from the 'Hindoos'. The later Anglicist strand refuted the Orientalist accounts and tried to present the Sikhs as 'mere Hindoos'. What is interesting about these two strands is that it reflects important 'fault lines' running through European culture at the time.[3] These 'fault lines' were themselves indicators of political and intellectual battles between European intellectuals and policy makers over the meaning of concepts such as 'freedom', 'religion' and 'secular' and whether (or how) such concepts could be applied to non-Western cultures.

Orientalist depictions of the Sikhs include short sketches by travel writers such as Henri Polier (1783), George Forster (1785) and James Browne (1785), and a longer essay by the noted Indologist Charles Wilkins (1788).[4] These accounts were primarily ethnographic in nature and commissioned either by Indian nobles or by Warren Hastings, then director of the East India Company. Wilkins speaks of the relative independence of the Sikhs, that their manners and customs were 'very unlike the other inhabitants of Hindostan', and that their rise to power during the last decades of the eighteenth century was due to the 'democratic elements in Sikh society', an observation that attests to the prevalence of the Khalsa form in the *misls*. Charles Wilkins presented the 'Seeks' as a third distinct community in North India, a 'sect of people who are distinguished from the worshippers of Brahm and the followers of Mahommed by the appellation Seek'.[5]

The next opportunity for the British to closely observe the Sikhs fell to Col. John Malcolm in the first decade of the nineteenth century, at a time when they had become firmly established as a military power under Maharaja Ranjit Singh. Funded by the East India Company, Malcolm's reconnaissance mission for them in the Punjab was published in 1812 as a short monograph 'Sketch of the Sikhs'.[6] For three decades it provided the only substantial introduction available until the publication of J. D. Cunningham's *History of the Sikhs* in 1848 which coincided with the fall of the Sikh kingdom and its annexation by the British.[7] Though more thoroughly researched than previous works, Cunningham's history was not acceptable to the British administration as it continued to present the Sikhs as an independent people different from 'Hindoos' and Muslims. More suited to the imperialist British sentiment were Anglicist accounts of Sikhs by missionaries such as William Ward and scholars such as James Mill and H. H. Wilson. These accounts argued that it was erroneous to regard Sikhs as a religion, that Sikhs were mere Hindoos, an unenlightened people.

After annexation

Although British attitudes towards the Sikhs betrayed a rising tone of hostility and arrogance in the aftermath of the Anglo-Sikh wars, fortunately for the defeated Sikhs, such sentiment did not convert into official policy on the ground. In fact, the Sikhs initially benefitted from British rule. A Board of Administration was set up under the direction of the Lawrence brothers (Henry and John) and around 56 highly experienced English civil servants who were drafted in from all over India to help govern Punjab. Recognizing the cultural diversity of the Punjab region (Hindus and Muslims greatly outnumbered the Sikhs), the Board maintained a strict policy of 'non-interference', or what amounted to secular governance, in regard to religious and cultural matters.[8] This policy worked smoothly in regard to matters pertaining to the public sphere such as economics, the military, transportation, communications and law, but not so well in regard to indigenous culture, which came under the private sphere.

Public sphere

The Khalsa army was disbanded and Punjab demilitarized. Those who had served in the Sikh armies were required to publicly surrender their weapons and return to agriculture or other pursuits. Those who held revenue-free lands (*jagirdars*) were allowed to decline particularly those seen as 'rebels'. Those Sikhs considered loyal to the British cause, for example Sikh aristocrats, especially those who had noted family lineages or were descended from the early Sikh Gurus, were given patronage and pensions. Groups such as the Udasis, who had maintained the historical gurdwaras during the eighteenth and early nineteenth centuries were allowed to retain proprietary control over lands and gurdwara buildings. The Administration went to considerable lengths to insert such 'loyalists' into the Golden Temple in order to exert as much control over the Sikh body-politic as possible.[9] One reason for this was the emergence of Sikh revivalist groups, such as the Nirankaris and the Namdharis, shortly after annexation. This revivalism was spurred by a growing disaffection within the ranks of ordinary Sikhs about the perceived decline of proper Sikh practices.

The Nirankari group was founded by Dyal Das who condemned the growing idol worship, obeisance to living gurus and influence of Brahmanic ritual that had crept into the Sikh Panth. He urged Sikhs to return their focus to a formless divine (*nirankar*) and described himself as a *nirankari*. Dyal Das was ostracized for his strict teachings by upper caste Sikhs and had to shift his residence several times. His work was continued by various successors into the twentieth century and eventually gathered a following of several thousands. However, they remained a fringe sect and when they eventually reverted to treating their leaders as living Gurus they came into conflict with mainstream Sikhs especially in the late 1970s.

The other revivalist group, the Namdharis founded by Baba Ram Singh, had more of a social impact due to the fact that they emphasized Khalsa identity and the authority of the Guru Granth Sahib.[10] One of their idiosyncratic practices was the loud and almost frenzied repetition of *nam* (hence the designation *namdhari*) which culminates in a frenzied howling or shrieking (*kuk*) of the name. Because of this practice this sect also became known as *kukas* (lit. howlers). Many of Ram Singh's followers subscribed to an apocryphal text, the *sau sakhi*, which foretold the decline of foreign rule and a return to Sikh rule. The British kept the *namdharis* under surveillance particularly at the time of the Indian Mutiny when Hindus and Muslims had rebelled against British rule. Thus when Ram Singh sent a circular to his followers asking them to congregate in 1857 at Amritsar, this was considered sufficiently threatening by the Administration to intern him. By the 1860s his following had grown to over 100,000 despite his internment.

British suspicions about Sikh loyalty largely subsided after the Indian Mutiny of 1857, when Sikh regiments showed loyalty to the British empire. As a result the remainder of the Khalsa armies were absorbed into the British Indian army. In the 1860s the Punjab Administration introduced land reforms to increase agricultural production and land revenues. Large irrigation projects were started creating the so-called canal colonies which prospered. As production increased so did the volume of trade. Initially the Sikh peasantry gained from this prosperity. However, colonial rule was also marked by economic exploitation as most of the agricultural produce was geared towards export needs which in turn were controlled by British banks and trading companies. The commercialization of agriculture also facilitated the growth of money-lending which was mostly in the hands of Hindu Khatris who charged high interest rates to peasant land holders. Between the commercial interests of the colonizer and the indigenous money lenders the peasantry was squeezed and by the 1880s had again become seriously disaffected.[11]

Private sphere (culture)

In regard to matters that concerned the cultural and social aspirations of the colonized, the results of the British policy of 'non-interference' were complex to say the least. While the British portrayed their governance as resolutely secular and balanced in its approach towards the different 'religions' of Punjab, they were seen by Indians as fundamentally Christian. The reason for this perception is not difficult to ascertain. It lies in the manifest change in the British Administration's understanding of secular governance that took place over a period of almost 70 years from the 1770s to the 1840s. In the early years of colonial encounter British Indologists in the pay of the East India Company had constructed India as a land of many religions often in conflict with one another (even though at first, Indian indigenous elites neither accepted nor reciprocated the term 'religion'). During this period the British Administration's notion of secularism reflected policy in the British metropole where state and religion had a harmonious relationship. Accordingly, in India, the British took over direct responsibility for the administration and upkeep of Hindu temples and rituals thereby creating a direct relationship between secular British rule and the Hindu 'religion'.[12] However, this partnership came under strong protest from politically influential Christian lobbies in Britain who demanded that Britain should be either neutral towards native (Hindu, Muslim, Sikh) institutions, or at least should support the Christian missionary project in India, something which the East India Company had been opposed to. By the late 1840s though, once the British had established direct rule over India, and with policymaking driven by politicians of a more evangelical bent of mind, the British Administration gave a *carte blanche* for Christian missionaries to enter India's public domain while continuing to maintain an outward policy of non-interference/secularism. What justified this double stance for the Administration was a combination of scholarly and political rhetoric according to which: (i) India had many 'religions', but these religions had fallen from their original state of vigour and purity; (ii) this fall into superstition and irrationality was the direct cause of 'Hindoos' loss of freedom first to Muslims and then to Europeans; (iii) to regain their freedom, so the rhetoric went, Indians needed to be civilized according to British customs and morals. They needed, in other words, to be reformed, either through the influence of Christianity, or the secular British state.[13]

Missionary activity had already begun during the last years of Maharajah Ranjit Singh's rule with the establishment of the

American Presbyterian Mission in Ludhiana, although it found few converts at that time. This changed immediately after annexation as important missionary groups such as the Church Missionary Society, Methodists, Episcopalians, the Salvation Army and some Roman Catholic orders set up centres and mission schools throughout Punjab with the active support of British officials in India and with substantial financial backing from the metropole. Their most important conversion was that of Maharajah Dalip Singh, the youngest son of Ranjit Singh and heir apparent to the Sikh kingdom. A spate of conversions of other aristocratic Sikh families in the 1860s caused shock and consternation throughout the Sikh community. The difficulties for indigenous communities were compounded by the Administration's policy on education. This policy put into operation the dictates of Macaulay's 1835 *Minute on Indian Education* by, on the one hand, delegitimizing indigenous education and forms of knowledge and languages, and on the other hand, actively promoting the teaching of 'secular' English literature in all government-sponsored schools – also known as Anglo-Vernacular Schools[14] which had been set up throughout North India. The purpose of these schools was to provide Indian native elites with a form of education that would help create a class of Indians whose mind set was more pliable so that it could break willingly with indigenous systems of education and become useful to the Empire. Given that most of the teachers in these Anglo-Vernacular schools were missionaries, and since the teaching of English literature simply relocated cultural values of the colonizer from overt Christian dogma into the supposedly neutral medium of literature, language and history, the natives remained suspicious of British policy. Nevertheless between the 1850s and the 1880s there was high demand for English education as a gateway to much-coveted government jobs.

Although the Administration's secular education policy made considerable inroads into the Sikh, Hindu and Muslim communities, the natives were not entirely fooled by the show of 'impartiality'. Instead each of these communities reacted by taking part in an alternative public sphere that was beginning to emerge. This development was exemplified by the emergence of voluntary Hindu, Sikh and Muslim organizations. Cities such as Calcutta in the 1820s and Banaras in the 1840s had already witnessed such a development with the formation of voluntary reformist societies such as the modernist

Brahmo Samaj and the more conservative Hindu Dharma Sabhas.[15] In Punjab during the 1870s this process was catalysed by the visit of the Hindu preacher Swami Dayanand Saraswati who published an influential polemicizing work, *Satyartha Prakash*.[16] Dayanand directly countered the missionaries by reinterpreting Hindu doctrine, refracting them through a Christian lens, thereby mimicking and adapting Christian frameworks in such a way that Hindus could claim that they possessed a monotheistic conception of God, a divinely revealed text, the Veda, and that they were descended from a pure original race, the Aryas. Moreover, Dayanand could claim a more ancient lineage for Hindu doctrine since the language of the Vedas, Sanskrit, was proven by Indologists to be older and purer than any of the European languages. And by arguing against caste and idol worship as later accretions, he neutralized one of the main weapons of Christian missionaries.

Initially Dayanand was welcomed by some Sikhs who found his monotheistic and anti-caste stance appealing. But this admiration was short lived as Dayanand made harsh and disparaging comments about Guru Nanak. Sikhs soon realized that Dayanand and the organization he had created in Punjab, the Arya Samaj, was an even greater threat to them than Christianity, as it was part of a massive and rising Hindu consciousness throughout India which tended to regard Sikhs and *Sikhi* as a minor sect of Hinduism. Feeling threatened, Sikh leaders convened meetings in Amritsar to oppose Dayanand's influence. These meetings culminated in the founding of a body called the Sri Guru Singh Sabha in 1873. This association marks the beginning of the most important voluntary body in Sikh history, a body that evolved into a movement whose success was premised on an engagement with the British state and with modernity per se. It is through the agency of this modernizing movement, the Singh Sabha, that the path of *Sikhi* originated by the Sikh Gurus, also known as the Sikh Panth, was further concretized into a 'religion' that came to be known as Sikhi*sm*.

The Singh Sabha Movement

The first Singh Sabha, the Sri Guru Singh Sabha, was founded in 1873 in Amritsar as a response to several different problems which faced the Sikhs at the time. The leaders of the Singh Sabha identified three main threats: (i) from Christian missionaries who continued to gain converts from within the Sikh community; (ii) the reverse proselytizing of the Arya Samaj and their campaign of purification (*shuddhi*) which was part of the rising tide of Hindu nationalist consciousness that was fomenting in India and which claimed Sikhs as a Hindu sect; (iii) the possibility of losing British patronage due to the actions of the Namdharis.

The Amritsar Singh Sabha was set up and backed by conservative Sikhs belonging to the Khatri caste, many of whom were descendents of the early Sikh Gurus. They included men such as Baba Khem Singh Bedi, a direct descendent of Guru Nanak, Thakar Singh Sandhanwalia, Avtar Singh Vahiria and Giani Gian Singh, a noted Sikh scholar of the time. The conservatism of this Amritsar-based group stemmed from the fact that they saw the Sikh Panth as one among the myriad streams constituting *sanatana dharma*, the so-called eternal tradition that identifies its source of authority as the Veda. These self-styled 'Sanatan Sikhs' can be traced to those groups that refused to take Khalsa initiation on the grounds that the *khande-ka-pahul* ceremony polluted their ritual boundaries and threatened their caste status which they regarded as primary. Though they resented the democratic tendency within the Khalsa groups, they continued to co-exist within the broader Sikh Panth even as they remained aloof from the mainstream Khalsa practices. Never relinquishing their claim to be natural leaders of the Panth, they regained their social prominence in the eighteenth and nineteenth centuries by taking over the main gurdwaras and other institutions vacated by the Khalsa Sikhs in their fight for survival against the Mughal state in the eighteenth century. Doctrinally the 'Sanatan Sikhs' considered Guru Nanak to be an incarnation or avatar of the Hindu deity Vishnu and thereby aligned Sikh traditions with the Brahmanical social structure and caste ideology. Thus the predominant concern of the conservative 'Sanatan Sikhs' was to protect the kind of social framework in which they had been nurtured. For these groups the principle of authority in Sikh tradition was invested in living gurus (as Baba Khem Singh Bedi liked to be regarded for example) rather than the principle of *shabad-guru* or Guru Granth–Guru Panth as upheld by the dominant Khalsa tradition.[17]

The conservative ideology of the Amritsar Singh Sabha invited stiff opposition within the Panth. This came primarily from Sikhs

who had strongly upheld the core Khalsa ideals and had benefitted from Western education and employment in such a way that
they were in a position to challenge the traditionalist elites represented by Khem Singh Bedi, Avtar Singh Vahiria and Thakur
Singh Sandhanwalia. They styled themselves as Tat Khalsa, or
advocates of the authentic Khalsa ideals after the Tat Khalsa of
the eighteenth century. These Tat Khalsa Sikhs, led by men such
as Gurmukh Singh, Harsha Singh Arora, Jawahir Singh and Giani
Ditt Singh became increasingly vocal in their opposition to the
'Sanatan Sikhs' and formed another branch of the Singh Sabha in
Lahore in 1879.[18]

Following the lead of the Lahore Singh Sabha many other
Sabhas were formed throughout Punjab. By 1899 there were Singh
Sabhas in every town and in many villages. Each of these associations modelled themselves either on the Lahore or Amritsar model.
However, the Lahore Singh Sabha proved to be far more successful
than its rival, to the extent that the term 'Singh Sabha' eventually
became synonymous with the Lahore group which was the dominant force in the modernization of the Sikh tradition. By the beginning of the twentieth century the two bodies eventually merged
into one, the Chief Khalsa Diwan (CKD), partly due to the need for
greater political coordination in the face of a more powerful common adversary, namely, the Arya Samaj as the main representative
of political Hinduism in Punjab. Indeed the nature of the Singh
Sabha's activities and the character of its modernizing zeal cannot
be properly understood without acknowledging that it was primarily, if not entirely, a response to the transformation of the term
'Hindu' from its original connotation as non-Muslim inhabitants
of India, to the master signifier of a specifically religious identity
embodied by the entity 'Hinduism'. What made this transformation threatening for the Sikhs was that it provided Hindus with a
form of identification not only at the provincial level (where they
already outnumbered Sikhs) but at the pan-continental level, effectively making India synonymous with 'Hindu' and 'Hinduism',
with the connotation that Sikhs were a tiny sect within a broader
pan-Hinduism. The Arya Samaj's systematic campaigns to reclaim
Sikhs as 'reformed Hindus' was evidence of this.

Accordingly the Singh Sabha's main activities focused on reviv-
ing an authentic Sikh consciousness on the Tat Khalsa model.
Much of their activity took place over a period of about 50 years

between the 1870s and 1920s. In the early phase between the 1870s and late 1890s the collective energies of some of the key reformist figures (such as Gurmukh Singh, Giani Ditt Singh, Mohan Singh Vaid, Bhagat Lakhshman Singh, Giani Hazara Singh, Kahn Singh Nabha and Bhai Vir Singh) were focused on: (i) redefining popular rituals and practices and distinguishing 'Sikh' from 'Hindu' or Muslim practices, and redefining an authentic Sikh praxis based on the Khalsa initiation and codes of conduct; (ii) setting up schools and colleges in towns and villages. Through the creative use of print media including tract publications and newspapers such as *Gurmukhi Akhbar* (Punjabi) and *The Khalsa* (English), these new leaders of the Singh Sabha were able to evolve a general consensus about the authentic nature of Sikh identity. They all agreed that the source of authentic *Sikhi* was the early Sikh tradition, specifically the period of the Sikh Gurus and immediately after. This tradition was embodied in authoritative Sikh literatures such as the Adi Granth, the compositions of Guru Gobind Singh (in the Dasam Granth), the works of Bhai Gurdas, selected *janamsakhis*, the *Gurbilas* literature and the *Rahitnamas*. Practices deemed un-Sikh included the worship of idols, the worship of superstitious cults such as Sakhi Sarvar, Gugga Pir and Hindu deities, their incarnations, marriage ceremonies conducted according to Vedic rites and officiated by a Brahmin. Authentic Sikh practice meant receiving Khalsa initiation, the adoption of the 5 K's and the names 'Singh' or 'Kaur'. More importantly, Sikh rites of birth, death and especially marriage came to acquire great importance. Sikh parents were encouraged to send their children to Khalsa schools where the teaching of Punjabi and Gurmukhi was compulsory.

Having been educated in Anglo-Vernacular mission schools, the Singh Sabha reformers were aware, however, that the success of such an extensive program of social reform depended on their ability to create a systematic corpus of literature that could provide doctrinal and historical elements necessary to persuade an increasingly literate Sikh populace. Central to this endeavour was the ability to interpret the meaning of Sikh scripture. True, there already existed a tradition of scriptural exegesis. However, a great deal of this material had been produced in the late eighteenth and early nineteenth centuries by scholars belonging to the Nirmala, Udasi and Giani schools whose interpretation was strongly influenced by Brahmanical philosophy that helped to sustain the conservative culture of the 'Sanatan Sikhs'. The Nirmala and Udasi schools had risen to prominence primarily because of the Khalsa's preoccupation with the quest for political power in the last decades of the eighteenth and early nineteenth centuries. Udasi and Nirmala scholars were routinely patronized by Sanatan Sikhs, the Sikh nobility, or were employed as *granthis* at Gurdwaras. From the Singh Sabha perspective, the Udasis and Nirmalas interpreted Sikh scripture from within a Brahmanic framework making it easy for the Arya Samajis to claim *Sikhi* as a reformed Hindu sect. Thus the efforts to renew the understanding of Sikh scripture and to recapture the original spirit of the Sikh Gurus' teaching became a cornerstone of their mission. This effort was conceived as a long-term project whose outcome would be the publication of a detailed series of commentaries on Sikh scripture.

Closer attention to some of these publications suggests that the exegetical project was motivated mainly as a reaction to the new era in which the representation of Sikh teachings through English had assumed a crucial importance. For the Sikhs this new era proved to be a rude awakening since their tradition had remained intrinsically connected to its Punjabi homeland, and there was never any strong incentive in earlier centuries to disturb the close association of scripture with liturgy by encouraging translations of the Adi Granth. But by the late 1870s, for the first time, Sikhs were forced to come face to face with the dangers as well as the possibilities of translation, where the stakes were nothing less than a displacement of indigenous categories in relation to Western or Anglophone categories.[19] One event in particular marked this new era of conceptual encounter with the West. This was the commissioning of an 'official' translation of the Adi Granth by the British Administration in Punjab, and its eventual publication in 1877 by the German Indologist Ernest Trumpp. Trumpp's translation can be considered as an event of cultural translation in the sense that it (continues to) cast a shadow on all modern translations and representations of Sikh scripture. For this reason alone it merits some brief attention.[20]

Trumpp's basic thesis was that although the 'chief point in Nanak's doctrine' was the 'unity of the Supreme Being', there were no reasonable grounds for differentiating the notion of God in the Adi Granth from orthodox Hindu philosophy. Clearly influenced by the Brahmanical leanings of his Nirmala collaborators,

Trumpp translated the first line of the Adi Granth by missing out the numeral '1', rendering the terms *ik oankar* by the syllable *om*. Since Hindu philosophers had long expounded the meaning of *om* as signifying the pantheistic unity of the Hindu deities, Brahma, Visnu and Shiva, it suggested that Nanak's notion of God was pantheistic, hence unable to transcend multiplicity and achieve a sufficiently monotheistic conception of divinity. Trumpp, in other words, designated the Adi Granth as lacking (i) theological transcendence and (ii) lacking systematic unity. Trumpp's thesis did several things at once. First, it suggested that the previous British accounts of 'Sikh doctrine' (written by men who had no training in the language of the Sikh scripture) as a 'moralizing deism' were mistaken. Secondly, that Guru Nanak's teaching was essentially Hindu in its orientation, and thirdly that 'Sikhism' could not be considered a proper religion as it did not have a 'sufficiently exalted idea of God'.[21] It could not prove the existence of God, and if it couldn't do this, there was no basis for any ethics and no possibility for the Sikhs to form some kind of self-government. As in the case of the 'Hindoos', the evidence of their own scripture justified the colonization of Sikhs by a European power. Fourthly, it shifted the conceptual terminology for representing Sikh scripture and its teachings into the domain of Western philosophical theology. It provided a conceptual framework that future translators could contest but not ignore, nor could they remain unaffected by it. In order to refute him it was necessary first to immerse oneself in and adopt the premises of Western-Christian thought.[22]

Trumpp's thesis had the potential to undermine the Administration's established view of the Sikhs as a distinct community with its own system of ethics and self-governance, a view that was strongly echoed by the Singh Sabha. As such it presented their leading scholars with a clearly defined task: to prove that their scripture could yield a 'sufficiently exalted concept of God' and a system of ethics. This task was incorporated into the long-term project of formulating new exegetical commentaries on Sikh scripture. One of the first commentaries to be commissioned from within the Sikh community was by the Raja of Faridkot, Bikram Singh. Its main writer was the 'Sanatan' Sikh, Badan Singh, whose work was published as late as 1905 in two volumes known as the *Faridkot Tika*. This work, however, had already been superseded by far more accessible interpretations by the Tat Khalsa intellectuals such as Kahn Singh

Nabha, Bhai Vir Singh and Principal Teja Singh. In the 1890s Kahn Singh Nabha published two important works: *Gurmat Prabhakhar* and *Gurmat Sudhakhar*, which contained a listing of key teachings by the Sikh Gurus arranged in alphabetical order and supported by relevant quotations. In 1898 Nabha published his influential tract on Sikh identity *Ham Hindu Nahin* (*We Are Not Hindus*). This was written in response to Sanatanists who had published a tract entitled *Sikh Hindu Hai* (*Sikhs Are Hindus*). Also at around this time Bhai Vir Singh, by far the most important literary figure in the Singh Sabha movement, had begun to publish a series of influential novels that recreated the heroic age of the Khalsa in the eighteenth century. Novels such as *Sundari*, *Bijai Singh*, *Satwant Kaur* and *Baba Naud Singh* helped to introduce the genre of historical fiction into Sikh and Punjabi literature.[23]

Although the Singh Sabha scholars wrote and published mainly in their native Punjabi language, there were some important collaborations with British Indologists that led to publications in English. The most important of these was the six-volume study of Sikh history and scripture by Max Arthur Macauliffe published in 1909 by the Clarendon Press. Unlike Trumpp, Macauliffe opted to disperse translated hymns from Sikh scripture within traditional narratives of the lives of the Sikh Gurus. Working closely with Kahn Singh Nabha and other Sikh *gianis* in the 1890s, Macauliffe's expressed aim was to controvert Trumpp's main charge that *Sikhi* was a mere pantheism and to reinstall it within the history of religions as an indigenous monotheism of India. But as Macauliffe himself admitted, even though his narrative faithfully mirrored the views of his Sikh reformist collaborators, the conceptual terminology of his critique of Trumpp was ultimately conditioned by the very schema used by his predecessor. No one, wrote Macauliffe, 'has succeeded in logically dissociating theism from pantheism', thereby suggesting that the moment when Sikh scripture is translated into a European language, must coexist in a terrain where all talk of religion or of God is automatically routed through categories of (Christian) philosophical theology. Thus the only difference between Macauliffe and Trumpp's translations was the position that each attributed to Sikhism in the evolution of religions, which for Macauliffe was a fully fledged theism, and for Trumpp a pantheism or amoral atheism. Macauliffe's translation helped the reformists to satisfy their desire – denied by

Trumpp – to prove a sufficiently exalted idea of God in the Sikh scriptures.[24]

For reformist intellectuals ultimate fulfillment of this desire could only be attained by proving that such an idea of God already existed within their own scripture and in its native language. This task was incorporated into the more systematic exegetical commentaries and shorter treatises produced during the mature phase of the Singh Sabha, some 40 or 50 years after its founding. Written by a new generation of scholars the most influential of these commentaries in modern Punjabi include Bhai Vir Singh's seven volume *Santhya Sri Guru Granth Sahib*, Teja Singh's four volume *Shahadarth Sri Guru Granth Sahib*, the ten volume *Sri Guru Granth Darpan* by Sahib Singh, and Jodh Singh's single volume *Gurmati Nirnai (Treatise on the Guru's Philosophy)*. *Gurmati Nirnai*, published in 1932, was particularly influential and could be regarded as the first systematic work of Sikh theology. Borrowing from Bhai Vir Singh's earlier work, Jodh Singh laid out a new schema for presenting Sikh teachings, one that began with a proof for the existence of God as a definition of a static immutable One that is ontologically separate from the world and man. In effect Jodh Singh had reproduced a Christian schema – not dissimilar to Thomas Aquinas' *Summa Theologica* – for representing the key ideas of the Sikh Gurus in short and easily reproducible form. *Gurmati Nirnai* packaged the essence of Sikh thought (*gurmat*) into a creedal form that: (i) provided in native Punjabi a very succinct access to a schema that could be reproduced with equal facility by Sikhs writing in Punjabi or English; (ii) by doing so it armed Sikh publicists, literary figures and preachers with an accessible creed that could be rapidly deployed to combat other creeds (Hindu, Muslim, Christian); (iii) it provided a way for later generations of Sikh scholars, especially those writing in English, to materialize a 'Sikh world view', and on the basis of this 'world view' to locate itself within the discourse of 'world religions'. Indeed it would be safe to suggest that this corpus of reformist publications was instrumental in transforming an amorphous *Sikhi* into the more concrete, boundarified entity that we call Sikh*ism* today.

Once this partly imagined, partly real entity Sikh*ism* had come into view, it was possible to reformulate a Sikh code of ethics and conduct. Bodies like the Chief Khalsa Diwan had tried to do this in the early decade of the twentieth century, but only got as far as producing a document called *Gurmat Prakash Bhag Sanskar* in

1915. However, this document was not ratified by the Sikh community until 1951 when the official Sikh Code of Conduct, or *Sikh
Rahitmaryada* was published. With the publication and ratification of the *Sikh Rahitmaryada*, the Sikhs finally had a document
that spelled out its core 'Beliefs and Practices' and outlined its
'world-view'. It represented the culmination of almost seven decades of work by Singh Sabha scholars.

In the early decades of the twentieth century, the main organs
for disseminating this modern Sikh world-view to the masses were
newspapers such as the Punjabi medium *Khalsa Samachar* (edited
by Bhai Vir Singh) and the English medium *Khalsa Advocate*. These
publications consistently projected a public image of the Sikhs as
a religious community, a separate religious identity, an emphasis
on the study of Sikh literature and history, an advocacy of Punjabi
language in the Gurmukhi script, and a separate marriage system
(*Anand Karaj*). There was also a trenchant critique of the management of gurdwaras by *mahants*, that is, *sahajdhari* Sikhs who had
received patronage by the British. In conjunction with the CKD as
the official representative body for Sikh affairs, newspapers and
publicists argued that the historical gurdwaras belonged to the
Panth and should never have been in the hereditary possession of
the *mahants*. But there was a problem translating this rhetoric into
action. For, while the CKD was definitely invested in safeguarding
the political rights of the Sikhs, great care was taken by its leaders
to work within the Administration's constitutional frameworks and
to continue expressions of loyalty to the British Government. In this
way, CKD leaders limited themselves to making pleas on behalf
of Sikhs to be allowed separate representations in municipalities,
local boards and provincial councils.[25] But what is patently clear
from the media of this period is that the religionization of the public
sphere in the late nineteenth century was morphing into grass-roots
political agitations by Sikhs in the early twentieth century fuelled
partly by a growing sense of dissatisfaction with British rule and by
a distressed peasantry in the heartlands of Punjab.

Disaffected spirits: The Ghadr Movement

British intelligence officers sensed this change in mood and pinned
it squarely on the influence of the Singh Sabha reformists. However,

the reformist movement was only one aspect of the disaffection among Sikhs. In the early years of the twentieth century there was an alarming rise in the rate of indebtedness among the peasantry that had been exacerbated by unethical money lenders. As land prices rose many Sikh farmers sold their land holdings. To alleviate this situation the British passed the Land Alienation Act in 1900, which to some extent safeguarded the interests of small cultivators, but this did not solve the problem of rural debt. In addition, Punjab was stricken with successive famines and an epidemic of Bubonic plague that claimed more than four million lives. The British were largely insensitive to these disasters and instead of taking further steps to reduce peasant debt they continued to inflict heavy punishment on debt defaulters.

In view of the CKD's pro-British stance, many in the peasantry saw them and their program of religionization as part of a broader colonial agenda. As a result of this disaffection, by 1906 some began to migrate to East Asian countries such as Burma, Hong Kong and the Philopines. Some migrated further afield to the Canadian west coast, specifically Vancouver. By 1909 there were over 5,000 Sikhs in Vancouver where they organized themselves under the auspices of a Khalsa Diwan Society and built a gurdwara in Abbottsford. Although the Vancouver Sikhs suffered widespread discrimination at the hands of Canadian whites, they retained strong emotional links with the homeland and continued to remain well informed about events in Punjab. Indeed they carried over the spirit of disaffection transforming it into bitter resentment against British rule and against the leadership of the CKD which was also coming increasingly under fire from Sikhs in Punjab at this time. In this regard, David Petrie reported in 1912 that he had gathered 'sufficient evidence to prove that a spirit of anti-British disaffection is common among Sikhs in Canada'.[26]

By 1913 a new organization, the Hindi Association of the Pacific Coast, had been formed and was given the popular name of Ghadr Party. The Ghadr Party in turn spawned a movement with the explicit aim of sending its workers back to Punjab to begin a revolution against the British, which they believed (wrongly as it turned out) was already underway in parts of India. The Ghadr Movement as it came to be known, was spear headed by Har Dyal, a Hindu, and Sohan Singh Bhakhna, a Jat Sikh. Its main organ was a weekly paper simply named *Ghadr*. The membership of the

Ghadr party was comprised almost entirely of Jat Sikhs. Many of
them did return to Punjab in 1914 to initiate a popular revolution
but were thwarted by a well-informed British intelligence. Many of
these Ghadrite Sikhs were either interned or deported back to their
villages in Punjab.

Two things stand out about the Ghadr movement. First,
while its ideologues and workers drew their inspiration from
the same sources as the Singh Sabha movement, namely the Sikh
Gurus and their tradition of resistance to oppression found in
the Khalsa, the Ghadr movement was not religious. Many have
simply described it as 'secular', and therefore different from the
'religious' Singh Sabha. But there is more to it than this. A different way of looking at the motivation of the Ghadr movement
is to suggest that it was perfectly possible to appropriate the
teachings of the Sikh Gurus in a non-religious manner, based
on the fact that these teachings cannot be encompassed within
the secular/religious binary. As we shall see later in this chapter,
it drew on an interpretation of *gurmat* that was not in consonance with the Singh Sabha's religious interpretation. This
strand of interpretation was already being articulated by writers such as Puran Singh and others who had close connections to
Singh Sabha ideologues such as Bhai Vir Singh, but interpreted
gurmat non-theistically. The Ghadrite Sikhs drew on something
like this strand and eventually merged it with the literary idiom
of Punjabi Marxism.

Although it failed to achieve its main objectives, the Ghadr
movement nevertheless helped to radicalize mainstream Sikh opinion against British rule and the CKD whose leadership was perceived to be too loyal to the colonizer. The CKD's emphasis on
working within the constitution had weakened the political position of the Sikhs *vis-à-vis* Muslims who had managed to obtain
separate electorates. When Sikhs pressed for separate electorates,
the Punjabi Hindus objected strongly, which in turn produced an
equally trenchant response from the more radical element of the
Sikhs. In an atmosphere dominated by calls for independence from
foreign rule, it was becoming obvious to many Sikhs that the only
way to make themselves heard was to by-pass the CKD and agitate
directly against the British.

In April 1919 an incident took place that further fuelled anti-
British sentiment among Indians and Sikhs. This was the Jallianwala

Bhag massacre. After many weeks of social unrest and agitation against British rule, Amritsar was placed under martial law. A large crowd had gathered at a park, Jallianwala Bhag, near the Golden Temple on the occasion of Baisakhi to listen to speeches. The park was surrounded and cordoned off by British troops under the command of Brigadier General Dyer who then ordered his men to open fire against the unarmed gathering. Around 400 people were shot and many more wounded in the assault. Since the vast majority of victims were Sikhs, the incident added urgency to calls for a new organizational body to represent Sikh interests. Following a general meeting of Sikhs convened at Lahore in 1919, a new political party known as the Central Sikh League was announced and formally inaugurated in Amritsar in July that year. At this meeting, the reformist impulse that had motivated the Singh Sabha movement, was passed into more radical hands in the shape of a new political party called the Akali Dal, whose creation inaugurated an era of non-violent agitation against British rule.

The Akalis and the Gurdwara Reform Movement[27]

The objectives of the newly formed Akali party were clearly set out in its print organ, the *Akali*. They included the need to bring Sikh educational facilities such as Khalsa College under control of the Sikh community, a call for Sikhs to participate in India's independence movement, and most importantly, the call to liberate Sikh shrines from the control of *mahants*, including most symbolically, the Golden Temple itself. By the early nineteenth century most gurdwaras were run by *mahants* (proprietors) who were able to misappropriate gurdwara income from public donations. Many of these *mahants* had adopted lifestyles considered immoral by pious Sikhs, and most had adopted practices that were at variance with mainstream Sikh tradition, including the display of idols alongside the Guru Granth Sahib and within the Harimandar itself. With British patronage the *mahants* effectively became owners of these temples.

In 1920 the Central Sikh League initiated moves to take back control of the Golden Temple, demanding that 'this foremost seat of Sikh faith should be placed in the hands of a representative

body of the Sikhs, constituted on an elective basis and responsible for its action to the Panth at large'.[28] By October 1920 the
Harimandar Sahib and the Akal Takht were handed back to the
CSL. When the British Administration tried to reappoint a committee of members chosen from the Sikh aristocracy, the CSL convened another general meeting in November which was attended
by more than 10,000 Sikhs, providing a clear signal to the British
that the Sikh masses were not with the *mahants*, the conservative 'Sanatan Sikhs' or the British. At this general meeting, 175
members were elected to form a managing committee for all Sikh
gurdwaras. The committee was given a comprehensive mandate as
implied by the name given to it: Shiromani Gurdwara Parbandhak
Committee (SGPC). Aided by its political functionary the Akali
Dal, also known as the Shiromani Akali Dal (SAD) or simply the
Akali Party, it was the SGPC that organized the movement for liberating all gurdwaras from the *mahants* and handing their control
back to the Sikh Panth. These two new organizations, spawned
by the Central Sikh League, began to carry out their mandate by
coordinating groups of volunteers known as Akali *jathas* to take
direct non-violent action to liberate the historic gurdwaras. They
were to play a pivotal role in Sikh politics throughout the twentieth
century and beyond.

Between January 1921 and May 1925, the SGPC and the SAD
successfully liberated a number of historic Gurdwaras. In January
1920 a band of 40 Akalis was sent to Tarn Taran to take control of
the Darbar Sahib there. Two Akalis were killed and several injured
in an altercation that ensued with the *mahant*. In February that
year, a hundred-strong Akali *jatha* was dispatched to Nankana
Sahib which was under the proprietorship of *mahant* Narain Das.
The British administrators advised Narain Das to make his own
arrangements for the security of the gurdwara. The *mahant* accordingly hired a large group of assassins to meet the Akali challenge.
Most of the 100 Akalis were killed and their bodies burned in the
vicinity of the gurdwara. Hearing of this atrocity, the SGPC sent
thousands of Akalis to Nankana Sahib. Narain Das was arrested
by the authorities along with 20 of his hired assassins, and the
gurdwara handed over to the SGPC.

Since the British had no real desire to see control of these important gurdwaras pass to the Akalis, they continued to support the
mahants for as long as possible. In the struggle to liberate Guru ka

Bhag near Ajnala in 1922, over 2,500 Akalis were arrested during a peaceful agitation. Many were badly injured by the British police who used *lathis* to stop the Akalis marching to their designated place. But the SGPC policy of non-violent agitation did not sit well with all Akalis. The behaviour of the British police at Guru ka Bhag forced some to take a more strident stance in the form of a militant group called the Babbar Akalis. These militants were drawn partly from the ranks of the Ghadr party and partly from the Akali party. Unlike the SGPC and Akali Dal, however, this group lacked the support of the masses and was soon infiltrated by British intelligence. Six Babbar Akalis were hanged by the authorities and others given varying prison sentences.

By 1923 the respective positions of the Akalis and the British had become more polarized and entrenched as things came to a head with the Jaito affair. When the British forced Maharajah Ripudamman Singh of Nabha, a key supporter of the Akalis, to abdicate his position, his case was taken up by the SGPC, who organized a *morcha* or non-violent agitation at Jaito, beginning with a non-stop reading of the Guru Granth Sahib, or *akhand path*. The *akhand path* was disrupted by the police and 59 Akalis were arrested and charged with conspiracy. From that moment onwards, the Jaito incident was transformed into a right-to-worship issue. The Akali Dal responded by sending an endless stream of *jathas* made up initially of 25, then 100, and finally 500 volunteers to court arrest. Many of those courting arrest were badly beaten by the British police. The Indian National Congress (INC) declared its full support for the Akali *morcha*. At one stage several INC leaders such as Jawaharlal Nehru, the future first Prime Minister of India, joined the movement and were arrested. The *jathas* continued to march to Jaito until 101 Akhand Paths had been completed in August 1925. The end result was that the Punjab Governor, Malcolm Hailey, was forced to concede to Akali demands by signing a bill in the legislative courts. This bill, the Sikh Gurdwaras Act of 1925, formally recognized the SGPC as the legal authority to manage and control Sikh gurdwaras. By the end of this five-year struggle to liberate the Sikh gurdwaras, 4,000 Akalis had died, over 2,000 were wounded and 30,000 men and women were jailed. Many others lost their jobs, and sympathizing Sikh soldiers were court-martialled for openly wearing symbols of the Sikh faith and black turbans.

Indian independence and partition

The Akalis had won a very important victory but it came at a cost. With the passing of the Sikh Gurdwaras Act of 1925, the SGPC and Akali Dal had become the single-most powerful Sikh institution, but it was now also formally identified as a religious body whose primary responsibility was for religious affairs. Clearly this had already been implicit within Singh Sabha politics from the 1870s onwards, but prior to 1925, even the foremost Tat Khalsa ideologues such as Kahn Singh Nabha had not envisioned any separation between religion and politics. For the Tat Khalsa ideologues, Sikhs were a Panth, and despite partially acceding to the ideology of modernity, the original meaning of the term Panth remained for them deeply resistant to any separation of religion and politics or religion and the secular, which was something that the colonizer had tried to impose on the Indian mind-set. In order to offset the religionization of the term Panth, which is how the British understood it and wanted it to be understood, Kahn Singh Nabha and his colleagues started to use the Persian term *qaum*, to emphasize that the Sikhs were a politico-spiritual community, or a nation in their own right alongside nations that comprised the Indian subcontinent. In this sense the Singh Sabha and the Akalis subscribed to a communitarian nationalism – the idea that the emerging Indian nation was made up of several communities each with its own sense of sovereignty that was not necessarily mutually exclusive of others. The Akalis were therefore prepared and able to work alongside bodies such as the INC which in its early stages also subscribed to a communitarian nationalism.[29]

The problem, however, came in the late 1920s and 1930s when the formation of an Indian State began to be seen as reality. Under pressure from religious parties such as the Hindu Mahasabha, and from the Muslim League who wanted a separate Muslim-dominated Pakistan, the INC, whose own party was predominantly Hindu, realized that its own claim to be truly representative of the 'Indian People' depended on presenting itself as a properly secular party and by doing so it would delegitimize the claim to representative power of religion-based parties such as the Hindu Mahasabha who would then be cast as 'communal' or 'sectarian'. To achieve this, however, the INC had to make the ideological transition from communitarian nationalism which was largely pushed by leaders such as Mohandas Gandhi, to a secular nationalism, thereby redefining itself in terms of Western European secularism, which recognized political representation only on the basis of the separation of religion from the secular state.

This was something that neither the Singh Sabha ideology nor the Akali strategists had bargained for. Moreover, the demographically small constituency of the Sikhs, combined with the Akalis' inability to move beyond 'religious' (or 'communal') representation, became more obvious when the creation of a Muslim-dominated Pakistan was becoming a distinct reality. Akali ideologues tried to come up with alternatives that would give Sikhs some measure of self-determination. One such idea was the notion of 'Khalistan' popularized in a pamphlet written by a Sikh doctor, V. S. Bhatti, in 1940. Bhatti's *Khalistan* was meant to act as a buffer state between Hindu-dominated India and Muslim-dominated Pakistan. The idea was dismissed by the Akali leadership on the grounds that it was a theocratic model. Two years later the Akalis floated their own model for a territorial entity that could ensure Sikh self-determination. It was called 'Azad Punjab' (or Free Punjab) which would have a demography comprising 40 per cent Muslims, 40 per cent Hindus and 20 per cent Sikhs.[30] Once again, though, this was a defensive scheme meant to counter-act the idea of Pakistan and the possibility that the Sikhs might have to live with a potentially hostile Muslim community. In the end, however, the Akali leader at the time, Master Tara Singh, was swayed by Nehru to cast his lot with the INC and the promise of an ostensibly secular India whose demography and politics was determined by a huge Hindu majority.

When partition happened in August 1947, Punjab was split into East and West, the former going to India, the latter to Pakistan. In the event there was a mass exodus of people as Sikhs and Hindus fled east towards India and Muslims west towards Pakistan. Major rioting and massacres occurred on both sides with total casualties estimated to be well over 1 million men, women and children. As they had feared, the Sikhs suffered the most in this painful, bloody and traumatic event. Not only did they lose many lives, but they lost some of their holiest shrines and historical gurdwaras, especially Nankana Sahib, the birthplace of Guru Nanak.

Sikhs in post-independence India

Immediately prior to the Partition the Akalis cast their lot with the INC on promises that their key concerns would be met. These included the need for Sikhs to have adequate political representation in the new Punjab, the promotion of Punjabi language in Gurmukhi script, and a measure of protection for the Sikh identity through some qualified form of sovereign status within the Indian Union. These concerns were simply aspects of a more deep-rooted anxiety over the position of the Sikhs as a tiny minority in a Hindu-dominated India. What Tara Singh simply overlooked in his negotiations with INC leaders such as Nehru, was that (i) Akali and Singh Sabha politics had pigeon-holed the Sikhs as a religious minority; (ii) to sign up to the Indian Union was to cede sovereignty to the new nation state which, by definition as a *secular* state, reserved the legal right to monopolize and concentrate sovereignty and power at its centre by defining itself in opposition to all religious or communal elements. For the next 50 years the Sikhs in India had to struggle with this problem.

In post-partition Punjab, Hindus constituted over 60 per cent of the total population with Sikhs at 35 per cent. Although this was a higher percentage than in British-ruled Punjab, Akalis sought to gain weight-age as a religious minority. This was categorically rejected by Punjabi Hindu leaders and was deeply resented by the Akalis. By 1948 the Akalis had realized that any politics based on religious identity was doomed from the outset due to their minoritarian status. The only way for them to gain a foothold in the political sphere was to evolve a more secular form of representation. The obvious choice was to push a marker of identity other than religion, one that Hindus might not oppose so much. The obvious choice was language, given that for Punjabi Hindus, Punjabi was still their mother tongue even though Hindi had been steadily gaining ground since the 1880s as the *lingua-franca* of the Indian nation. Accordingly, a language formula was evolved through the offices of Bhim Sen Sachar, the Hindu Chief Minister of Punjab. The Sachar Formula as it came to be known, created distinct Punjabi and Hindi zones that allowed Punjabi to be taught at the primary school level. But this scheme was bitterly opposed by the Arya Samaj who encouraged Punjabi Hindus to deny that Punjabi was their mother tongue and instead identify with Hindi.

From then on the demand for a Punjabi-speaking state (or Punjabi Suba) took centre stage with the Akalis, who put great effort into clarifying that the language-based demand was democratic, secular, and benefitted non-Sikhs and Sikhs alike. During the 1951 census, a majority of Hindus returned Hindi as their mother tongue even though many of them only spoke Punjabi. This led to the defeat of the Akalis in 1952. It would take another 14 years of intense political effort, agitations and the assassination of a Chief Minister, Partap Singh Kairon, before a Punjabi Suba was inaugurated in 1966 according to the recommendations of a Parliamentary committee comprising among others, Nehru's daughter Indira Gandhi who had become Prime Minister a year earlier.

Although the Akali Dal was able to form a government in 1966, the Akalis were not allowed to exercise power without constant interference from the Congress Party, ruled by Indira Gandhi, whose main priority as far as Punjab was concerned, was to keep the Hindu support base of the Congress appeased. Under pressure of electoral considerations the central government left out many Punjabi villages and the new capital Chandigarh which was jointly awarded to Punjab and Haryana, with the Union-Government exercising control over river-waters, irrigation projects and power in Punjab. Despite this handicap, Punjab underwent a 'green revolution' between the 1960s and 1970s pioneered by Jat Sikh farmers, becoming India's granary and supplier of river-water to other states. Sikhs also played a major role in three wars: in 1962 with China, and in 1967 and 1971 with Pakistan. The government's indifference towards Sikh issues and the inability of the Akalis to be allowed to exercise power in their own state continued to foster bitterness and many began to revive different ideas about autonomy.

After again losing the state elections in 1972 to Congress, the Akalis decided to radically rethink their strategy by chalking out a new policy program at a meeting that took place in Anandpur Sahib during the Baisakhi of 1973. Generally referred to as the Anandpur Sahib Resolution (ASR), this would come to be regarded as the most controversial resolution to be passed by the Shiromani Akali Dal in their history. Even though it was redrafted several times between 1973 and 1978, the main aims of the ASR were certainly laudable. They included advocacy for a truly federal constitution against the increasing tendency of the ruling Congress party to centralize power (which it had done by continually amending the Indian Constitution), plus a secular demand for greater power for Punjab. Although the ASR was a clearly defined document, it also created several problems for the Akalis. Its main problem was that it was couched in the terminology of religious nationalism. Its preamble spoke of the 'propagation of religion and Sikh tenets, the condemnation of atheism . . .' and that its 'primary task is to inculcate a sense of Divinity among Sikhs' to be achieved by 'training theologians, publishing religious literature and Amrit Parchar'.[31] These strong religious undertones were sufficient for the opponents of the Akalis, who included the ruling Congress, Punjabi Marxists and Hindu right wing parties (such as the Arya Samaj and the Jan Sangh) to declare that the ASR was a covert demand for a Sikh homeland based on a Sikh theocracy that was incompatible with India's secular democracy. Despite their efforts to the contrary, Akali politics would continue to be painted as 'religious' or 'sectarian' by the Indian media. Secondly, parts of the ASR sub-preamble which stipulated the pre-eminence of the 'voice of Khalsa Sikhs' in the Panth, gave credence to more sectarian elements within internal Sikh politics, which would harm the Akali interests over the next two decades.

The period from 1974 to 1977 was a turbulent one for Indira Gandhi's ruling Congress Party.[32] Faced with massive civil disobedience throughout the country against the state's penchant for centralizing power and weakening the provinces, Mrs Gandhi declared an Emergency in 1975 effectively stalling the democratic process. In response the Akalis launched a massive campaign of non-violent civil disobedience, in which 40,000 Akalis courted arrest, including many of its leadership. After the Emergency was withdrawn in 1977, the Congress was routed at the polls and the Akalis were able to form a coalition government. But any gains made by the Akalis during these years were quickly reversed when Indira Gandhi returned to power in 1980. Between 1980 and 1983 a familiar struggle ensued between the Akalis and the Congress, but by this time the political stakes had risen sharply.

In July 1981 the Akali Dal president, Sant Harchand Singh Longowal was empowered by a World Sikh Conference to plan an agitation for Sikh rights (*dharamyudh morcha*) based on the

Anandpur Sahib Resolution. Major non-violent agitations were launched. In response Indira Gandhi adopted different tactics partly because Congress now faced a more potent threat to its electoral base at the national and provincial levels. This threat came from the return of religious nationalist movements into the political arena in the late 1970s spearheaded by the so-called Sangh Parivar or family of right wing organizations that included the Bhartiya Janata Party (BJP), the Rashtrya Swayam Sevak Sangh (RSS) and Vishva Hindu Parishad (VHP). This family of organizations had successfully reorganized the Hindu networks along religious lines and unified the vast Hindu vote bank against the secular Congress through the stigmatization of non-Hindu minorities. Besieged by minorities such as the Sikhs, Muslims and Communists at the provincial level and by the rise of Hindu fundamentalism at the national level, Indira Gandhi was caught in a serious dilemma. For while Muslims were part of an important vote bank for Congress, they could not afford to alienate mainstream Hindus who previously had voted for Congress, comprised the vast majority of Indian voters and were increasingly being affected by Hindu nationalist rhetoric which was stridently anti-Muslim.

Congress' solution to this dilemma was to divert the attention of the Hindu voting bloc by recreating the figure of a new internal enemy of the Hindus: the Sikhs. Indira Gandhi and her policy makers did this by derailing the Akali Dal's ostensibly secular and non-violent stance. This was achieved by creation or promotion of fringe elements within the Sikh and Hindu communities. These fringe elements included: (i) a hitherto unknown organization called Dal Khalsa, believed to have had covert connections with the prominent Congress figures such as Giani Zail Singh, a former Chief Minister and later President of India; the right wing newspaper editor Lala Jagat Narayan whose newspaper was known for its anti-Sikh vitriol; (iii) the charismatic Sikh preacher Sant Jarnail Singh Bhindranwale who was head of an important but marginal Sikh missionary institution, the Damdami Taksaal. Giani Zail Singh initially tried to use Bhindranwale to split the popular support base of the Akalis and to derail their agitations; (iv) the former Congress minister and expatriate Jagjit Singh Chauhan, who from his London headquarters instigated the call for a separate Sikh state, Khalistan. Chauhan was rumoured to be an operative of the Indian government's secret services, and was specifically assigned the task of undermining popular Sikh support for the Akalis. Although there was no support for Chauhan among Sikhs in Punjab and the diaspora for Chauhan, his call for Khalistan was quickly taken up especially by the Hindu media who connected it with the Sikhs in general, while turning a blind eye to police brutality against ordinary Sikhs and especially against those who supported the agitation in general and the Akalis in particular. The presence of these figures combined to catalyse the fires of communal politics in Punjab.

Bhindranwale, however, quickly discovered the Congress' true motives and turned against his would-be promoters. In 1982 he rejoined the Akalis and his presence initially strengthened their agitation but the alliance did not last long. The ruling Congress Party systematically allowed the law-and-order situation to deteriorate to dangerous levels and, with the Indian media largely on their side, was able to manufacture a scenario where tensions between Hindus and Sikhs were allowed to grow, with scholars, media and politicians portraying the situation as a 'Hindu Sikh conflict'.[33] Bhindranwale in particular was given excessive coverage in the media to the extent that his presence soon overshadowed that of the Akalis. By 1983 Bhindranwale had grown powerful enough to challenge the Akalis directly and in late 1983 he moved into the Akal Takht accompanied by militant organizations such as the All India Students Federation led by Amrik Singh, and the Babbar Khalsa. Once lodged in the Akal Takht these organizations began to accumulate weapons in an attempt to counter the brutal excesses of the Punjab police and Hindu fundamentalists. This was done under the watchful eye of the authorities who made no attempt to stop the stockpiling of weapons, leading many to speculate that the situation had been carefully controlled by intelligence agencies as part of a bigger plan.

Once Bhindranwale had broken with the Akalis and decided to openly confront the secular government through the force of arms, this provided the perfect opportunity for Congress policy makers to create a persona for him as the archetypal religious fundamentalist broadly representing Sikh aspirations. Bhindranwale's name and image became synonymous with the spectre of secessionism and communalism. By neatly conflating the image of Bhindranwale as the arch 'Sikh terrorist' with the 'Punjab problem', 'Khalistan' and the 'Hindu–Sikh conflict', the Sikhs as a whole came to be perceived as the enemy within, ready at any moment to collude with the 'foreign hand' of India's arch enemy and neighbour, Pakistan. It also provided a pretext for Indira Gandhi to declare Punjab a disturbed region, to impose Presidential rule and to take military action against Bhindranwale, which resulted in the Indian army's attack on the Golden Temple complex on 5 June 1984. During three days of intense fighting more than 4,000 people were killed as a result of the army's assault, code-named Operation Blue Star.

For Indira Gandhi it solved the Akali problem, as many in her party saw it. More importantly, though, it undermined the electoral campaign of her main political rivals, the BJP, as the Hindu vote-bank migrated back to Congress. But the Indian Prime Minister also made a fatal miscalculation. The attack on their holiest shrine and the army's destruction of the Akal Tahkt, the seat of temporal authority for Sikhs, enraged Sikhs throughout the world who saw it as an attack on their sovereignty. In October 1984 Indira Gandhi was assassinated by her Sikh bodyguards in a revenge attack. This was followed by three days of state-orchestrated pogroms against the Sikhs throughout India but especially in New Delhi where over 3,000 Sikhs were killed by mobs of rampaging Hindus.

These events gave rise to the belief among many Sikhs that only an independent Sikh state could safeguard their sovereignty. Dispersed militant groups were quickly reformed to begin a war of 'national self-determination'. The Akali leader Sant Longowal was assassinated shortly after he had accepted a peace accord with Rajiv Gandhi. This effectively put the Akalis out of the picture for almost eight years as Sikh politics began to be dictated by the militant groups. Two years later in April 1986, a specially convened global meeting of Sikhs (*Sarbat Khalsa*) was held at the Akal Takht and dominated by the main militant groups. The outcome of this meeting, attended by more than 80,000 Sikhs, was the formal declaration of a struggle for an independent Sikh state, Khalistan. This declaration concretized the idea of a Sikh nation or *qaum* that had been in the making for almost a century, albeit an imagined nation that was in search of statehood. The armed struggle for Khalistan was largely financed by functionaries of the militant groups in the Sikh diaspora, especially in Canada, the United Kingdom and the United States.

The Indian government reacted to the declaration of Khalistan by implementing a politics of 'violent control' which further undermined Akali position and unleashed a vicious counter-insurgency targeting the militant groups throughout Punjab. A cycle of terror gripped Punjab for almost eight years until it was quickly brought to an end by the systematic elimination of the militant leaders and their organizations. Part of the reason for the rapid demise of the Khalistan movement was that it had lost much of its initial support among the masses in Punjab and the militant organizations had no grass roots political presence, which continued to be dominated by the Akalis. Conservative estimates suggest that more than 80,000 people lost their lives in Punjab during 10 violent years from 1982 to 1992. Although the violence in Punjab subsided after the early 1990s, its root causes have not been addressed. As we shall see in Chapter 7, the region is again simmering with political and social discontent despite its full-fledged transition into capitalism.

PART TWO

Teachings and Practices

CHAPTER FOUR

Way of Life

In a memorable sketch from the popular UK comedy series *Goodness Gracious Me*, a Sikh boy beset with existential angst asks his father: 'Dad, what does it mean to be a Sikh?' The father looks at the boy somewhat incredulously and replies: 'Its very simple! You have man; you have a *pagh* [turban]. Put *pagh* on man, you have Sikh!' Unconvinced, the boy presses his father: 'But dad, what about the Guru Granth Sahib, what about the philosophy. . . .?'

The sketch is light hearted, of course, but it raises a more serious issue that most Sikhs will have faced at one time or another, namely, that the basic structure of a Sikh's life is ostensibly no different from that of non-Sikhs. They get up, go to work or school for the day, rejoin their families and then retire at night. But what is it that constitutes a *Sikh* way of life? And why?

Fortunately, this is not such a difficult question to answer since, as we have already seen, a fairly distinct pattern of life had begun to evolve in the time of Guru Nanak himself, and continued to develop in the hands of his successor Gurus. The fourth Guru Ram Das, for example, refers to a form of practice that is as old as the Kartarpur community and modelled on Guru Nanak's own way of life:

> He who calls himself the Guru's Sikh (gursikh) should rise early and meditate on the Name. That Sikh should rise early and bathe his mind in the nectar of the Guru's Word. By repeating the Lord's Name according to the Guru's teaching (gurmat), his misdeeds will be wiped clean. . . . (GGS, p. 305)

For the tenth Guru, Gobind Singh, the only person he recognized as his Sikh was the one who lived a life of discipline (*raini rahe soi sikh mera*). The evolution of this form of discipline continued until it was given a more formalized structure in the twentieth century, specifically in the shape of the *Sikh Rahit Maryada* (Sikh Code of Conduct) first published in 1954. In its four main sections the *Sikh Rahit Maryada* addresses the duties expected of Sikhs. These relate to: (i) individual devotional discipline, (ii) corporate observance, (iii) rituals, ceremonies and festivals, (iv) Panthic discipline, especially in regard to the rite of Khalsa initiation.

Although the *Sikh Rahit Maryada* is a relatively recent document, and despite all the profound changes wrought by modernity, its injunctions show a clear continuity between the life style advocated by the Sikh Gurus and modern Sikh lifestyles. This continuity can be seen in the presence of the Guru in all Sikh practices and projects. Perhaps more than any other aspect it is the centrality of the figure of the Guru that lends consistency and a certain uniqueness to all Sikh practices and way of life. Although the Guru is no longer a human presence but a physical text, or even a virtual text available on the internet, its proximity to the individual and to the corporate Sikh consciousness has not changed. It is this essential relationship between Sikh and Guru, and thus the centrality of the Guru Granth Sahib, that must be borne in mind as we look at Sikh practices in closer detail. To do that, however, we need to take a closer look at the central role of Sikh scripture, primarily the Guru Granth Sahib, and to a lesser extent the Dasam Granth, in the Sikh way of life.

Sikh scripture

Guru Granth Sahib

As we have already noted, shortly before his death in 1708, the tenth Guru, Gobind Singh, transferred the title of Guru to the text of the Adi Granth which he had expanded by the inclusion of Guru Tegh Bahadur's hymns and a couplet of his own. This was a unique development, rich in its implications, since the Guru Granth Sahib, was now to be acknowledged as the basis for spiritual and temporal authority. Sikhs were to live their lives in response to it and it was to be central to all that happened in Sikh life.

The Guru Granth Sahib has no real parallel in other Indian traditions. Its immense importance in the Sikh way of life is most obviously manifested in the central place given to the Sikh scripture in the physical layout of a Gurdwara. While it is in no sense a book containing the sort of laws and rules characteristic of the Abrahamic scriptures, the Guru Granth Sahib as a hymnal and as the focus of private congregational and communal devotion, naturally dictates much of the liturgy. It also provides the text of the unbroken readings of the entire scripture by teams of readers (*akhand path*), which has become a popular feature of modern Sikhism, not to speak of its role as an infallible reference text, whether for counsel in times of difficulty, or as an aid in determining the name to be given to a newborn child. If the status of the Guru Granth Sahib as the primary scripture of the Sikhs is a very special one, this is due in no small way to the character of its contents and organization. In its modern form, which dates from after the introduction of the printing press into nineteenth-century Punjab, it has a standard format of 1,430 pages (see Figure 4.1). It is printed in the

FIGURE 4.1 *A Sikh woman reading from the Guru Granth Sahib.*
(Courtesy of Manvir Singh)

Gurumukhi script with the text printed in continuous lines, with breaks only for major new sections.[1]

Structurally the Guru Granth is composed of three main sections of unequal length (see Figure 4.2). The first is a relatively brief opening section consisting of hymns used for liturgical practices. This section contains works that a devout Sikh will recite or sing each day: the *Japji* by Guru Nanak which is prescribed for recitation in the early morning hours and the hymns by the Gurus prescribed for the evening prayers (*Rahiras*) and the night prayer (*Sohilla*). The somewhat longer final section (pp. 1353–1430) contains collections of shorter verses by the Gurus and others, along with poems of praise in honor of the Gurus composed by their court poets, the Bhatts.[2]

The main body of the scripture (pp. 14–1353) is a vast collection of hymns. As illustrated above its primary arrangement is by means of the *raga* or musical measure in which they are to be performed. Within the primary category of the 31 main *ragas* which are distinguished as separate headings (equivalent to what might be considered 'chapters' in a typical book), the hymns of the Gurus are next organized by their poetic form, beginning with the shortest, which may occupy only a few lines of text, and gradually progressing to much longer compositions, which may each take up

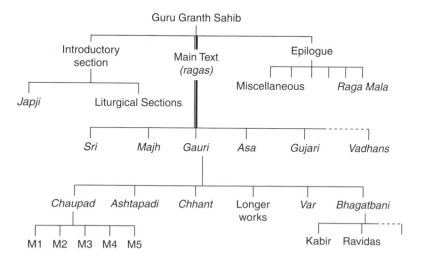

FIGURE 4.2 *Structural organization of hymns in the Guru Granth Sahib.*

several pages. It is within these categories that authorship is finally distinguished beginning with the hymns of Guru Nanak, followed by those of other Gurus in chronological order. Since all the Gurus used the poetic signature 'Nanak', their compositions are distinguished by the codeword Mohalla, abbreviated as M, so that the hymns of Guru Nanak himself are labelled as M1, those of the second and third Guru as M2 and M3 respectively, and so on. After the hymns of the Gurus, most *ragas* then conclude with shorter groups of hymns by non-Sikh poets of the pre-Guru period, such as Kabir, Namdev, Ravidas and Farid. These authors are generically known as *bhagats*.[3]

In total, the Guru Granth Sahib contains some 6,000 separate compositions. Of the Sikh Gurus whose works are included in the Sikh scriptures, Guru Nanak has 974 compositions, Guru Angad 62, Guru Amar Das 907, Guru Ramdas 679, Guru Arjan 2218 and Guru Tegh Bahadur 116. Of the *bhagats*, Kabir has the greatest number, 541, although many of these are very short verses. In the formation of the Adi Granth as a whole, the key figure is Guru Arjan, by far the largest contributor.[4] Indeed the organizational structure of the Guru Granth Sahib as a collection stands as testimony to his skill as its chief redactor.

As mentioned above the Guru Granth's main body of text (1,430 pages) is arranged not according to concept or narrative but according to musical measures known as *ragas*. A *raga* (along with the *tala* or rhythm) is a traditional melodic type in Hindustani music, consisting of a theme that expresses an aspect of spiritual feeling and sets forth a tonal system on which variations are improvised within a prescribed framework of typical progressions, melodic formulas and rhythmic patterns (*talas*). The Sikh Gurus were well versed in contemporary styles of Indian music. For example, popular portraits of Guru Nanak depict his constant companion Mardana as a trained musician specializing in the stringed instrument called *rabab*. Guru Nanak and his successors wished their hymns to be sung to *ragas* that expressed the emotions of the text, and the performance style to be compatible with the meaning of the hymn.

Far from being supplementary to the text, the role of the *raga* and *tala* is central to its organization, since according to Indian aesthetic theory, each musical *raga* in combination with *tala* evokes a mood or expression that has its own distinctive flavour (*rasa*), which may vary across a spectrum that ranges from adoration and rejoicing to desolation and entreaty. To render the *raga* correctly in performance (*kirtan*) is to correctly express one mood or set of emotions and not another. In order to reproduce a certain mood, traditions of Sikh musicology, variously known as *gurbani kirtan* or *gurmat sangeet*, stress the performance rules and melodic material as the best way of maintaining the individual properties of the *raga* and of allowing the finer aspect of the hymn to emerge.[5]

Each hymn is therefore set to a predefined *raga* and when it is sung the nature and feelings associated with the *raga* affect the lyrical interpretation of the text. Sikh music thus has some limitation placed on it so that the aesthetic-spiritual aspect of the performance can be maintained. In performance, therefore, the purpose of setting the Guru's words to a *raga* and *tala* is to make an impression on the ego or self-consciousness of the listener's mind in such a way that it is forced into dialogue with its unconscious aspect, the heart or soul. When these two different aspects of the mind speak to each other, it is said to be attuned to the oneness of all existence. The Gurus aimed to convey experience through feelings and moods because they make up an aspect of consciousness which cannot be reduced to conceptuality, and it is always important to remember the significance of this lyrical dimension when approaching the record of the Gurus' teaching which is contained within the text of their hymns as they appear, silently, on the printed page.

All the compositions of the Gurus are in poetic verse. At the most general level their verse can be defined by common characteristics, shared with most medieval Indian poetry. It is composed in shorts units, with the end of each line marked by strong rhyme, and with longer lines generally being broken by a marked *caesura*. Since there is no grammatical run-off from line to line, each self-contained syntactic unit has to be quite short, thus favouring a typically condensed and direct style of expression which relies on such devices as parallelism and varied repetition for its cumulative effects. The verse of the Sikh Gurus is not strictly bound by the exact metrical rules of Hindi poetics, and individual lines or half-lines are often expanded by a word or phrase which is additional to the strict metrical count. This feature is particularly common in the case of the author's signature (*chhap*) which is a standard mark of closure in all Indian poetic genres. As mentioned above, all the Gurus (except Guru Gobind Singh) use the signature 'Nanak', typically as a vocative self-address in the sense of 'O Nanak', or more explicitly spelled out as 'Nanak says'.[6]

Four main categories of poetic form can be distinguished. The most numerous are the hymns used for musical performance, generally called *shabad*. These consist of a number of short rhyming stanzas. The theme is set by the refrain, whose significance is emphasized by its often being composed in a different metre from the body of the hymn, and by its being followed in the text by the mark *rahao* (pause). The refrain usually comes after the first stanza. The last verse is marked by the poetic signature 'Nanak'. Within any hymn the metre and rhyme schemes are normally constant. Hymns are generally further arranged in short four-line stanzas (*chaupadas*), or on eight-line stanzas (*ashtpadis*). Apart from the *shabads*, there are much longer hymns comprising a category known as the *var* or ballad, a genre typically used for heroic narrative in Punjabi folk poetry and adapted by the Gurus for more extended and systematic expression of their teachings. Another category of poetic expression is the *shalok*, which is typically much shorter than *var* or *shabad*. A *shalok* normally consists of a pair of rhyming lines, each divided by strong internal *caesura*, making four syntactic units in total. The form of *shalok* is essentially suited for oral repetition or remembrance, rather than for musical performance.[7]

The Dasam Granth

Although the canonical status of the Guru Granth as an authentic record of the teachings of the Sikh Gurus remains unquestioned, there is by comparison, a much lesser degree of consensus among the Sikh community when it comes to the other book of scripture, the Dasam Granth, which is associated with the tenth Guru, Gobind Singh.[8]

With its 1,428 pages of Gurmukhi type, the modern printed editions of the Dasam Granth look similar to the Guru Granth Sahib. But this is a very different kind of book. In place of the skillful arrangement of hymns by different authors within the Guru Granth Sahib, the Dasam Granth consists of a miscellany of different items, many of which do not seem to be placed in any particular logical order, and few of which are unambiguously marked as the work of the Tenth Master himself (Patshahi 10). Its original compilation is supposed to have been undertaken by Guru Gobind Singh's close disciple Bhai Mani Singh, but once again, the manuscript evidence suggests that the collection and eventual finalization of its contents was a more gradual process.

The Dasam Granth enjoyed considerable scriptural authority during the eighteenth and early nineteenth centuries. During this period, as we have noted, while the Khalsa Panth was largely preoccupied either with survival or with the conquest of Punjab, the upkeep, scholarship and exegesis of Sikh institutions fell into the hands of Udasi and Nirmala sects, whose social and ideological leanings were closer to the Brahmanic *sanatana dharma*, rather than the teachings of the Sikh Gurus. However, the status of the Dasam Granth began to be challenged with the rise of the Singh Sabha reform movement in the late nineteenth century. Much of the Dasam Granth proved difficult to accommodate within the reformist scheme, since by far the largest part of its contents are devoted either to lengthy poetic reworkings of Puranic sources of what was seen to be distinctively Hindu mythology, or else to a vast collection of 'Tales of Deceit' (*Charitropakhyan*) from a whole variety of sources. By contrast, devotional hymns of the kind that make up the Guru Granth Sahib are relatively few in the Dasam Granth. The modern tendency has therefore been to reserve canonical status only for the explicitly devotional hymns and autobiographical poems which can be safely attributed to Guru Gobind Singh himself, and insofar as these hymns are compatible with the modern Sikh definition of scripture, which is based primarily upon the supremely authoritative Guru Granth Sahib.[9]

Individual discipline

Most Sikhs observe a daily routine known as *nitnem* (lit. repetition of a rule) that is based on the model of Guru Nanak's discipline of *nam simaran* (repetition of the Name). First the Sikh must arise early, typically before sunrise, bathe and then sing the following hymns from the scripture: Guru Nanak's *Japji* and Guru Gobind Singh's *Jaap* and the ten *Savayyas*. This can take anywhere between 30 minutes to an hour to complete and many even begin reciting the *Japji* as they bathe. During the day the Sikh is expected to work for his or her living. Secondly, at sunset he or she should repeat the selection known as *Rahiras*, and finally, just before retiring to bed the *Sohila*. A form of prayer called *ardas* (lit. petition) is recited at the conclusion of the morning and evening recitations. Many people, especially women, also recite *Sukhmani* – a long and beautiful hymn composed by Guru Arjan which extols the virtues of the Beloved's Name. Many Sikhs will endeavour to memorize these compositions, a task that is made easier by the strong poetic rhyming in all of them. Typically, though, many Sikhs use a *gutka* or small prayer book, containing these and other compositions such as *Asa ki Var*, for recitation. The *nitnem* can be performed individually, as a family, or as member of a gurdwara *sangat* (congregation). In whatever way it is practiced, the purpose of *nitnem* is to calm the mind by bringing the Name constantly to mind.

The Gurdwara

Wherever Sikhs have settled they have built gurdwaras. The term gurdwara literally means a door to the Guru, and is any place which houses the Guru Granth Sahib and provides a place for Sikhs to come together as community to worship or to conduct more worldly affairs pertaining to the interests of the community. Gurdwaras can be as simple as a room in a Sikh's house (Figure 4.3). Indeed many gurdwaras started out this way particularly in the diaspora. Or they can be more elaborate buildings rising high above the surrounding buildings in a Punjabi village or in towns and cities in India and the West. There are also historic gurdwaras that were built to mark the important events in Sikh history. Whatever its size, shape or status, no building can be designated as gurdwara without the copy of the Guru Granth Sahib which is given a central place within its precinct.

Over time gurdwaras evolved into much more than places of worship. Typically they are open to all Sikhs and non-Sikhs without restriction as long as certain rules and etiquette are adhered to. Devotees are thus able to come and go as they please.

All gurdwaras have a community kitchen or *langar* and most will serve meals on a regular basis. The larger gurdwaras also have rooms for devotees and visitors to stay overnight particularly during major festivals. Most gurdwaras also serve as centres of

FIGURE 4.3 *A room in a Sikh home with a Guru Granth Sahib.*
(Courtesy of Damanvir Kaur)

education and heritage transmission particularly the teaching of Punjabi. Increasingly more and more offer facilities for old people. Gurdwaras are in every sense community centres as much as they are places of worship.

As far as possible the architecture of individual gurdwaras is modelled on the Harimandir Sahib (Figure 4.4). Many of the larger ones will have an impressive gold- or white-coloured dome. Somewhere in the outer precincts a triangular Nishaan Sahib (or emblem of the Khalsa) borne on a tall mast clad in saffron-coloured cloth flies high above the Gurdwara signalling its presence and its sovereign status. Each year on Baisakhi day, the Nishaan Sahib and its cladding is ceremonially removed and replaced by members of the local *sangat*.[10]

Inside a typical gurdwara (Figure 4.5) there will be a large main room or *divan*-hall – so called because it is the room where the Guru Granth Sahib is housed under a *palki* or canopy. The volume itself is laid out on a lectern over which a white cloth is spread with cushions to support it. Once the Guru Granth is ritually installed and opened for reading, a *granthi* (reader) or any member of the *sangat* carrying a *chaur* (or fly whisk) must be in attendance. The *divan* hall is used mainly for collective worship centred around *kirtan* or hymn singing led by a group of professional singers (*kirtani jatha*) or by members of the *sangat* who are proficient in the performance of *gurbani kirtan*. In addition to the *divan* hall there will be a *langar* room or dining hall with an attached kitchen.

FIGURE 4.4 *The Harimandar Sahib or 'Golden Temple'.*
(Courtesy of Nirinjan Khalsa)

FIGURE 4.5 *Layout inside a typical Gurdwara.*
(Courtesy of Damanvir Kaur)

    To ensure the regularity of services, respectful observance of the
Granth Sahib and for generally maintaining the premises, gurdwaras generally employ a suitably trained person to perform such
tasks. In recognition of the need for such personnel, especially in
the late twentieth century, the SGPC created colleges where the
Sikhs could undergo training for such positions. The personnel so
trained are called *granthis* (readers of the Granth). Despite this
honorific title, it should be noted that *granthis* do not constitute a
clergy in the Christian sense. They are not priests, for as we have
seen in earlier chapters, there is no ordination in *Sikh*ism. *Granthis*
are usually married, have families, and are accordingly housed in
buildings adjacent to the gurdwaras. Although most *granthis* are
men, the office is certainly open to women.
    Visits to gurdwaras by non-Sikhs are a common occurrence
these days particularly in the diaspora. What might one expect to
hear and see on such a visit? The first thing is basic etiquette. Sikhs
and non-Sikhs alike are required to cover their heads, remove their
shoes and wash their hands as they enter the gurdwara. Tobacco

and intoxicants such as alcohol are strictly forbidden. Once in the *divan* hall, one must present oneself before the Guru Granth Sahib and bow before the scripture with forehead touching the floor (*matha tekna*). One then joins the assembled *sangat* taking a seat on the floor facing the Guru Granth Sahib. Women usually sit on the left hand side of the hall and men on the right hand side, although this is neither mandatory nor strictly enforced. A gangway divides the men and women, and allows others to approach the Guru Granth. As mentioned above, people of any faith, or no faith at all, caste, nationality, can join the *sangat* providing that etiquette is adhered to, and no distinction is made between Sikh and non-Sikh. All are equal in the eyes of the Guru.

Once seated, all members of the *sangat* are expected to maintain a respectful level of silence and to focus attention on the service itself. The main service lasts between two and three hours, typically beginning in the late morning, around 11 a.m., and finishing at around 1.30 p.m. The order of service follows the following pattern.[11] It begins with a ritual opening of the Guru Granth Sahib. This is followed by an extended period of *kirtan* led by a *kirtani jatha* specially invited for the occasion, or a *jatha* from the *sangat* itself. This is then followed by a *katha* (exegetical sermon) which may explain the verses or speak about a related matter. Once the sermon is over, the *kirtani jatha* will sing the first five verses from Guru Amar Das' hymn Anand Sahib. The *granthi* then conducts the *ardas* after which he will take *hukam* which is done by opening the Guru Granth Sahib at random and reading the hymn which appears at the top of the left hand page. The *hukam* can be regarded as an ethical instruction for the day. Once the *hukam* is taken, the *granthi* will begin to ritually close the Guru Granth by wrapping it in cloth. During this time, *karah parshad* (sacred food prepared in an iron pan) is served to all present by volunteers from the *sangat*. *Karah parshad* is prepared beforehand by mixing whole meal flour with sugar and clarified butter (*ghee*). After taking *karah parshad* the *sangat* disperses and moves towards the *langar* hall to partake of a meal. Members of the congregation will seat themselves on the floor in designated orderly lines (*pangat*) and will be served traditional Punjabi vegetarian food by other members of the *sangat*. If the service happens to take place in the evening, the fully draped Guru Granth Sahib will be solemnly carried by the *granthi* (who will have placed the Granth on his head, rested on a small cushion) accompanied by members of the *sangat* to a small chamber. Here a final closing ritual called *sukhasan* (lit. taking position for the night) will be performed. This consists of singing Guru Nanak's *arati* hymn followed by the *Kirtan Sohilla*.

Rituals

Some Sikhs argue that rituals should have no place in the Sikh way of life. The Guru Granth Sahib itself is full of quotes about the uselessness of ritual. A good example is the following:

> *Rituals and ceremonies are chains of the mind*
> *Cursed is the ritual that makes us forget the Beloved.*
> (AG, p. 590)

But what exactly is a ritual? According to one definition, rituals are actions repeated in regular and predictable ways, often comprising forms of repetition, commitment, intentional pattern, tradition, memory and performance.[12] On the basis of this definition, one might ask whether there are forms of repetition that Sikhs enact or perform that might justify this definition? The answer would have to be an unqualified yes! The basic and prescribed forms of repetition centre around the practice of *nam simran* (loving remembrance of the Name) either by chanting or more importantly through the practice of *gurbani kirtan*, singing the hymns of the Gurus. In fact these two basic forms of repetition derive from the time of Guru Nanak himself.

Another mode of daily practice that would certainly qualify as ritual is the elaborate adoration of the Guru Granth Sahib, a practice that is becoming more solidified as it is broadcast daily on Indian TV channels from Amritsar and on local Sikh TV channels in the diaspora. Due to this televisualization, it could be argued that the Guru Granth Sahib is now treated as a visual and sonic icon. One might conceive the difference between these forms of repetition and practice as different forms of devotion, interior versus exterior, thereby designating two different types of ritual. But this would be misleading, for Sikhs do not necessarily distinguish between the inner and the outer, or between sacred and profane.

How, then, are we to understand the teaching of the Sikh Gurus, all of whom appear to criticize rituals over and again in their writings, even though they themselves laid the foundations for many of the forms of repetition that were to evolve later? Were they merely criticizing Hindu or Muslim rituals only to make room for newer Sikh rituals? Closer examination of the Gurus' attitude towards ritual and ceremony suggests that they did not regard them as fundamentally wrong, only as potentially distracting. Sikhs were being warned that ritual could become an end in itself rather than a means for self-realization, which depends crucially on the work of self-surrender or self-negation. The question of ritual and its purpose in *Sikhi* becomes one of enabling the devotee to recognize in the midst of temporal existence, ways in which the passage of time affords the possibilities for renewing and reasserting life itself through self negation or self-surrender, and meaningful action. This principle comes to the fore in certain rituals that mark the journey of an individual Sikh as he or she negotiates the different stages of the life cycle.

Rites of the life cycle (*sanskaras*)

As we noted in Chapter Two, while key Sikh rites of passage such as birth, death, marriage and initiation ceremonies have their origins in early Sikh tradition, they underwent important changes in the late nineteenth and early twentieth centuries as Sikh reformists sought to establish firmer boundaries between Sikh versus Hindu and Muslim rites of passage. New elements were added to marriage and death ceremonies. The *Amrit* ceremony (initiation into the Khalsa order) was by and large retained according to earlier form with minor changes. The modernized forms of these rites of passage have been followed over a century and have become part and parcel of normative Sikh tradition.

(i) Birth and name giving (janam sanskar)

Although the safe birth of a child becomes an occasion for much rejoicing, in traditional Sikh families the preparation of the child's environment begins while the mother is still pregnant. During the last few months of pregnancy it is common for Sikh women to imbibe the sounds and strains of *kirtan* and *nam simaran*. The recitation of hymns such as *Sukhmani* are considered particularly efficacious. Those who are unable to recite themselves, can instead listen to recordings of *kirtan* and *path*. Behind this prenatal practice is the strong belief that the aesthetic–spiritual orientations of the child begin well before birth, and that immersion in the sounds and strains of *gurbani* helps to shape the developing consciousness of the unborn child in a particular direction.

When a child is born, the occasion is marked by a simple *Amrit* ceremony. *Amrit* (nectar) is prepared by dissolving sugar crystals in water stirred with a *kirpan*, while reciting the first five stanzas of Japji. A few drops are then administered to the child and the remainder drunk by the mother. When the mother is well enough to walk, her family will take her to the gurdwara carrying with them some *karah pashad* prepared beforehand. At the gurdwara, the *granthi* will open the Guru Granth Sahib at random and the child will be given a name beginning with the letter that appears on the left hand page where the Granth opens. The parents can take a name directly from the Guru Granth Sahib itself (beginning with this letter), or they can opt to make up their own name often using combinations of words used in the Guru Granth Sahib. As far as naming is concerned there is no gender differentiation. The same name can be given to girls and to boys. Only the second name differentiates the child's gender: Kaur for girls and Singh for boys. The child is also given its first *kara* or iron bracelet. The naming ceremony ends with a *kirtan*, followed by recitation of *ardas* and customary participation in *langar*. More often than not, the family will invite friends or relatives to such an occasion. It should be noted that those families who have a Guru Granth Sahib in their home often opt to do it at home.

(ii) Tying the turban (dastar bandi)

When a Sikh boy reaches a suitable age (between 12 and 16) he is taken to the gurdwara for a *dastar bandi* ceremony. This is usually quite a simple ceremony. Following an *ardas* in the presence of the Guru Granth Sahib, the *granthi* or another respected Sikh ceremonially ties on his first turban. The ceremony signifies the respect that is accorded to the turban in Sikh tradition. Again, the ceremony can also be conducted at home providing a Guru Granth Sahib is available.

(iii) Khalsa initiation: *Amrit sanskar or khande ka pahul*

At some point in their lives, many Sikhs both female and male, are inspired to undergo initiation into the Khalsa order. To go through with this initiation ceremony today indicates that he or she is willing to make a special commitment to a stricter way of life. In the current context this means following a *rahit* or code of conduct as strictly as possible. The *amrit* ceremony itself replays the original event of the Khalsa's creation in 1699. It is open to anyone, although those who receive *khande ka pahul* should be old enough to comprehend the meaning of the ceremony. Initiation can take place at any time of the year, although Baisakhi is the preferred occasion for obvious reasons, and in any location that a Guru Granth Sahib is present, the gurdwara being an obvious choice.

Contemporary initiation practices are fairly uniform and try to enact the 1699 event as closely as possible. Required for the initiation are five Khalsa Sikhs who can enact the role of the *panj piare* (Five Beloved Ones) and conduct the ceremony, and two others, one of whom sits with the open copy of the Guru Granth Sahib, while the other stands guard at the door of the initiation room. No one will be allowed into this room during the ceremony and any windows or similar openings will be covered with a cloth to ensure the strictest privacy. Prior to the ceremony, new initiates and the *panj piare* are required to bathe and wash their hair. The initiates must wear the five Ks (*kesh, kanga, kara, kirpan, kacch*) and must remove all ornaments.

The ceremony begins with an address by one of the *panj piaras* outlining the importance of the ceremony and a *hukam* is taken from the Guru Granth Sahib. Taking a large iron bowl containing water, the *panj piaras* then stir-in sugar crystals with a double-edged sword (*khanda*). Gathering around the bowl they adopt the heroic posture (*vir asan*) by going down on one knee and begin to recite the prescribed hymns of the Sikh Gurus: *Japji, Jaap,* the ten *Swayyas, Benati Chaupei* and six stanzas from *Anand Sahib.* The *amrit* or *pahul* continues to be stirred in the meantime. When the recitation is complete, the initiates are asked to adopt the *vir asan* and to cup their hands in order to receive the *amrit* from the *panj piare* who will stand over the initiate. Each initiate will be given five handfuls of *amrit* to drink and each time the *panj piare* will utter: *waheguru ji ka khalsa, waheguru ji ki fateh* (the Khalsa belongs to Waheguru and to Waheguru belongs the victory). The initiates then have to reciprocate this call. After this the *panj piare* will sprinkle *amrit* into the opened eyes of the initiates and into their hair. The iron bowl is then taken to each of the initiates who must drink directly from the bowl itself. The opening lines of Guru Nanak's Japji (*mool manter*) are then repeated by everyone present, after which one of the *panj piare* will explain the meaning and importance of the *rahit*, or code of conduct, which they are required to obey.

Marriage (*anand karaj*)

The Sikh wedding is unique in a number of ways. It requires only the presence of the Guru Granth Sahib, someone (of either sex) to read the required hymns, and the bride and bridegroom to walk around the Guru Granth four times. It requires no services to be performed by a priest, and does not even have to take place in a gurdwara. It can be performed in a home or any appropriate public space such as a community hall.

Marriage remains one of the most joyous social events for any Sikh family. Celebrations take place over several days and it can be one of the most memorable days in a Sikh's life. Guru Ram Das named it *anand karaj* – the blissful activity. Having said that, marriage continues to be a relatively conservative institution with most marriages still being arranged or assisted by parents and close relatives. At the very least, even with the large increase in matrimonial websites, young Sikhs are expected to gain parental consent and approval for their choice of partner, who should ideally be a Sikh, although marriages between Sikhs and non-Sikhs are not uncommon these days.

Traditionally the first step in the making of a marriage is for the parents of the daughter or son to ask a trusted relative or friend (called a *vichola* or intermediary) to find a suitable spouse for their child. The *vichola* works discretely making inquiries among known families and will try to match the profiles of the prospective partners and their families. When a suitable candidate is found the *vichola* arranges a meeting of the two families so that the prospective partners and their families can meet each other. If the two parties are not satisfied the *vichola* will begin another search. In the last two or three decades it has become increasingly common for prospective families to meet directly through matrimonial columns in Punjabi newspapers, or more recently, through Sikh and Punjabi internet sites. But even with these new tools many families have continued to use a *vichola* to help make the first approaches.

If the prospective partners and families agree, then preparations for a marriage can begin, the first step being the fixing of a wedding date. Typically there are several steps that lead up to the wedding day. These main ones are as follows, although it should be noted that some of these are actually Punjabi in origin rather than strictly Sikh: (i) an engagement (*kurmai* or *thaka*); (ii) prenuptial ceremonies including an *akhand path*, *shagan*, *sangeet*, *mehndhi* and *choora*; (iii) the wedding procession which includes *sehra bandhi*, reception of the *baraat* and the milni; (iv) the marriage ceremony itself or *anand karaj*, followed by a *doli*; (v) the reception.

For the engagement (*kurmai*) the families assemble either at the groom's residence or at a gurdwara. To seal the engagement an *ardas* will be offered and the girl's parents will offer to the prospective husband an iron bracelet (*kara*), a *kirpan* and Punjabi sweets (*mithai*). In addition, many Sikhs also exchange rings at this stage although this is not essential. On the day of the wedding the bridegroom arrives at the gurdwara accompanied by the *baraat* or wedding party comprised of relatives, friends and invited guests. The *baraat* is formally received by the bride's family and relatives in a greeting ceremony called *milni*. After the *milni* an *ardas* will be offered, and both parties partake of breakfast before proceeding to the wedding ceremony or *anand karaj*.

For the *anand karaj* the congregation assembles in the presence of the Guru Granth Sahib (Figure 4.6). As *kirtan* is performed by a *ragi jatha* the groom will be seated first and waits for his prospective bride to join him on his left in front of the Guru Granth. The *granthi* conducting the ceremony will ask the couple and the *sangat* to arise for *ardas*, after which the couple will receive instruction

FIGURE 4.6 *Anand Karaj or Sikh marriage ceremony showing a couple seated in front of the Guru Granth Sahib.*
(Courtesy of Pardeep Singh)

on the Guru's teaching about the institution of marriage and its importance. After they assent to this instruction, they will then be seated and the bride's father or other senior relative will place one end of a scarf (*palla*) in the bride's hand and place the other end in the groom's hand. This is an emotional ceremony signifying that the father has given his daughter away to her prospective husband, and the formation of a new bond between husband and wife. The *granthi* will then read the first four stanzas comprising Guru Ram Das' *lavan* hymn, sung in *raga Suhi* by the *kitani jatha*. As the singing of the hymn begins, the couple will arise and walk slowly and solemnly around the Guru Granth Sahib, with the bride following the groom, aiming to complete one circuit in the time that it takes to sing one stanza. The process is repeated three times, so that the couple will have made four clockwise transits around the Guru Granth Sahib. By prostrating themselves in front of the Guru, the couple signal their binding to each other through the Word of scripture. The ceremony will conclude with a singing of Guru Amardas' hymn *Anand Sahib* and the distribution of *karah parshad*.

After a wedding banquet which can be elaborate or as simple as a gurdwara *langar*, the bride and groom depart for a reception either at the bride's house or at a marriage hall where the two families and guests celebrate the occasion with traditional Punjabi music and dance. Once the banquet is over, the bride is taken back to her home from where she will formally depart from her parents' home. This leave-taking is called *doli* which refers to the wooden sedan-like structure in which the bride was escorted in by-gone days (this is now replaced by an adorned car). The *doli* is a tearful occasion as the bride takes leave of her parents and gets back into the car which will take her and her husband to her new home.

Death ceremony (*antam sanskar*)

The theme of death is a powerful and pervasive one in the writing and teachings of the Sikh Gurus. This is not because the Gurus were pessimistic about this world, but because for them, the processes of life and death, creation and destruction, are inseparable. If one is born, one must also die. Mortality is not something to be morbid about, but rather a constant reminder that one should cherish life and not be deluded by the false pretences of the ego. As Guru Nanak so poignantly reminds us about the last stages of life:

> The ninth stage sees shortness of breath and white hair,
> In the tenth the body burns till only ashes are left.
> As the funeral party utters laments,
> Life came, and is gone, and so too has one's fame,
> Leaving only the offerings for crows.
> Nanak, the love of the self-led is blind
> Without the true Guru the world drowns in darkness.
>
> (GGS, p. 137)

> Death does not wait for auspicious days,
> Or ask whether it's the light or dark side of the month.
> Some are treated harshly, others well cared for.
> Some leave armies and mansions to the sound of drums.
> Nanak, this heap of dust returns to dust.
>
> (GGS, p. 1254)

In accordance with this teaching the death rites are a relatively simple and dignified affair. Those mourning the loss of a loved one are expected to maintain a state of mental equipoise, and not to indulge in loud lamentation. Like Hindus, Buddhists and Jains, Sikhs practice cremation. The cremation ceremony is a family occasion. Members of the family wash and clothe the body in clean garments and the five Ks. In India the body is laid in a bier and taken to the cremation ground where the pyre will be lit by the eldest son or by a close relative. In Western countries the body is laid in a coffin and taken in a hearse to the nearest crematorium. As the cremation fire is lit and made ready to receive the body, *kirtan sohila* is sung, followed by a recitation of *ardas* in which blessings are sought for the departed soul. When the party returns to the home of the deceased, the mourners wash their hands and *karah parshad* is distributed. Once the cremation is over, it is customary for a complete reading of the Guru Granth Sahib to be undertaken in the house of the deceased. This reading must be completed in ten days. Mourners sit quietly and listen. It is customary for mourners not to wear bright clothes and women usually wear white. In India the immediate family members return to the cremation grounds after 48 hours to retrieve the ashes, which are then placed in the flowing waters of a nearby river or stream, very often the river Sutlej. Sikhs in the diaspora usually take the ashes back to Punjab where they will be disposed of at Kiratpur into the Sutlej.

Gurpurbs and festivals

In Sikh tradition *gurpurbs* and festivals are celebrated on the lunar dates of the Indian calendar. Although they overlap in many ways there is also something of a difference between them. *Gurpurbs* (lit. the day of the Guru) celebrate significant events associated with the lives of the ten Gurus. The main *gurpurbs* are the birth of Guru Nanak (in November), the birth of Guru Gobind Singh (late December or early January) and the martyrdoms of Guru Arjan (early June) and Guru Tegh Bahadur (November). *Gurpurb* celebrations involve the decoration of gurdwaras where Sikh gather in large numbers for festivities or mourning, depending on the occasion. In Punjab's major cities processions are held that include colourful floats carrying the Guru Granth Sahib. These processions

FIGURE 4.7 *A Sikh procession in London led by the Panj Piare on Baisakhi Day.*
(Courtesy of Daljit Singh)

often wind through city streets where people come out to pay homage to the Guru Granth and greet the marchers.

Sikh festivals, on the other hand, overlap with cultural events celebrated throughout India. The main Sikh festivals are Baisakhi, Divali and Hola Mohalla.

In India Baisakhi follows a solar calendar and so falls on or around 13 April each year. For Hindus, Baisakhi is a grain harvest festival marking the close of one agricultural cycle and the beginning of a new one. Sikhs also follow this tradition but for them Baisakhi has acquired historical associations since Guru Gobind Singh created the Khalsa on this day. As a result Sikhs celebrate Baisakhi as a historical birth anniversary for their community with Anandpur being a major centre of festive activity and celebration.

Unlike Baisakhi, the date for the Divali festival varies because it follows the lunar cycle, but it generally falls in October. For Hindus, Divali is the festival of light, when oil lamps are lit to adorn homes and sweets are distributed to friends and neighbours. Sikhs too light up their homes and gurdwaras, and distribute sweets. But whereas Hindus associate Divali with the return of the beloved after a period of separation (specifically the return of Ram Chandra and Sita after their exile in South India) as narrated in the Ramayana and Mahabharata, Sikhs celebrate Divali for the return of the sixth Guru, Hargobind, after a period of imprisonment under the Mughal emperor Jahangir. According to the popular versions of this story, Guru Hargobind refused to leave prison unless 52 Hindu princes were also freed. Jahangir agreed to release only as many of them as could hold onto Hargobind's clothing.

The festival of Hola Mohalla also follows a lunar cycle. It takes place at the end of March or the beginning of April. It is held a day after the Hindu festival of Holi (the festival of colours) when Hindus splash coloured powder on anyone or anything in sight. For Hindus, the splashing of colours lowers (but does not remove completely) the strictness of social norms, which includes gaps between age, gender, status and caste. Together, the rich and poor, women and men, enjoy each other's presence on this joyous day. No one expects polite behaviour; as a result, the atmosphere is filled with excitement, fun and joy. For the Sikh Gurus this festival had little significance because of the emphasis in their teachings on social egalitarianism. Instead, Guru Gobind Singh directed the attention of Sikhs away from Holi by instituting a different festival of Hola Mohalla, which provided an opportunity for Sikhs to engage in military exercises and mock battles, athletic competitions and literary contests.

CHAPTER FIVE

Sikh Philosophy

Introduction

Why 'Sikh philosophy?' What exactly does the term 'Sikh phi losophy' designate? One often hears of 'Buddhist philosophy' or 'Hindu philosophy' for which there are well-established indigenous traditions and famous exegetes. But rarely does one hear the term 'Sikh philosophy'. It is almost never used by Western scholars of Sikh studies, whose preference has been for the cognate term 'Sikh theology'.[1] By contrast one almost never hears of 'Buddhist theology' or 'Hindu theology'. This may be because there are indigenous categories (*darshanas* and *shastras* in the Hindu context or *dhamma/dharma* in Buddhist context) that broadly correspond to the Western category of 'philosophy'. Yet the Sikh lexicon has similar categories such as *dharam* (signifying moral order) and especially the term *gurmat* which refers to the instruction or teaching of the Guru and broadly corresponds to the term 'philosophy'.

But this raises two questions. First, why the preference for 'Sikh theology' in much of modern Sikh studies scholarship? Second, is 'Sikh philosophy' anything other than a secularized version of Sikh theology?

To answer the first question, categories such as *gurmat and dharam* took on a theological signification in the late nineteenth and early twentieth centuries in the attempt of Singh Sabha scholars to erect definitive boundaries between an emergent and politically active Hinduism and the Sikh tradition, by constituting *Sikhi*(sm) as an entity that corresponded to the Western definition of proper religion. They did this by reformulating the idea of direct inner experience that is so central to the teaching of Sikh scripture, in terms of a revelation from a personal God.

No doubt there are secondary sources such as the *Purantan Janamsakhi* which present Guru Nanak's attainment of spiritual perfection in terms of the revelation model. The Singh Sabha scholars Christianized the *janamsakhi* version of the Sultanpur experience by formulating extensive written commentaries on Sikh scripture in the form of proofs for the existence of God. The purpose of these commentaries was to ideologically separate what they considered as Sikh 'revelation' from the impersonal Vedic revelation based on an eternal cosmic sound.

As we have seen in Chapter 1 the problem with the *janamsakhi/* revelation model is two-fold however. First, while Guru Nanak himself says nothing about *this* pivotal experience at Sultanpur, he does say a great deal about how direct experience and spiritual perfection can be attained by anybody and at anytime. It is a theme that is repeatedly stressed in the Adi Granth by his successor Gurus, and their emphasis is not on hearing voices from God, but on changing the nature of the human mind. Secondly, the Purantan Janamsakhi is itself not at all consistent about the revelation model. Read closely, one can find strong suggestions of other, non-theological (or simply philosophical) ways of explaining direct experience or attainment of perfection that are far more consistent with the teachings of the Sikh Gurus as we find them in the Adi Granth. The emphasis here is on *explaining* or better still *interpreting*, which should give us a hint as to why I prefer the term 'Sikh philosophy' over 'Sikh theology', even though both have inherent limitations.[2] As a mode of explanation or interpretation Sikh philosophy does not remain in thrall to its 'original' context, nor, paradoxically, does it ever lose sight of that 'original' context. 'Sikh theology' could not do this because it worked within the constraints of the peculiarly Western discourse of ontotheology,[3] whose logic effectively subsumed much of modern Sikh thinking and practice. After its encounter with the West, modern *Sikhi*sm could therefore only develop in one direction – culturally, politically and intellectually.[4]

In answer to the second question, the simple answer is that 'Sikh philosophy' is far from a secularized theology. Unlike other disciplines philosophy has the capacity to self-reflexively engage with its own categories in such a way that it is able to refuse the very distinction between religion and the secular that is so entrenched in the Western system of thought. In fact there is already a living system of Sikh reasoning and thought. It is not difficult to show that this indigenous mode of thinking has, and continues, to resist the religion-secular distinction, despite the Singh Sabha's religious apologetic. Many Sikh writers, including Puran Singh in the early twentieth century, and Harinder Singh Mahboob in the late twentieth century, or prominent *kathakars* such as Sant Singh Maskin or Darshan Singh Ragi, exemplify this tendency towards the 'philosophical' defined primarily through concepts and categories inherent within the teachings of the Sikh Gurus. Because of its inherent self-reflexivity, Sikh philosophy has much greater potential for evolving conceptual frameworks for interpreting the teachings of the Sikh Gurus, adapting them to the lived experience of individual Sikhs and to different cultural environments and for conceptually engaging non-Sikh cultures.

But before turning our attention to what these concepts might look like, we need to consider two further objections to the term 'Sikh philosophy'. The obvious one is that philosophy is a western discipline and therefore unsuited both for the study of Sikh literature and of the Sikh life-world. This may be rebutted on the grounds that philosophy is no more Western than sociology, history, anthropology or other disciplines whose presence is now well established in Sikh studies. In fact the field of Sikh studies can itself be considered a form of ongoing engagement with the West, one that began in the colonial period and whose mark is firmly imprinted in all literature influenced by Singh Sabha scholarship. This encounter with Western thought and its categories is as much a reality for those who think and write in Punjabi as it is for those who write in English. If anything, 'philosophy' provides better access to understanding the framework and mechanisms of this encounter.

A second objection may be that one of the primary sources for Sikh philosophy, the Adi Granth, is not set out as a philosophical treatise or as legal codes to be read silently, but as poetry intended to be sung or recited individually or in groups. While the range and power of these teachings are immediately evident to those who participate in the practices of *kirtan* and *nam simaran*, the aesthetic framing of the hymns in the classical *raga* and *talas* of North Indian music, poses some resistance to any formal systemization, for example, in the form of philosophical conceptualization. This is especially the case when we try to render the content of these teachings in modern English, although modern Punjabi is no less problematic. It could therefore be argued that that there is nothing to think about since the literature is purely devotional.[5] If so, then surely the term 'Sikh theology' is the most suitable frame whether one likes it or not.

The rebuttal to this argument is relatively straightforward. The source literature is indeed poetic in nature, but there is a vast body of secondary literature that expounds and explicates the teachings of the Adi Granth through *modes of reasoning* that happen to be current in any social context. Moreover, there are well established and vibrant living traditions of oral exegesis of the Adi Granth (often simply referred to as *gurmat vichar*, or *gurbani viakhia*) that also expound its core teachings, again, using modes of reasoning that are conventional at any particular time and social context.[6] While these traditions are not doing 'philosophy' in the strictly academic sense of the term, they do perform a certain kind of conceptualization that helps ordinary Sikhs to think about, to reflect upon, important aspects of the Gurus' teachings, and to relate them to the everyday world that they live in, that is, to their lived experience. This work of thinking-about (*vichar, viakhia*), which inevitably involves forms of public reasoning, suggest that an implicit philosophical endeavour has always been underway since the time of the Sikh Gurus, one that became more explicit in the work of modern Sikh scholars. Sikh philosophy is therefore a more pragmatic term in that it links Sikh subjectivity or lived-experience directly to the task of interpreting Sikh scripture on a daily basis.

The authority of experience

Having raised and answered these objections, we are in a better position to gauge what the basic elements of Sikh philosophy might be, including, of course, a possible starting point. The problem of finding a starting point is no trivial matter, for it is connected to the question of authority of a particular discourse, in this case, the discourse of Sikh philosophy. Fortunately, the question of authority is fairly well established in the writings of the Sikh Gurus and especially in Guru Nanak's most important composition, the Japji. As early as the first few stanzas of this hymn, it becomes obvious that it is nothing less than Guru Nanak's own testimony about the nature of his authority and the direct experience that authorizes it. Thus any discourse going by the name 'Sikh philosophy' would have to ground itself in relation to this direct experience and the possibility that others today can experience something similar, here and now. In other words Sikh philosophy would have to locate its authority within an existential as opposed to an epistemological (=transcendental) perspective. Which means that what the Sikh Gurus directly experienced, and what they exhorted their followers to try and achieve, was not the experience of a transcendental deity, but first and foremost, an experience of living within this world – an experience that is strictly within the horizon of life and death, or mortality. This is not to get rid of a personal 'God'. Indeed reference to a 'personal God' who takes infinite names, abounds in the hymns of the Gurus. Rather, it is to suggest that the notion of personal deity is the result of an experience that comes up against the limits of language[7] and should therefore be understood in a radically different way. It means that the object of the Gurus' teaching (hence the subject matter of what we call Sikh philosophy) is existence itself, and that this existence, which is identical to non-existence, is neither different from, nor the same as, what we ordinarily term by 'God'. The perspective that I am seeking should not only be suited to Sikh and non-Sikh sensibilities alike, but more importantly it should allow readers to connect their own lived experiences today to the poetry of the Sikh Gurus, to begin to understand why they felt it necessary to produce such writings, and to apply these to the contemporary world.

Perhaps the best way to explain this is to reconsider Guru Nanak's own testimony on the matter in the first few stanzas of this hymn, where he succinctly outlines the foundational elements of his teaching and any future Sikh philosophy. He begins by elaborating on the nature of the One, which is depicted as a symbol expressive of the nature of reality. His main point about the One is that in order to achieve a perfected awareness of the nature of reality as One, it has to be *experienced* all the time, rather than simply comprehended. Paradoxically, however, the very experience of this One disorients the functioning of what we call 'reality'. The experience of the One reveals a gaping hole in our knowledge of the One, such that knowledge and experience cannot be in the same place. To speak about this in conventional language, to bring experience into words, something has to give way. What gives way is our self, or ego, which has to shatter and be reformed but not in the place where it was before. This is the point that Guru Nanak is trying to make in the five stanzas that follow the *mul mantar*, where he goes on to articulate some of the key concepts that become foundational to Sikh philosophy.

Evidently then, the work of 'Sikh philosophy' cannot simply be located either in the realms of epistemology or ontology in the sense that Western philosophy demarcates these terms.[8] The discourse of 'Sikh philosophy', insofar as we conduct this discourse through Anglophone categories, must therefore be grounded in the encounter between concepts, Sikh and Western, and, as we shall see in the following interpretation of the first five stanzas, it points to a mode of thinking in which conceptuality is intrinsically linked to affect. In what follows I will try to outline how the basic 'philosophical' move made in the first five stanzas – a move which it needs to be stressed is at once affective and conceptual – orients the relationship between *key terms* (such as *hukam*, *nam*, *shabad*, *guru*, *anhad nad*) and gives rise to *themes* (such as temporality, the nature of consciousness, action and grace) within the teachings of the Sikh Gurus that are existential-affective as opposed to merely conceptual and therefore speak to a lived existence.

The One: Experiencing reality as non-dual

The Japji is recited daily by pious Sikhs and its opening formula, the *mul mantar* or foundational statement, is repeatedly invoked in shortened form on almost every page of the Guru Granth Sahib. For Sikhs the *mul mantar* serves as a kind of creedal statement that expresses through rich symbolism the experience undergone by Guru Nanak. Of special importance is the opening phrase *ik oankar* (lit: One, whose expression emerges as Word) which consists of the numeral 1, a figure that is universally recognizable across cultures and languages and stands for the Absolute. This is followed by the sign *oan* (lit. the unfolding or emergence of the Word), and completed by the extended sign – *kar* which connects *oan* to the next two words in the *mul mantar*: *sat(i)* (from the Sanskrit *satya* meaning existence or being) followed by *nam* (lit.

the Name). The verse following the *mul mantar* further elaborates the nature of the Absolute One as:

Repeat:
True in the beginning, true before time began
True even now, Nanak, ever will be true.[9]

However, an important question arises here. If, as Nanak claims, the truth of this Absolute One can be experienced here and now, what is it that stops each and every person from realizing this all the time? What stops us repeating such an experience of the One or of being One? More importantly, *how* could such an experience be repeated?

The answer for Guru Nanak is relatively straightforward. From the standpoint of someone who has actualized Oneness in his or her own existence, the Absolute is One (*ik*) and the One is Absolute. But our normal, everyday consciousness is such that it keeps us fundamentally separated from this One. Our everyday consciousness, which also generates our sense of normality, creates a wall or barrier that prevents us from actualizing Oneness in our lived existence.[10] The cause of this barrier is that we are fundamentally deluded about the true nature of Oneness.

What does this mean? What Nanak seems to be suggesting is that the numeral One is not a numeral among other numerals. Rather, One is simultaneously the most unique and the most deceitful. One is most unique in the sense that there is no other like it insofar as it names the truth of existence itself (*satnam*); it is a '1' that cannot be owned or appropriated and thereby made part of a series of numbers (1+n). On the other hand, '1' is the most deceitful.[11] This '1' is the basis of knowledge as calculation which evaluates, measures each '1' against every other '1' and thus sets up a difference between them based on this evaluation. It is the '1' that we regard as everyday normality but which is in fact mediated through the structure of the ego, the self which asserts its being on the basis of individuation (*haumai* or self-attachment as the mechanism of a subject which returns the self to self, generating the sense of 'I am my own self' or 'I am self-existent'). This oneness makes ego the prior basis of all relationality. The fundamental problem with this '1' is that it projects itself as an infinite proximity between the numeral '1' as the signifier of unity and identity, and the word 'I'

as the signifier of the self's identity. For Nanak, the correspondence between numeral and word, '1' and 'I', is deceitful insofar as
it reproduces this self as an identity that sets itself up in opposition
to anything that is different. The ego thereby maintains its existence by erecting barriers against the outside world. It sees itself
as a subject fundamentally separated from everything else which
becomes an object for it. Nanak likens the subject–object mode of
relating to delusion (*bharam*) created by duality (*dubida*: seeing the
'1' as two).[12]

But the problem, as Nanak sees it, goes much further than the
simple assumption that the ego is the source of duality/deceit. For
as he explains in the first stanza of Japji, from the standpoint of
ego, the Absolute '1' cannot be attained either through conceptual
thought or through ritual purity no matter how much one repeats
such thinking or ritual.[13] Nor can the Absolute '1' be obtained by
practicing silent austerities[14] since these too fail to silence the ego's
constant chatter, nor indeed by satisfying one's innermost cravings.[15] The ego works by routing our experience of the Absolute '1'
through all manner of repetition: concepts, rituals or austerities.
Consequently the Absolute '1' always fails to be experienced as
such; the nearest we get is to re-present it as an object or an idol
to constantly gratify the ego's desire for permanence. How then
does one overcome egotism? How can the ego's illusory barriers be
broken?[16] How does one become self-realized?[17]

Nanak answers this in the first and second stanzas of Japji. The
ego's boundary is broken by orienting the self towards an imperative
that is always already inscribed with(in) the self and within the nature
of all existence.[18] Nanak's name for this imperative is *hukam* – a very
simple word that ordinarily means an order or command. But how is
one to recognize this imperative? Where is it located? And if it could
be located, how does one go about actualizing it? Nanak's answer to
these questions is deceptively simple. He states:

> O Nanak, to recognize this imperative (hukam), for it to take
> effect,
> Let the ego not say: 'I am myself'.[19]

Let the ego *not say* 'I am myself'. Notice here how Nanak insists
on two things simultaneously: (i) the emphasis on a certain kind
of speech where one speaks by not saying, or by avoiding saying

something; and (ii) a psychic structure, the ego or 'I am', correspond-ing to a certain kind of language-use centred around self-possession, so that the psycho-linguistic structure in question can be described as an 'I am my-self' (haumai). But what exactly does this imperative mean: that one should not say I am myself? Is this then an imper-ative to say silent, to stop speaking altogether? If so, why would Nanak and other mystics like him want to say so much, as is evident by how much they wrote? In any case Nanak has already mentioned in an earlier stanza that silence is not the answer to his problem. Rather, what Nanak seems to suggest is that there is a *different way* of speaking. To better understand this, it may be helpful to rephrase the imperative as: 'Let ego *say* I am not' which might then be inter-preted as: speak/think/act in such a way that your existence stops revolving around, and thereby stops inscribing, the psychic forma-tion 'I am my-self', but instead revolves around a different psychic formation: 'I am not'. In other words, the ego must become silent so that one can resist saying 'I am *my*-self' even as ego continues to be formed. For Nanak this silencing of the ego is not to be understood literally. Silence refers to a process of ego-loss, a self-enforced with-drawal of ego at the very moment that the self names itself as 'I' and thus starts to become an origin or absolute centre in relation to all other existing things including others.

So man's fundamental problem, according to Nanak, lies in not understanding the nature of the ego and its intrinsic connection to language. Interestingly, though, he suggests that the remedy to this problem also lies in the very constitution of the ego.[20] If, as we have seen, ego constructs itself by a certain kind of language use (in the form of self-naming or the assertion of one's existence as the centre of all reality: 'I am my-self'), Nanak argues that it is also possible for ego to *re*-construct itself by perfecting its relationship to lan-guage, thereby perfecting the potential that all humans have for speech/thought/action. A question immediately arises here. How do we go about changing the way we normally relate to language in order to bring about the required change in the constitution of the ego? Note that this is a chicken-and-egg question. For we could equally well ask: how to bring about ego-loss in order to effect a change in our relationship to language?

Answers to these questions are not given directly by the Sikh Gurus. More often than not references to language and ego-loss are woven into the fabric of their poetic verse. Nevertheless, because of the sheer repetition of these two themes it is possible to formulate the beginnings of a response – a response that will enable us to highlight and briefly discuss some of the leading themes in the teachings of the Sikh Gurus. It will be helpful to return to the question of ego-loss and rejoin the question of language when we discuss the themes.

So how does one go from ego to ego-loss? From saying 'I am myself' to 'I might not be', or 'I might not be in possession of my-self?' From the certainty of 'I exist' to the uncertainty of 'I might not exist?' Is it even practical or useful to ask such a question? Logically speaking, would it not lead us into self-annihilation? Fortunately there is a time-honoured way of asking this question without falling into the abyss. The way to do this would be to introduce a modicum of self-doubt into the over-confident assertion of *haumai* (I am my-self), so that one asks instead: *Why* do I exist? For Guru Nanak, to ask the question *why* about one's own self, is to have accepted the working of the imperative (*hukam*) that had been inscribed within the self from the moment it came into existence. Indeed, this *hukam* is inscribed in the very nature of existence itself in the form of a universal law: everything that exists must eventually fall into non-existence. As the law of existence *hukam* governs both cosmos and consciousness at the same time. To recognize and imbibe *hukam* into one's existence in the form of the question 'Why do I exist?', as Nanak suggests, begins the process of decentring the ordinary ego-centric standpoint from where we give meaning to and evaluate all things in relation to our own individual consciousness and our own lives. To recognize *hukam* is to recognize the shortness of life and the ever-presence of death in life.

As the law of impermanence, the inevitability of returning to one's origin, *hukam* is a central category in the teachings of the Sikh Gurus reminding us not only of the mutual imbrications of macrocosm and microcosm, of cosmos and psyche, but also of the ego's confrontation with time. *Hukam* comprises a structure-without-structure around which revolve all other themes in the teachings of the Sikh Gurus. Some of the larger themes will be introduced below.

Time and impermanence

As we have noted above, the recurrent message in Guru Nanak's *Japji*, indeed throughout the Adi Granth, is to experience Oneness by re-uniting the ego with non-ego, by recognizing and imbibing *hukam* – the law of impermanence. *Hukam* reminds us that the very element in which separation and unification can take place is time. Not surprisingly the theme of time is one of the most pervasive in Sikh scripture. However, the Gurus do not treat time as a category or entity distinct from the phenomenal world and from existing beings. The reason for this is that time can only be 'known' as *aporia*, an irresolvable contradiction, where each moment disappears in the very moment that it appears. As such, time itself escapes the subject-object opposition generated by ego-centrism. By itself time is simultaneously subjective and objective.

For example, ordinarily we think of time as a static grid or a screen on which subjects appear to move between set coordinates, for example from past to future. From this dualistic perspective, time is perceived as always out-there, someone else's time, but never 'my time'. To collapse this dualism Guru Nanak adopts the well-rehearsed strategy of shrinking the entire passage of human life into a single night, depicting the night's progression in terms of infancy, childhood, youth and old age.

> A momentary guest, man comes into this world to sort things out.
> But the fool is trapped by worldly greed
> Till, seized by death, he repents when he departs.
>
> The reaper, when he comes, cuts both ripe and unripe,
> He makes his preparations, picking up his scythe,
> For once the farmer orders, the crop is cut and weighed.
>
> The first watch is wasted on busyness, the next in sleep,
> The third in idle talk, and in the fourth dawn breaks,
> The One from which life springs is never once remembered.

To the person who refuses to confront the true nature of time as impermanent here and now ('one dies of course, but not me, not yet'), the Gurus project the true nature of time as one's own mortality that is always already there and cannot be deferred. Through this depiction one is existentially confronted with the presence of death here in this very moment of my existence. Reversing our normal everyday understanding, the Gurus show how, from the perspective of impermanence, the usual secure optimism of daylight and the waking state turn out to be illusions, whereas night and the dreaming state are better indicators of reality.

The nature of time as the ultimate equalizer of fortunes is evident in many hymns which show that if one rises, one must ultimately fall, irrespective of whether that happens in one's own lifetime, as shown by the plight of the princesses who fell victim to Babur's marauding army:

> The Princesses' hair once parted with vermillion
> Is scissored off from heads now covered with dust,
> They, who once had palaces, now have nowhere to sit.
>
> The wealth and looks they flaunted have become their foes,
> Dishonoured now by soldiers they're carried off.
> Pain and pleasure are given according to the Lord's command.

or whether it occurs after one's life has been lived, portrayed below in Shaikh Farid's autere verse:

> Umbrella-shaded kings, whose praise
> Their bards to drum beats cried,
> Are gone to clumber in their graves,
> With orphans at their side.

Time, however, is nothing if not paradoxical. According to the Gurus, it is neither real nor illusory, yet it is both; neither subjective nor objective, yet both. One the one hand time is the matrix in which the self is forged but ultimately trapped. Having forgotten its true nature as impermanent and becoming attached to worldly projects, beauty, youth and wealth, it suffers and grieves when these things are lost. On the other hand, given that the locus of one's existence in time is the body, time is a gift. Likening the temporal body to a full blooded mare, the Guru urges man to saddle up and ride life in order to cross the sea of existence:

> The body's a mare fashioned by the Lord.
> How blessed is this human existence which through virtue is
>   bestowed.

While ordinarily people lament the passing of time, grieving for things lost, and suffering pain when attachments are broken, the Guru teaches that attachment and suffering result only from the ego's habitual obstruction of the natural flow of time. By accepting time's impermanence as our own essence and seeing every attempt to control time as ultimately illusory like the waves of the sea, which are here one moment, gone the next, one can be released from suffering which the Gurus refer to through the metaphors of the cycle of births and death. But if one learns to cultivate a mindfulness of *hukam* through the practice of constant remembrance of the Name, one can learn to renounce self-attachment as the insidious obstacle to the flow of time. With the obstruction removed the mind is freed from its self-imposed bindings, from its immersion in the cycle of birth and death and from the anxiety of being born into one life-form after another.

Mind, consciousness, ego

If all of existence is sustained by *hukam*, the law of impermanence, then human consciousness (or mind) too is subject to this inexorable law. But as the Sikh Gurus constantly remind us, humans develop a tendency to resist this natural law. Instead of aligning our consciousness with *hukam*, we become attached to worldly things including our own egos, in the process increasing the separation of ego from its source. For Nanak this is man's fundamental problem. Nevertheless, he suggests that the solution to this problem also lies in the very nature and constitution of the ego.[21] How can this be possible?

To grasp what Nanak is saying here it is helpful to look more carefully at the term *man* (pronounced 'mun') which refers to the totality of consciousness prior to its being split through the function of the self-conscious ego, and for which the corresponding English terms would be psyche, mind, memory, consciousness, heart, etc. *Man* (or mind) has two aspects for the Sikh Gurus. There is on the one hand the mind-as-ego which causes the split or separation in the first place. As self-conscious, mind-as-ego possesses a discriminatory awareness, a sense of duality which grasps or rejects something external. Fundamentally, it is that which falsely posits an other (*duja*) as the basis of external reference and projects itself as the basis of normative reality. From Nanak's perspective, this mind-as-ego is afflicted by a chronic sickness (*diragh rog*). This happens to be the aspect of mind that calculates, desires, manipulates, flares up in anger and indulges in negative emotions. It needs to constantly assert and reaffirm its existence by fragmenting, conceptualizing and solidifying our experience of the temporal world. In fact Nanak refers to the ego-mind as *man pardesi* – the mind that has become a foreigner to itself. By creating a defensive boundary around itself it becomes estranged from what Nanak refers to as its true home, its beloved 'object', ego-less mind, or simply mind-as-other. Yet even though it is the one estranged from its beloved, the mind-as-ego disavows its own estrangement by positing that from which it is separated as stranger, as the other. In other words it projects its own activity and its guilt onto its other. Though separated by ego activity, however, the two aspects are intimately drawn to each other like lover and beloved. Together these aspects comprise a psychic whole.[22]

The split (but ultimately unified) nature of *man* raises questions about the 'standpoint' from which Nanak enunciates and particularly to his signature (the proper name 'Nanak') which accompanies all of his hymns. Who is it that speaks in these invocations? Precisely to whom is Nanak's utterance addressed? Who is the other of Nanak's speech? Is it God? Is it the reader? The answer to both of these must be an emphatic no! Rather Nanak almost always speaks to his own mind, addressing it at times through tender love as when he says 'my beloved mind', at times by cajoling it 'my foolish mind' or at other times beseeching it as a lover beseeches her beloved not to leave her. However, because almost every hymn in the Adi Granth ends with the invocation 'O Nanak' the impression may be given that through the use of his proper name, Nanak is signatory to his own words, that these words belong to the person Nanak, thereby marking them with a seal of authority? In which case Nanak's enunciation would be just another form of communication from A to B (where B might be another person, the reader, or God). Closer scrutiny shows that Nanak's speech is primarily directed to himself, to his own mind. More specifically Nanak's enunciation is invariably directed towards the ego-mind, and comes from his unconscious mind (the mind which is at home) as a form of supplication which beseeches his conscious ego-mind (the mind which has become a stranger to itself) to join together in union.

If the ego-mind responds to the supplication of the unconscious mind, it can do so only through the gesture of renunciation. By renouncing its self-naming as 'I', it can unite with its (beloved) other from which it has come to be separated. This gesture of withdrawal is deeply traumatic for the ego-mind, for it requires the ego to cross the very barrier which it has erected as its own defence. Such a crossing constitutes a death (ego-loss). However, what is absolutely clear in the Gurus' teachings is that they do not advocate any kind of annihilation of the ego or its repression through excessive discipline, for as Nanak says, the ego contains its own cure (*daru bi is mahi*)! Its cure is contained within it as its most intimate kernel, namely its beloved other. Because the nature of ego is intrinsically time, the cure involves a struggle not against the world but a struggle to exist within the world while being connected to the unconscious mind. This struggle, however, can only be waged through the language of love ('Beloved mind, come back to me', etc.). If ego-mind is to come back it must cross its own boundary, and in so doing it must die to itself.

Action and grace

Once the nature of ego and time are understood to be intrinsically linked, a rather more interesting and complex picture of ethical action emerges than the stereotypical opposition between a passive *karma* and an active notion of divine grace. For as Guru Nanak states in the Japji, 'Through deeds we've done we get this garment [of human existence], through grace we reach the door of liberation' (1.4). The Punjabi term for *karma*, as it occurs in the writings of the Sikh Gurus, is *karam*. It has three central connotations. First, it means to do, to perform, accomplish, make, to cause or effect. Second, when associated with the term *avagavan* (lit. coming and going, the cycle of births and deaths) it stands for fate, destiny, predestination, transmigration, insofar as all of these result from one's actions or deeds. The third meaning of *karam*, which happens to be derived from Arabic sources, is conceptually synonymous with the terms *nadar* and *kirpa* (implying grace) and the Persian term *hukam* (order/command/will/call, etc.).

In Vedic (orthodox Hindu) philosophy *karma* corresponds to something like a psycho-physical law according to which every action – physical or mental – has its own consequence which must be faced either in this life or in lives to come. The term thus corresponds to doctrines and processes of reincarnation and transmigration. In order to reap the consequences of one's previous *karma*, an individual self (*jiva*) has to take another birth, but in the very process of acting out this consequence, the *jiva* creates further chains of actions that incur further debt thereby setting in motion an endless cycle of birth–action–death–rebirth, etc. This cycle works on the principle of obligatory debt referred to variously as the karmic cycle or the wheel of alternating birth and death (*janam maran ka chakar*). The production of fresh *karma* keeps the wheel in endless motion until the chain is broken through the eradication of *karma* (= debt) and the *jiva* eventually attains liberation (*mukti*) from the karmic cycle.

Now, while the Sikh understanding of this process clearly acknowledges the traditional Indian articulation as a backdrop, there are some very important differences. Indeed the difference between the traditional Indic (or Brahmanic) concept of *karma* and the Sikh articulation of it, encapsulated within the linked terms *karam/nadar/hukam*, boils down to very different concepts of time. Accordingly the interlinked notions of *karam, nadar* and *hukam* often appear in the same hymn, underscoring the essentially paradoxical unity between them:

The deeds you do won't help you in the end,
For you reap whatever you've sown.
There is no other to protect you then,
Besides the saving grace shown by the Lord.
(Ramkali M5, p. 898)

In the writings of the Sikh Gurus, the Vedic notion of *karma* is replaced by the term *hukam*, the imperative that is inherent within the nature of existence. Instead of *karma* the Gurus speak of *karam*, deeds or actions that are aligned either with or against the working of *hukam*. Existence itself is depicted by the Gurus as an unfolding of the One, a writing (*lekh*) that is held in place by a fabric of space, time and cause (the so-called three qualities or *tin gun*). The metaphor of writing signifies the nature of the One as a non-static or continually flowing action. Thus any action committed by an individual ego, which by definition is already separated from the One, works against the flow of nature, effectively creating eddies that attempt to freeze the flux of existence. By working against the flow of *hukam*, every egotistical action leaves traces of its signature (*kar, karni*) within the temporal fabric. Instead of simply arising and passing out of existence as would be required by *hukam*, these karmic traces accumulate and prolong the separation between ego and the One.

As the context in which actions are performed, the operation of *hukam* can be likened to the law of conservation of energy, with the proviso that it is not limited by physical nature but includes the non-physical or psychic aspect of sentient beings such as thoughts, speech, desires and feelings. Thus 'good' and 'bad' rebirths are not rewards or punishments but are consequences of specific actions. An action is like a seed which must bear fruit either in this life or the next:

> We reap as we have sown, we eat as we have earned,
> No check is made of those who are marked as approved.
>
> We are all classified according to our deeds,
> The breath without remembrance is drawn to no avail.
>
> (Suhi M1, p. 730)

What determines the nature of a karmic seed, however, is the nature of a particular action. Moreover, each and every action, even when this action is intentional as in thought, speech, desire or feeling, is imprinted into the temporal fabric of the self through the work of memory. These imprints are confirmed tendencies which can be regarded as being somewhat like psychic genes. Actions repeated over time turn into tendencies or habits carried by an individual through this life into the next, unless a way is found to secure release from the imprinting process. Indeed there are certain meritorious actions, such as self-surrender, ego-loss, dying to the self, which, if performed, stop the imprinting process:

> We repeat that same act
> Prescribed from the beginning.
> But who can estimate the act
> Of surrender to the Guru?
>
> (Asa M1, p. 420)

As the most meritorious of all actions, self-surrender, requires the intervention of a *satguru* either in person or in Word. The person

who surrenders his or her mind to the guru is called a *gurmukh* –
lit. one whose being is turned towards the guru and who no longer
performs actions from the standpoint of ego:

> All wear the cloak of lust and wrath
>   On entering the world.
> Some see the light while others die
>   As the command dictates.
> There is no end to birth and death,
>   Possessed by other love.
> Bound in chains they transmigrate
>   There is nothing they can do.
> The guru comes to those on whom God's mercy is bestowed.
>   They turn away to die in life
> With spontaneity.
>
> (M3, p. 1414)

In contrast to the *gurmukh* stand the self-centred (*manmukh*) who
continue to act from the standpoint of ego. The actions of a *gurmukh* arise spontaneously.

The intertwined nature of *karam* and *nadar*, of the *gurmukh* and
manmukh, is perhaps best illustrated by references in the Gurus'
hymns to transmigration and the cycle of births and deaths. Insofar
as both the *gurmukh* and the self-willed must perform actions in
time, the cycle of births and deaths provides a mythical perspective
on time and life which gives rise to sympathy and respect for all living
beings. That all existing things are subject to birth, death and passage between different forms means that everything that is and that
happens is absolutely interconnected. This interconnectedness of all
existence is the only proper starting point for ethical thinking.

Birha: The state of fusion–separation

An important consequence of the concept of mind as Nanak elaborates it is that it both refines and negates the monotheistic concept of self/God as a relationship between inside and outside. In
Nanak's teaching this relationship is played out through the movement of love between lover (unconscious mind as non-ego) and
beloved (mind-as-ego). Monotheism in the strict sense becomes

almost redundant in the movement and crossings of love. Or when this love relationship is consummated (fusion), its outward manifestation is as an existence in the world that is radically interconnected to all others. This death of ego mind, or its capitulation to the embrace of the lover (unconscious mind), is constituted as a realization that our singularity is punctuated by the presence of other existing beings, not simply humans. A fact which opens up the possibility of ethics and politics based on a state of mind that keeps its two halves fused together in a state of balance. Let us try and unpack these ideas a little more carefully.

Part of the problem of monotheism, as we have already noted, is that it remains within a standpoint from which reality is perceived dualistically in terms of either/or oppositions: One/many, existence/non-existence, form/formlessness, good/evil, etc. Such a standpoint however replaces the immediate experience of the One with the dualistic representation of that experience. For Nanak the One cannot be attained by simply annihilating such oppositions or by elevating one term over another. Rather the unity proper to the Absolute must remain a paradox, that is, as the minimal coincidence of self with other. Nanak's term for this coincidence of self and other is *birha*. Resisting all description except through paradox, *birha* signifies a link between self and other that exists only in erasing itself. *Birha* is a point at which self and other touch and fuse but are ever in danger of separating.[13] In *birha* separation is the same as union and vice versa. To speak of this state the Gurus invoke the intensely emotional imagery of the virgin bride who anticipates the embrace of her husband on her wedding night, or the wife's longing for her husband's return from a far-off land. Bride, virgin, wife are simply metaphors for a self which is individuated and which pines for the union with the other. The emotion invoked here is that of intensely painful longing combined with the ecstasy of fusion. The pain signifies the minimal link to the self which cannot be broken for otherwise fusion would mean annihilation of self and world. Hence, self and therefore separation always remain but within ecstasy. Alternatively, the ecstasy of fusion is always there but tinged with the pain of separation. This state of fusion–separation where knowledge becomes non-knowledge is not a metaphysical ideal but a lived reality, a state of liberation, in which the liberated person *instinctively* avoids relating to everything else in terms of subject–object duality. Such a realized person no longer re-presents the Absolute since the conscious distinction between self and other, I and not-I, lover and beloved, *nirgun* (non-existence or a being that cannot be predicated) and *sargun* (existence or a being that can be predicated) has disappeared leaving an ecstatic and purely spontaneous form of existence (*sahaj*: literally equipoise).

In the writings of the Sikh Gurus, a person who maintains this state of *birha* and its attendant balance of separation–fusion, self–other, action–inaction, attachment–detachment in the course of daily life is known as *gurmukh* (literally one whose speech is centred around the Guru-Word, the unconscious Word, the *sat-guru*). The *gurmukh* lives in stark contradiction to the *manmukh* (one whose existence is self-centred). The distinction between *gur-mukh* and *manmukh* is more than just an ethical one since 'ethic' implies some minimal binding to some norm or duty. Rather the distinction implies a freedom from the bindings of the self, which gives rise not to an annihilation of self but to a spontaneity of speech–thought–action. Whether this transition is viewed epistemologically as a shift from duality to Oneness or existentially from *manmukh* to *gurmukh*, the transition itself revolves around the efficacy of the Name (*nam*) which is both the object of love and the means of loving attachment to one's beloved. The term *nam* names the impossible point of contact between self–other, separation–fusion. Attunement to *nam* constitutes a wordless communication between self and other which corresponds to the primordial love through which all existent things relate to each other before individuation takes over.

In Guru Nanak's hymns *nam* is not a particular word or mantra. It is inscribed within, yet manifests as speech in which traces of ego are constantly erased as they arise. As the constituting link between interiority and worldly action, *nam* arises involuntarily in the *gur-mukh's* speech through the practice of constantly holding in mind the remembrance of death (*nam simaran*). But *nam* cannot be obtained through self-effort alone. Its attainment depends on the grace or favourable glance (*kirpa, nadar*) of a spiritual preceptor or a guru.

Guru as word: *shabad, nam, satguru*

As one of the central terms in the Sikh lexicon, the term 'guru' takes on theologico-political connotations that go well beyond its meaning and application in the broader South Asian context, where it is limited to a teacher of worldly knowledge or a conveyor of spiritual insights. In Sikh tradition the term guru automatically incorporates this earlier meaning, referring thereby to the personality of Guru Nanak and his nine successor Gurus. Metaphorically it refers to the same principle of spirituality manifested in all ten Gurus; practically it serves to indicate the authority vested in the name 'Nanak'. Thus the hymns of the different Gurus in the Adi Granth are cited according to their respective composers as sequential locations (*mohala*) for the manifestation of the name 'Nanak'. Just before the death of the tenth Nanak, Guru Gobind Singh, spiritual authority was vested in the Adi Granth (henceforth Guru Granth Sahib), leading to the doctrine of scripture or Word as Guru (*shabad-guru*).

The logic of this doctrine notwithstanding, the question arises as to who was Nanak's guru? Who or what was his source of ultimate authority? It may be helpful here to look at several ways in which Nanak himself answers this question:

The Word is my guru, my mind attuned to it is its disciple.
I stay detached through the Unspoken Word.
(Siddh Gosht, p. 544)

I narrate the Word of my Beloved as it comes to me.
(Tilang M1 5, p. 722)

Elsewhere Nanak says: 'I myself do not know how to speak, For as I am commanded, so I speak'. What is interesting here is that despite speaking much, Nanak says categorically that *he* cannot speak. His self is silent. Rather, he claims, it is the Word that speaks not Nanak. As we have noted in the discussions above, in order to be vested with authority, Nanak must silence the speech of his ego (the faculty that says 'I am') by renouncing his claim to authority over what is spoken. Nanak's renunciation of authority is indicative of the fact that his own preceptor was not a human guru but an impersonal principle: the Word (*shabad*) which Nanak also calls *satguru* (lit. the true authority) a term that implies a personal relation to the Word. Personal or impersonal, only the Word speaks truly about the nature of existence.

A variation on the terms *shabad* and *satguru* is the term *anhad shabad* or *anhad nad* (lit. the 'unspoken Word' or 'unstruck Sound') inherited by the Sikh Gurus from their predecessors such as Kabir who in turn borrows the term from the Siddhas and Naths, the expert practitioners of Hatha Yoga. According to Nath usage *anhad shabad* refers to the 'Eternal Sound' that is heard at the climax of the Hatha Yoga process. In the context of the Sikh Gurus the term refers to words or language that is not tainted by traces of ego, and therefore not like ordinary communication between egos in which words are merely labels for things.

As *anhad shabad* the Word itself speaks or resounds without being spoken. This sounds like a tautology but actually indicates a mode of communication in which ego no longer controls the production of words, nor indeed the process of making words into things. Removed from the grasp of ego, words are no longer given value according to their degree of correspondence to things, but instead arise from an internalized mode of speech that occurs between conscious (ego) and unconsious (non-ego) mind. The unspoken Word arises from a mode of communication in which the mind speaks with itself, giving the impression of a departure from the standards of everyday social reality in which speech is meaningful if it makes sense to everybody. The point of this seemingly impossible communication is to rejoin the two aspects of the dualistic mind separated by ego sense. Devoid of ego-traces the Word that is so minted in the mind appears as an expression of wonder (*vismad*) at the nature of existence, that things exist at all rather than nothing. Just as all creation simply happens without asking why, so the unspoken Word arises without connection to intention, desire or will.

Thus Guru Nanak's authority, what makes him Guru or *gurmukh*, is derived from the *satguru =shabad*. But *satguru* as *shabad-guru* manifests only when the ego erases its own traces but without annihilating itself. This self-erasure is another name for the love between self and other that enables them to be One even in separation. Thus Nanak's authority is derived his own experience of the One.

This experience is authoritative in as much as it entails a radical re-orientation of consciousness which constitutes what is normally

understood as liberation. Thus the liberative reorientation of consciousness that the Sikh Gurus are looking for must happen primarily at the level of language or Word (*shabad*), such that one's
ordinary relationship to language, which is based on self-naming
where the 'I' is attached to a primary identification to its own
image and name, is transformed by its attunement to the Word as
nam (the Name). *Nam* is the link by means of which all existing
things acknowledge their non-existent source, as well as the means
by which each self acknowledges its link to its voided other.

Nam: Beyond the personal and the impersonal

As the Sikh Gurus articulate it, insofar as *nām* cannot simply be
reduced to God's Name, or to the names of individual gods, it illustrates the paradox of the One and the Many. Throughout the Adi
Granth, *nam* serves to replace what is named in other (especially
religious and philosophical) traditions as 'God' whose name is no
more than a tool for calling this entity to mind at will. In contradistinction, *nam* makes superfluous the need for such an entity and
thereby constitutes the single most important term for deriving a
post-theistic *gurmat*. For the Gurus, any 'God' or 'god' that is outside of the ego is to remain subject to the operation of *maya*, the
veil of illusion generated by the ego. Although 'God' is referred to
as the highest or ultimate, etc., these superlatives still only refer
to a highest or ultimate entity which remains within a scale determined by man. Thus, whereas 'God' is liable to be turned into an
idol, and therefore never experienced as such, *nam* signifies that
divinity can only be experienced through the meeting of eternity
and time, absolute and finite. *Nam* is therefore not so much an
indicator of transcendental experience as it is of the possibility of
all possible experience. The term *nam* is as much theological as it
is political. To see how this might be the case, it is helpful to relate
our discussion of *nam* to two other terms used by Guru Nanak to
refer to his experience of the One: the terms *nirgun* and *sargun*.

Nirgun: the experience of the divine as ineffable, without
qualities, beyond naming, signifies the divinity's detachment or
non-existence; hence either 'God' has no Name or God's Name is

the signifier of emptiness. *Sargun*: 'God' has infinite names, corresponding to infinite attributes, and insofar signifies absolute fullness, or a full involvement of the divinity in all things. Yet for
Nanak these two opposing terms are also the same: *nirgun aap
sargun bi ohi* (being absent the same One is also fully present, or,
the one detached is the same as the one involved).[24] So 'God' is
beyond yet 'God' actualizes himself through the relation of equivalence, and therefore substitutability, between all names and things.
As there is an equivalence between all things, so God's ineffability/
absence and his fullness/presence are different aspects of the same
formless one: *sargun nirgun nirankar.*[25]

Nam therefore names this equivalential connection
(*sargun-nirgun*) as an ineffable fullness, which is to say that *nam* is
a signifier of emptiness, an empty signifier. So what we regard as an
entity called 'God' is better termed *nam*, such that *nam* implies an
entity that is involved in the world but is at the same time absent.
Only *nam* can signify this impossible relation between absence/
presence, non-existence/existence, empty/full, etc. And *nam* can
do this not because it has any metaphysical characteristics, but
precisely because it is part of an already existing discursive network of signifiers, a symbolic order that we call language. *Nam*, in
other words, is part of the fabric of ordinary and everyday experience. *Nam* therefore helps us make sense of the divine paradox
(*nirgun-sargun*) by putting the impossible, the beyond, the absent, to
play in the context of finitude.[26] I can only experience the Absolute
as utterly empty (*nirgun*) if I can project it into the contingent, everyday experience of particulars (*sargun*) and therefore be involved
in the world. Consequently *nam*, as experience, is to experience the
detachment (*nirgun*) while living, speaking, and being involved in
ordinary worldly experience (*sargun*). If something is experienced
by the mystic, then this experience, if it is not to remain abstract
or detached, must actualize itself through attachment to a particular, to that which is finite and, therefore, to contingent events. If
nam names the mystical experience that desires ultimate fullness,
then *nam* must accompany all positive experience. This is also the
condition of all authority, of all sovereignty and consequently of
the political. Authority or sovereignty is such only if it is radically
empty or represented through the empty signifier that is *nam*.

This is why the Gurus prefer *nam*, a term which names the intricate link or experience between self and other. In contradistinction

to the 'I' generated by ego's cravings which operates an economy of narcissism precisely to gain a return to oneself, hence self-ownership as the beginning of ownership of the other, Name is the only capital that cannot be reduced to the status of a thing and circulated in an economy of exchange. Nanak's instruction in this regard is very pragmatic: one cannot simply escape the economic nature of one's existence in the world driven by the self's desire to make everything its own property. But it is possible to change the very nature of this economy by transforming narcissistic self-love into a love of the Name.

Moreover the Gurus suggest a practice for transforming the ego-based economy of ordinary life in which we accumulate knowledge, exchange entities, transact commerce, reasonable rules, plans and projects, rites and rituals. This practice is *nam simaran*: the constant holding in remembrance of the Name, which goes beyond mechanical repetition to become a spontaneous form of love between self and other. The paradoxical dialectic here between appropriation of *nam* and disappropriation of ego becomes more evident from the etymology of the word *simaran*. Derived from the Indo-European root *smr-* (to remember, hold in mind) the term has traditionally been understood to resonate with the Sanskrit terms *mr-* and *marana*, to die or pass away, suggesting that *simaran* is a form of remembrance which automatically lets go or renounces. Stated differently, *simaran* is first of all remembrance of one's own mortality, of the ego's death, remembering which one awakens to the Name. *Nam simaran* is therefore the condition of experience of finitude. Alternatively, the experience of finitude is the condition for the experience of *nam*. Because *nam simaran* is not a metaphysical concept but a concrete sacrificial practice for transforming memory, as that function of mind which weaves time into the structures that manipulate our existence and thinking, it can also be viewed as a way of transforming worldly time and existence. It provides a means for the individual to participate and make changes in the world. *Nam simaran* is as inherently political as it is spiritual. As a result such conceptual dualities as those between religion and politics, mysticism and violence become superfluous. This is evident in the lives of the Sikh Gurus for whom there was no contradiction between mystical experience and the life of a soldier, householder or political leader.

PART THREE

Pluralism and Its Challenges

CHAPTER SIX

Sikh Ethics

For guidance on ethics and morals Sikhs look to a number of scriptural and other sources which include the Guru Granth Sahib, accepted portions of the Dasam Granth, the janamsakhis, the writings of Bhai Gurdas, the Rahitnamas and a relatively recent document, the *Sikh Rahit Maryada* (SRM) (Sikh Code of Conduct). These sources in turn fall into two qualitatively different categories. By far the most important are the scriptural sources, particularly the Guru Granth Sahib. However, the moral teachings contained in the Guru Granth are non normative or universal in the sense that they provide a guidance to humanity in general and not just to a specific community. On the other hand, the Rahitnamas and the SRM are basically life-rules, organizational duties or codes of conduct that provide guidance on how Sikhs ought to live.

As noted in earlier chapters, the Rahitnamas are essentially codes that were formulated after the creation of the Khalsa. The compilers of these codes were faced with the need to consolidate differences and tensions within the early Sikh community by providing some form of internal discipline. Some of the codes came into being when the early Khalsa community was actively engaged in a battle for survival in the early part of the eighteenth century. For Khalsa Sikhs the main ethical duty is a quest for justice on behalf of the weak, the needy or those whose basic rights have been disregarded by unscrupulous states or rulers. To maintain some elementary public form corresponding to certain ethical principles, Khalsa Sikhs pledge themselves to fulfil certain obligations such as wearing the five Ks, uphold prohibitions against cutting

hair, shun the use of tobacco or other intoxicants and avoid marrying non-Sikhs. During the late nineteenth and early twentieth
centuries, and particularly under the modernizing influence of the
Singh Sabha, the Khalsa way of life regained and even surpassed
its earlier hegemonic position. Considerable effort was put into
consolidating the earlier Rahitnamas into a more coherent code
of conduct applicable to Sikh society and more in line with the
Guru Granth Sahib. These efforts culminated in the formulation
and ratification of the SRM in 1954 by the Shiromani Gurdwara
Parbandhak Committee.

Although the code outlined in the SRM continues to strongly
influence the conduct of Sikhs, its limitations are all too evident. The
conceptual framing of the SRM (see Chapter Three) belongs to the
colonial period where the competition between religious identities
took precedence over other considerations. Such a conceptual framing
may have produced the desired effect in Punjab, but it is proving to be
completely inadequate for contemporary life in the major metropo-
lises of India and in the Western diasporas where Punjabi tradition
and life style directly encounters a post-secular politics, technology,
environmental concerns and pluralism on a scale not seen before.

To provide answers to increasingly complex ethical dilemmas
Sikhs are beginning to by-pass the SRM and look at new ways of
interpreting primary sources such as the Guru Granth Sahib. In
fact it is generally accepted that if the codes of conduct conflict
with the precepts of the Guru Granth, or if they are simply silent,
they should be disregarded in relation to the former. However, as
we learned in the previous chapter, Sikh scripture is resistant to a
conceptual logic based on metaphysical rationality or representa-
tional thinking. As such it does not allow the reader to form absolute responses to issues that many of us are concerned with. This
is partly because of the strong poetic and musical framing of the
text which resists metaphysical schematizations such as God/Man/
World that privilege a transcendental deity over life itself. In such
schemas, which are routinely associated with 'religions' and their
belief systems, life itself is valued only in relation to its transcendental or sacred ground.

To the uninitiated reader the Guru Granth's lack of rigid ideology and categorical imperatives ('you *must* do this . . .') can be
disconcerting. But this does not necessarily mean the absence of
a system of moral thinking in the teachings of the Sikh Gurus

(*gurmat*). Indeed, as outlined in the previous chapter, Guru Nanak actually spells out something like a 'moral standard' in the opening lines of the Japji, even though it cannot be made to coincide with societal norms of morality. Nanak identifies his moral standard as self-realization (*sachiara*), the struggle to remain faithful to the truth of an experience of Oneness whose manifestation is ego-loss, and to therefore act and live according to a natural imperative (*hukam rajai chalana*) that undergirds any social law. The moral standpoint is not grounded in belief or standpoint. Rather it is best considered as a general principle or sovereign imperative (*hukam*) which enjoins that whatever the duties or discipline entailed by one's station (*rajai/raza*), these ought to be performed to the best of one's ability until one can progress to a higher station and so on. We can therefore consider the moral 'standard' as a way of performing actions such that in each act performed or duty fulfilled, we actively appropriate the sovereign imperative (*hukam*) that is inscribed into life itself, indeed into all existence. Because *hukam* is immanent within life (*hukmai andar sab koe, bahar hukam na koe*), it replaces the need for transcendental ground, be that a deity or otherwise. In other words, because of the immanence of *hukam*, life is revalued for itself and not as a supplement to 'the sacred'. Life itself is sovereign and cannot be captured within metaphysical distinctions such as sacred versus profane and sacred versus secular. This *hukam*, inscribed into all life, is the imperative to negate the ego which says 'I am'. If left untended, the sense of 'I am'-ness becomes a disease engendered by five propensities that might be regarded as 'moral evils'. The Sikh Gurus refer to them as the 'five enemies' or 'five thieves': (i) *kam* (concupiscence, lust or simply craving); (ii) *krodh* (anger or wrath); (iii) *lobh* (covetousness or the desire to possess what belongs to others); (iv) *moh* (attachment or delusion); (v) *ahankar* (egotistical pride). Guru Arjan provides a telling description of each of these 'thieves', referring to them as psychic entities or persons that lead the mind astray:

> Attachment (*moh*), mightiest of enemies,
> Whose power breaks the strongest men!
> How you beguile gods and men,
> All demigods, birds and beasts.
>> Salute the One who made the world,
>> Nanak, seek refuge with the Lord.

Lust *(kam)*, you deliver man to hell,
And make him roam through many births!
O stealer of thoughts, found in all worlds,
Destroyer of pious observance!
The pleasure you give is brief,
You take away all wealth and peace.
            The company of saints removes
            Your fear, O Nanak, through the Lord.

Anger *(krodh)*, the basis of all strife,
In whom there is no tenderness!
All creatures in your power
Act like monkeys made to dance.
Your company makes man debased
And subject to death's punishments.
            O protector of the weak
            Nanak, from anger save us all!

Greed *(lobh)*, close companion of the great,
Your surges make so many twitch!
You make them race and run around,
Lurch and roll unsteadily.
You are without respect for friend,
For guru, parents or for kin.
You're known as the one who makes man do
And eat and make what he should not.
            O save me, save me, Nanak says,
            I look to your protection, Lord.

Ego *(ahankar)*, the root of birth and death,
You are the very soul of sin!
Betraying friends, you give foes strength,
As you extend illusion's net.
You weary man with birth and death
With knowing many joys and pains.
With roaming in doubt's wilderness
With facing mortal illnesses.
            The only doctor is the Lord,
            O Nanak, whose Name we repeat.
                                    (GGS, p. 1358)

Essentially these 'five enemies' are psychic propensities of the self that either attract the person towards something (maybe an object or an action), or repel the person away from what is wholesome. They are better understood not as biological or primitive instincts, but as learned dispositions or habitual frames of mind that can take on a life of their own. If left unchecked these propensities keep the individual in a state of restlessness. The person whose being is motivated by these five enemies will continue to disregard *hukam* and in doing so will inscribe ego into his or her being, thereby perpetuating the cycle of attachment to one's own ego. Such a person is called *manmukh* (lit. self-willed).

However, as Guru Nanak reminds us in the first stanzas of his Japji, the 'five enemies' cannot be controlled through ascetic practices, ritual cleansing or by philosophically reflecting about them. Rather they must be regulated by inculcating and actively practicing virtues such as wisdom (*gian*), truthfulness (*sach*), justice (*niaon*), temperance (*sanjam*), courage (*nidar*), humility (*garibi, nimarta*) and contentment (*santokh*). Those who actively appropriate such virtues are able to inscribe *hukam* into their very being as ego-loss. They actively resist saying 'I am' and instead balance this egotistical propensity by being able to say 'I am not', and thereby elevate themselves beyond the self-willed rationalist morality of societal norms (*manmukh*). Appropriating *hukam* (the sovereign imperative that resists being rationalized into a system of knowledge) forces the individual to think and act almost like an aesthete or artist. Such a person who is freed and empowered to challenge existing values, freed to create new values rather than blindly following social rules, is known as *gurmukh*.

Hence Guru Nanak's moral standard of ego-loss, the *gurmukh*, takes us beyond socially sanctioned oppositional norms such as good versus evil, wrong versus right and violence versus peace. It questions the very frameworks in which we operate even as it allows us to make deliberate, conscious choices in both mundane challenges of everyday life and the more extraordinary quandaries that face human beings today. Consequently the Gurus' teachings are entirely practical and applicable to all life situations, actual or possible. They allow the person to determine how best to live from day to day in an ever-changing world.

To understand how this moral 'standard' of ego-loss might work in actual practice, it will be helpful to pluck scenarios or questions out of the stream of everyday life in order to engage the more abstract theory outlined above and in the previous chapter. Some of the scenarios are real, some fictional, others based on interviews with Sikh practitioners who have faced such issues, yet all of them involve real, somewhat cold and often uncomfortable consequences. The scenarios will be organized around a set of questions that reflect the key moral and ethical issues.

Good and evil

Basic questions: Does it make sense to speak of good versus evil or 'good' versus 'bad' persons in Sikhi? Does a gurmukh have to be a member of the Sikh community? Can someone be an atheist and still strive for the gurmukh stage? Why do bad things happen to good people?

The word 'good' has relatively little meaning in Sikh ethics unless it is understood in relation to the problem of self-centredness. Thus one might be deemed good in the sense that one diligently follows one's value or belief system which may or may not be associated with a particular set of life-rules or code of conduct (*rahit*). And this may indeed involve respect or tolerance towards others. But according to *gurmat* (the Guru's philosophy) one might still be a *manmukh* (self-centred individual), whereas the aim in *Sikhi* is to achieve the state of consciousness known as *gurmukh* – one who has experienced self-realization or Oneness by shattering his or her ego. There is therefore no essential goodness or badness. It is more accurate to speak of good and bad actions. For a *gurmukh* dualities such as 'good' and bad' have only relative meaning. To become a *gurmukh* one has to undergo self-transformation by overcoming the five psychic vices: *kam* (lust), *krodh* (anger), *lobh* (greed), *moh* (attachment), *ahankar* (pride).

A *gurmukh* certainly does not have to belong to the Sikh community. The term *gurmukh* refers to a state of consciousness which can be achieved by anyone. Hence Sikhs might be fervently religious but still be no closer to overcoming the *manmukh* stage of existence. Overcoming *manmukh* existence involves a radical transformation of one's mind, and there is no reason why this could not be done by non-Sikhs as long as they remain focused on the desire to attain spiritual unity. Thus one can technically be an 'atheist' and still strive for a *gurmukh* state, since the basis of *Sikhi* has little or nothing to do with the artificial categories 'theism' or 'atheism' or with belief in a divine deity.

Bad things can certainly happen to good people. Again, the problem is with the terms 'good' and 'bad'. *Sikhi* teaches the equal acceptance of good and bad as part of the happening of *hukam* (the law of existence). Only a *manmukh* laments if bad things happen to him or her, and celebrates if good things happen. To a *gurmukh* who strives to attain a state of mental equipoise at all times, all that happens is acceptable as equally sweet (*tera kia mitha lagai*).

Use of force

Basic questions: Can violence or killing be justified? Can war be justified? To what extent is martyrdom acceptable? Is capital punishment acceptable?

In *Sikhi* there is no metaphysical contradiction between violence and peace. These are relative terms. True violence is the self's assertion of its separateness, its individuality, by forgetting that all existence is within *hukam*. True peace is attained by violently struggling against the self's tendency towards individuation, its tendency to believe that it exists outside of *hukam*. However, killing can only be justified as a very last resort when all other means have been exhausted, or when the lives of innocent people, including one's own life, are threatened. As explained in Chapters Two and Three, there are examples in Sikh history when the taking of life has been justified, for example, when it has been beneficial to a larger number of people or to the survival of a way of life. So, if one is forced to take the life of another, or that of an animal, in self-defence, it should be done from a state of mind motivated by virtuous instincts such as compassion and the intention to protect others, rather than anger or pride. Thus one must not kill simply to protect one's possessions or for the sake of revenge as these are tendencies motivated by egotism. Accordingly, war can only ever be justified as a last resort when the innocent and defenceless are under attack from oppressors. Under such circumstances, to not raise the sword, to simply stand by and watch others persecuted would be regarded as nothing more than self-preservation, a pretentious form of ego-indulgence and would constitute a greater evil.

The opposite of this tendency is provided by the figure of the martyr (*shahid*) who is able to offer his or her own body for the benefit
of others in a pure and selfless action. The martyr is therefore one
who has most struggled with his own self and is able to imbibe the
principle of *hukam*: to not inscribe ego on oneself, the one who is
most able to surrender the self. According to the paradoxical logic
of *hukam*, there is no consensus among Sikhs either for or against
capital punishment.

Behavior, value and culture

Basic questions: What is the value of marriage and family? Is sex
outside marriage permissible? Is it moral to have more than one
spouse at one time? Is divorce acceptable? Is the decline of mar-
riage a good or bad thing?

   Although there is no religious or other imperative to 'go forth
and multiply', Sikhs are by and large family-orientated irrespective
of their piety. Due to their relative prosperity the norm for Sikh
families is two to three children. Pious Sikhs will often say that
preference for family life, as opposed to, say, the path of reclusive
asceticism (*sanyasa*), derives from the need to translate the three
central precepts of *nam japna*, *wand chakna* and *kirt karana* into
the practice of everyday life. To properly imbibe these precepts and
achieve the ultimate goal of liberation through self-realization,
Sikhs are strongly encouraged to adopt the life of a householder
(*grihasta*).

   With the exception of the child-Guru, Harkrishan (who died
at the age of 9), all of the Sikh Gurus took spouses, had children
and lived lives that combined the roles of householder, warrior and
spiritual preceptor. However, the Gurus were fully aware that this
would also be the most demanding way to live. It was much easier to run away from social issues, by renouncing family ties and
becoming an ascetic.

   In order to lead a life which allows full expression of one's
emotional, psychological and biological impulses, *Sikh*ism encour-
ages and generally follows a heteronormative model of marriage.
However, because the joint or extended family is still the prevalent
norm within North Indian society and to a lesser extent in the
Western Sikh diaspora, marriage is not a private affair between

two individuals. Rather it involves the joining of two families who become connected through the individuals. The concept of marriage in *Sikhism* is not based on a social contract but aims at the fusion of two souls into one. It is therefore analogous to the union of man with the divine which is also the goal of Sikh spirituality. In this union man is the lover (hence female) while the divine is the beloved (hence male). Marriage is the institution where spirituality is consummated:

> *They are not man and wife who have physical contact only.*
> *Only they are truly married who have one spirit in two bodies.*
> (GGS, p. 788)

Physical consummation is therefore to be considered a necessary step towards a broader goal of awakening spiritual desire and longing for detachment within the very institution which joins two individuals. Such attachment, which is to be attained while being attached to another, is likened to the 'blissful state' in which the mind attains union with the beloved. Given this emphasis, it is not difficult to see why sex outside of marriage is forbidden. For the Gurus, while denial of the sexual instinct is certainly unhealthy, sexual activity should not be indulged in for the purpose of procreation. Rather it should be enjoyed between man and wife in a deeply committed relationship.

While monogamy is certainly the norm, there are occasions where taking more than one wife has been sanctioned. The obvious examples are those of the sixth Guru, Hargobind, and the tenth Guru, Gobind Singh, who, under strong pressure from their parents and relatives, both remarried after the deaths of their first wives. Another circumstance that would allow a divergence from monogamy is where one's brother dies and the remaining brother takes the widow into his own household in order to protect her and her family. But the final decision in such cases is always with the woman.

Given the sentiment that the institution of marriage has to be entered into as a lifelong commitment, divorce is something to be avoided as far as is reasonably possible. However Sikhs also recognize that this ideal may be severely strained in certain cases, particularly when one partner or his/her children may be suffering unnecessarily due to domestic violence or related issues. In

such cases marriages are allowed to be dissolved and remarriage
allowed.

Gender: Equality and difference

*Basic Questions: Are the roles played by men and women a moral
issue? What value do Sikhs place on the notion of equality of the
sexes?*
The answer to these questions depends on how we apply the moral
standard of ego-loss. The real issue, then, is whether both women
and men can become *gurmukh*, and the answer to this question has
to be an emphatic yes! This would then suggest that the roles played
by men and women should never become a moral issue. Nevertheless,
in keeping with societal norms men and women have played different
roles. But if the moral standard is not biological but spiritual, there is
nothing, scripturally or otherwise, to stop a reversal of these societal
roles. The question of 'equality' is more complex, however, and to
answer it we need to look at historical and contemporary examples.
The Sikh Gurus gave woman an exalted place within society
echoing the strong emphasis on practicing spirituality within a
worldly setting. In a much quoted verse, Guru Nanak castigates
medieval Indian society for looking down on women because they
menstruated or bore children. Even more vehement was the Guru's
condemnation of *sati*, the self-immolation of women at the funeral
pyres of their husbands.

We are born from a woman, and in a woman we grow.
We're engaged to and wed a woman.
We take a woman as lifelong partner, and from the woman
  comes family.
If one woman dies we seek another.
Without woman there is no social bond.
So why denigrate woman when she gives birth to kings?
Woman herself is born of woman, none comes into the world
  without her.

(GGS, p. 473)

Other Sikh Gurus further emphasized the status of woman. Guru
Amar Das forbade women to veil their faces while Guru Gobind

Singh invited his spouse to become part of the ceremony for initiating Sikhs into the order of the Khalsa. In keeping with this, monogamy is therefore the preferred and predominant model. Widow remarriage is a relatively prevalent occurrence in contemporary Sikh society, although many other Sikh women choose not to remarry and remain single.

The representation of Sikhs in contemporary media – bearded and turbaned men carrying swords, cases of female infanticide, combined with a growing chorus of voices advocating more women's equality – has given the impression that Sikh society is fundamentally patriarchal. Appearances can be deceptive, however. Closer scrutiny suggests that the role and status of women is more diverse and influential than is suggested by the media imagery. If the somewhat simplistic feminist notion of 'equality' with men is the goal being sought then Sikhism does not fare all that badly. Women have exactly the same access to religious teachings and practices as men. In fact the transmission of basic spiritual and moral precepts to the next generation usually begins with women in their role as mothers. Though rarely acknowledged the teachings of the Sikh Gurus suggest that women have an innately greater spiritual potential than men. This is partly because the central obstacle in spiritual attainment is not simply the ego but the conflation of the ego with the attributes of maleness which hinders one's ability to tap the reservoir of emotions and moods necessary for achieving a balanced state of mind. Moreover, the nature and concept of 'God' or the divine in the teachings of the Sikh Gurus is not necessarily male. Divinity has equally feminine attributes.

Historically, women have risen to the highest positions in Sikh society. The tenth Guru's spouse, Mata Sundari, not only played a key role in the creation of a new spiritual-cum-military order (the Khalsa), but after the Guru's death led the Sikh community in spiritual and political matters, far longer than any male Sikh Guru. Other women such as Rani Jindan (the spouse of the Sikh ruler, Maharajah Ranjit Singh) wielded enormous power in the Sikh kingdom prior to British rule. In recent years, Bibi Jagir Kaur was elected the jathedar of the Akal Takht, the highest ecclesiastical position in Sikhism. In short, there is no teaching in the scriptures or anywhere else that prevents women from achieving, social, political or spiritual ascendancy. Nor are the roles played by men and women a moral issue. Factors that prevent women from doing so are primarily ingrained in the social and patriarchal fabric of North Indian society, particularly caste. Contrary to what is often thought, Westernization has had an ambivalent effect on women's status in Sikh society. Although women have found and taken advantage of greater access to education and professions, colonialism also helped to foster a certain hyper-masculinity, thus further entrenching the notion that masculinity is normative because God is male.

Sexuality

Basic questions: Is transgendering immoral? Is homosexuality immoral? Should gay marriages be recognized by the State?

According to the value system of modern Sikhism as prescribed by the Sikh Code of Conduct (1954), Sikhs are expected to live in a family environment in order to properly nurture their children. Most Sikhs interpret the family structure to be based on a heteronormative model of sexuality. Because the heteronormative model has gained a moral sanction, alternative models of family have been discouraged. Many Sikhs have interpreted this to mean that homosexuality cannot result in procreation and is therefore unnatural. However, such a judgment bears a strongly Christian, and especially Catholic imprint, which believes in natural law: 'what is natural is what is moral'. This can be seen in recent statements by Sikh religious leaders who not only openly condemned homosexuality as unnatural but seemed to justify their stance by reference to 'other major world religions'.

As a result of these strictures many Sikhs who have homosexual desires have tried to enforce upon themselves a 'normalization' of their sexuality by believing that what they experience is merely lust, and as a remedy marrying a member of the opposite sex and having children. Such a process of forcing homosexuals to go underground, as it were, has led to a belief among many Sikhs that there are no homosexual Sikhs. This belief has, in turn, caused distress to those Sikhs who happened to find themselves attracted to members of the same sex.

However, a closer look at the primary source of Sikh ethics, the Guru Granth Sahib, shows that while the question of homosexuality has not been explicitly discussed, there is no justification whatsoever for castigating and banning homosexuality. In fact homosexuality need not even be regarded a moral issue given the fact that South Asian culture has by and large been traditionally tolerant towards the question of homosexuality seeing it as one of manifestations of ecstatic and erotic mysticism. Trans-sexuality and gender crossing is a well-known aspect of mystical enunciation particularly in those movements influenced by *bhakti* and Sufism. More recently many Sikhs have called for new ways of interpreting Sikh scripture on the question of gender and sexuality which give greater credence to the trans-gendered 'standpoint' of devotional love that is central to the Sikh Gurus' teachings. Recent research suggests that such new interpretations are likely to complicate the issue considerably as the Sikh Guru's writings on love and eroticism may challenge the peculiarly modern perceptions of sexuality.

Diet, drugs, alcohol and tobacco

Basic questions: What is the Sikh stance on eating meat? Is the food a person eats a moral concern? Is there anything inherently wrong with drug use? Is the use of substances to produce an altered state desirable and/or part of common human experience, or does it defile the natural state of the body?

Despite the fact that communal eating and the sharing of food has been and continues to be so central to the Sikh way of life, the current Sikh Code of Conduct (SRM) has left the question of dietary rules unresolved or ambiguous at best. This is perhaps not surprising when we consider that the primary source of Sikh ethics, the Guru Granth Sahib, does not provide hard-and-fast rules concerning diet. Instead it offers more philosophical and pragmatic advice about avoiding or eating in moderation such foods that could potentially harm the body and mind.

Nevertheless, Sikh communities throughout the world have adopted a fairly consistent attitude towards certain kinds of food. For example, as a rule, no meat or intoxicants are served in Sikh gurdwaras, all of which have a communal kitchen attached to them. Foods prepared within the gurdwara have to use wholesome natural products, primarily milk, wheat or corn flour and vegetables. A variety of Punjabi tea is also served in many Western gurdwaras but this is not the norm. Sikhs initiated into certain Khalsa orders are strictly vegetarian with the exception of sects like the Nihangs. The Sikh Code of Conduct does not prohibit meat eating but it does state that animals should be slaughtered as humanely as possible with a single blow. Only beef is strictly avoided as most Sikhs come from a rural background. Since the cow, buffalo and ox were central to the livelihoods of many rural Sikhs, these animals are treated with respect and never slaughtered for consumption.

As far as drug, tobacco and alcohol use is concerned the Sikh stance is fairly straightforward. Tobacco and drug use is strictly forbidden. The Gurus encouraged their disciples to practice natural methods to control and cultivate the potential of the senses. Each of the senses provides a particular pathway to states of consciousness that leads to the experience of Oneness. But to achieve this state the senses also have to be directed by the primary virtues. At the same time one must avoid being directed by the primary vices of *kam, krodh, lob, moh, ahankar*, etc. which redirect the senses towards worldly things, leading to craving, addiction and ultimately an increase the egocentric state of *manmukhta*. The vices simply add fuel to the fire. Drugs taken for so-called recreational uses may lead to fleeting experiences of ecstasy, but in as much as these drug-induced states are accompanied by hallucinatory and delusional states of mind, they also run the risk of long-term damage to the body through long-term addiction. Drug use is therefore to be avoided except where they are prescribed by competent physicians for treatment of a specific illness. Now there are sects such as the neo-Nihangs and certain Sant *deras* who have used opium to enhance certain mental powers but this practice is forbidden in mainstream Sikhism. In so far as alcohol dulls the senses its use is also to be avoided as far as possible, although in practice the strictures on alcohol are less strictly observed by many Sikhs.

Life and death

Basic questions: What are the Sikh teachings on life and death? How do these determine Sikh attitudes towards issues such as abortion, prenatal testing, suicide and euthanasia? Are contraception and reproductive technologies compatible with Sikh principles?

Death is a powerful and abiding theme in the teachings of the Sikh Gurus and more broadly within South Asian spirituality.

Despite saying much about the fact and phenomenon of death, however, the Sikh Gurus also acknowledge that death is and will remain a constant mystery, an irresolvable contradiction, not least because death is intrinsically connected to life and existence rather than being opposed to it. Death and life are often mentioned and discussed in the same verse and often in the same line. In this sense the Sikh Gurus perceive death differently from modern science which defines death as 'the permanent cessation of the vital function in the bodies of animals and plants' or, simply, as the end of life caused by stoppage of the means of sustenance to body cells. In Sikh teachings death underlies existence from the very start of one's life, or as Bhagat Kabir says to the woman swollen with pride at the birth of her son: 'the foolish woman does not realize that death was already there from the moment her son was born, for as he grows older he grows ever closer to death'. Or as Guru Nanak says 'we entered this world with death written as our fate':

His steps have become shaky, his feet and hands slip, the skin of his body has shrivelled. Eyes become dim, ears deaf, but the self-centred man still doesn't know the Name.

What have you gained by coming into this world, blind man? You remembered not the Lord, nor served the Guru. You depart having lost even the merit that you brought into this world. (GGS, p. 1126)

Affections are dead, love is dead, hatred and wrangling are dead too. Color has faded, beauty is gone and the body writhes in agony. Whence did he come, where did he go? What was he, what wasn't he? The self-centred ones talked incessantly and immersed themselves in their pleasures. But, says Nanak, without the Name, their honor is split from head to toe. (GGS p. 1287)

Far from being expressions of morbidity and nihilism, such verses are meant to remind man of his attachment to worldly things and to his own self-centred nature, and that the unavoidable event of death marks the end not of the body but of the very self and identity that one has so carefully nourished throughout one's life. Contemplating both together, one truly comprehends the phenomenon of life and death (*maran jivan ki sojhi pae*).

Suicide and euthanasia

Basic Question: Does Sikhi endorse the hastening of one's death or the death of another?

Sikhs believe that human birth is a precious gift, an opportunity with which to harness the body's potential for adoring the Name and serving others. Life is a field upon which the self can properly experience the twin registers of *sukh* (pleasure/enjoyment/happiness) and *dukh* (pain or suffering) as thoroughly intertwined. Although one's existence may be imbued with pain, Sikh teaching emphasizes that one should not reject pain by labelling it bad, but rather accept it with the same demeanour that one accepts pleasure. From such a perspective, many Sikhs argue that taking one's own life is ethically wrong because the impulse to annihilate oneself emanates primarily and paradoxically from a deep-seated self-attachment, the desire to cling to one's own life as if it were one's own to begin with.[1] Moreover, suicide far from solving anything only creates more pain for those left behind.

The case of euthanasia is more complex, however. To begin with, it is necessary to differentiate between active and passive euthanasia. Whereas active euthanasia implies the intentional hastening of death by a deliberate act, passive euthanasia can refer to the intentional hastening of death through a deliberate omission or withdrawal of things that might otherwise sustain life, for example, food, medical treatment or an artificial life-support mechanism. Furthermore, euthanasia can be carried out against the wishes of the patient or actually be requested by the patient and undertaken by a third party who might be a doctor or other accomplice. The modern and conventional Sikh response to euthanasia is to say that the decision to kill or ascribe death to a person in pain or undergoing other forms of suffering is based on delusion. The causal root of delusion can be traced to one or another of the five vices spoken of in Sikh scripture [*kam* (lust), *krodh* (anger), *lobh* (coveteousness), *moh* (attachment), *ahamkar* (pride)].[2] In such cases, the argument goes, the dying person and/or the person assisting the dying person, should use the process of dying as an opportunity to reflect on the nature of self-attachment and other psychological charges associated with the five vices. The idea here is that as long as there is life, there is always hope. Sikhs contemplating euthanasia should look at the whole picture, as it were, and try to make the appropriate distinctions between ending life and not artificially prolonging a terminal state. For those who contemplate assisting the death of another, the emphasis of this argument is to provide greater care and service for others who are less fortunate.

While this theory works perfectly well in the cases where the motive for hastening death is bodily pain or a similar type of suffering, nevertheless, a complication can be seen to arise when we stretch the motives for hastening death. The complication arises if we take into account historically important cases of Sikhs refusing to live in order to serve a 'higher' or nobler cause. The obvious example is the person who hastens his or her own death in order to save others from a fate that they themselves may not have contemplated. For example, the possibility of an entire community being enslaved or becoming subservient to more powerful external socio-political forces. Two of the Sikh Gurus (Arjan and Tegh Bahadur) willingly chose to be tortured and die rather than prolong their own lives and comforts, and in so doing condemn their fellow men and women to subservience and misery. Their deaths had a powerful emancipatory force on the community. There are numerous other examples in early and modern Sikh history. Of course, such death is normally classified as martyrdom. But how distinct, philosophically and spiritually, is the concept of martyrdom from other types of death, especially when the idea of a good or proper death is so strong in Sikh scripture? My point here is that health practitioners may need to be aware, on the one hand, of the psychological motivations for an individual's hastening death, and on the other, of the deeply spiritual and often ambivalent nature of Sikh teachings on death.

Abortion

Basic Question: Under what circumstances, if any, is abortion acceptable?

The modern Sikh Code of Conduct and related historical sources are silent about the question of abortion. As a result individual Sikhs and Sikh communities in Punjab and in the Western diaspora have had to work out relevant responses based on their interpretation of the teachings of the Sikh Gurus or by resorting to existing Punjabi cultural norms and shared traditions.

When one turns to Sikh scripture, however, the issue of abortion is not specifically mentioned although there are many references to the conception of life, the nature of sentient beings and the transmigration of the soul. In consonance with prevalent North Indian cultural beliefs and practices, many Sikhs share a culture and world view that includes ideas of karma, rebirth, and collective as opposed to individual identity. Unlike the linear notion of time held by Judaism, Christianity and Islam, many Sikhs (like Hindus and Buddhists) believe that time is non-linear and consequently birth and death are repeated for each person in continuous cycles. The desires, thoughts and actions one does in a particular lifetime leave their traces in the memory of an individual. These traces influence the circumstances and predispositions experienced in future lives. Accordingly there is no absolute beginning or end. More importantly, from such a perspective, the moment of conception is the rebirth of a fully developed person who has lived in previous lifetimes. To terminate a birth through abortion would be tantamount to refusing a soul entry into a particular body and sending it back into the cycle of birth and deaths – a choice that is not ours to make. Sikh scripture does indeed make reference to karmic theory, as for example in the first verse of a famous hymn composed by Guru Nanak:

In the first watch of night, my trader friend
You were thrown into the womb, where upside down
Your thoughts and prayers became fixed on the Lord.
Upside down your prayers and devotion were completed.
Each helpless creature must endure its written fate.
Nanak, in the night's first watch you were sent to the
womb.

(GGS, p. 74)

Consequently those Sikhs who interpret the Gurus' teachings as inseparable from the broader North Indian cultural world-view, tend to take a firm position that abortion is wrong as it interferes in the divine schema. If conception has taken place, the argument goes, it would be wrong to deliberately induce miscarriage and abortion. Based as it is on a purely metaphysical standpoint, however, such a view is increasingly recognized by Sikhs today as idealistic, and unable to provide suitable answers to instances such as: (i) a threat to the mother's physical health if continuing pregnancy were to lead to her death, or if it were to physically harm the mother but not cause her death; (ii) a threat to the mother's psychological health, if, for example, the pregnancy is due to rape or incest, or if there is an adverse medical condition; (iii) problems with the foetus' health, for example if the foetus is malformed or has contracted a disease such as HIV; (iv) when a woman simply wishes to exercise her 'right to choose' as to whether or not to abort the foetus.

Because the vast majority of scriptural teachings avoid such metaphysical standpoints as at the very least unhelpful, most Sikhs influenced by the modern reformist tradition tend to interpret the Guru's teachings in a more pragmatic fashion. Thus, if one follows the above hymn through to completion, it becomes obvious that the Guru has a more pragmatic and existential notion of the nature of time that is firmly rooted in an acceptance of impermanence:

In the night's fourth watch, my trader friend,
The reaper comes into the field.
None is informed, my trader friend
When death will come to send them off.
When death comes to send them off
Is known to the Lord and no one else.
Your family's lamentation is false
For the dead one is no longer their kin.
What you get in the end is only that
On which you fastened so much love.
Says Nanak: In the nights fourth watch, my soul
The reaper harvested the field.

(GGS, p. 74)

Consequently neither modern Sikh society nor its ecclesiastical structure has been overly concerned to lay down hard and fast rules in regard to issues such as abortion. Nevertheless, if there are strictures regarding abortion which would be binding on all Sikhs, it would be that abortion should not be linked to any kind of personal gain, economic or otherwise, nor driven by selfish motives or by the five vices.

A poignant example of the way that the doctrinal ambiguity can have negative social consequences can be seen in the continuing prevalence of female foeticide in many Sikh (and North Indian) couples.[3] This stems from a general bias in North Indian society favouring males over females. The roots of this bias stem from the patriarchal nature of North Indian society in which women are viewed as economic liabilities. As a result, when they get married sons receive a dowry along with their wife, which adds to the family prestige and wealth. For daughters the case is reverse. One result of this cultural belief/practice is an evident decrease in the female population especially in Punjab. As a social practice it has reached alarming proportions in the diaspora, where large numbers of Punjabi Sikh women especially in Canada and Britain have succumbed either to greed or to the pressures of the extended family system and seek early termination of the pregnancy. There are increasing signs, however, that the political, social and spiritual empowerment of women in Sikhism may help to curb this unhealthy trend.

Contraception and reproductive technologies

Although contraception and abortion are often linked together they are two rather different issues. In the case of contraception, birth control takes place before pregnancy begins. So, until the sperm fertilizes the egg there is no form of life that can be killed. However, the issue becomes a little more complicated when we consider forms of birth control that act after the egg has been fertilized but prior to pregnancy becoming established. A good example is the 'morning-after pill'. These birth control pills work by stopping eggs being released, inhibiting sperm or preventing the implantation of a fertilized egg.[4]

For Sikhs there are a number of interlinked issues to consider. How is life defined, particularly in Sikh scripture? If one could define life as such, at what point does life actually begin in the reproductive timetable? And is there a moral difference between not starting a life (contraception) and ending one (abortion)? As we have seen, although the scriptures are non-committal on this topic there are hints that the definition of life is relatively fluid and would incorporate a continuum that includes non-sentient and sentient forms. According to the writings of the Sikh Gurus, then, a properly moral issue can only arise when the new life-form becomes sentient. Even though sentience includes both unconscious and conscious states of existence, the crucial point of origin may not necessarily be the physical joining of sperm and ovum but happens at a later stage, that is, when the foetus becomes sentient. The difficulty of pinning this process down might explain why Sikhs are not unnecessarily concerned about contraception except insofar as it becomes a process that is both driven by and leads to an increase in the five vices. In addition it is also helpful to remember that women in rural India have long used alternative methods, techniques and traditional remedies to prevent contraception and carry out abortions. Thus contraception and abortion are not linked strongly to religious concerns as they are in other cultures.

Nevertheless, the current prevalence of female foeticide in many Sikh and Punjabi households highlights the way in which reproductive technologies, such as those that enable parents to predict the sex of the foetus, can and have been routinely used for unethical purposes. Given the strong emphasis in Sikhism on the family, the use of research and technology is generally considered an asset and has rarely, if ever, raised ethical issues. With the Sikh Code of Conduct being generally silent on the issue of technology, Sikhs by and large, are likely to welcome new technologies such as *in vitro* fertilization which can give a woman the chance to bear children. Although issues such as genetic engineering have not been routinely discussed in the community, given the non-dogmatic nature of the Guru Granth Sahib, Sikhs are unlikely to be opposed to such research given its potential to predict and eradicate cases of chronic disease such as Parkinsons, multiple sclerosis (MS), Downs syndrome and certain types of cancer.

Health and disease

Disease according to its modern conception is an unhealthy condition, an illness or sickness of the body and mind. Such a definition presupposes that the body has a normal condition which is health and wholeness. Health, in turn, has been defined by the World Health Organization as a 'state of complete physical, mental and social well-being and not merely the absence of disease or infirmity' but is more narrowly conceived by many practicing physicians as the body's physical display of vital statistics determined by medical science.[5]

While such definitions are perfectly acceptable to Sikh philosophy, it is also far too narrow. Its narrowness results on the one hand from having reduced the idea of health only to what can be seen, measured and replicated according to scientific criteria, and on the other hand, from having determined health as opposed to disease. Health is the condition of the self, and by definition, that which must remain healthy in order to be self. And it does this by constantly staving off diseases of the body and mind. In the teachings of the Sikh Gurus, however, health and disease are ontologically connected. This is because body and mind are considered to be part of a continuum rather than opposed as matter versus spirit. Health is therefore imaginary if only because it is temporary. The real state of our being is dis-ease. In this sense, disease is not episodic but chronic. Dis-ease is a condition of existing in time and the world but without being in tune with its ebbs and flows, and without realizing its transitory nature. Therefore loss of self and the collapse of the body are normative conditions.

In Sikh scripture, disease is always 'causally' connected not to a bodily mis-function, but to the way in which man fundamentally exists in the world – namely, the state of ego. It is when man asserts 'I am myself' (*haumain*) and turns this enunciation of his state of being into a defensive posture resistant to the flows of nature that is the root cause of all disease, bodily and mental. Thus Guru Nanak says:

> *Ego is given to man as his disease.*
> *Disease affects all creatures that arise in the world*
> *Except those who remain detached.*
> *Man is born in sickness*
> *In sickness he wanders through birth after birth.*
> *Captive to disease he finds no rest,*
> *Without the Guru sickness never stops.*
>
> (GGS, p. 1140)

In a sense this may seem to suggest that disease is incurable, or, that it is not ultimately important to cure disease since any cure will be temporary. To the modern sensibility such a standpoint may seem overly resignatory, perhaps even nihilistic. In fact it provides a certain conditioning for the mind to perceive disease (rather than the person who is marked with disease) not as a terrifying other that must be stigmatized and isolated, but rather as something or someone who is already part of myself. Does this mean, then, that disease is simply illusory? If so, what would be the idea of a cure and of medicine?

A closer look at Sikh practices and attitudes towards health practices, however, suggests a very reasoned approach to the question of disease. The Sikh Gurus, for example, vehemently rejected all manner of superstitious practices prevalent in South Asian culture such as belief that disease is caused by the 'evil eye' (*buri nazar*), black magic (*jadu-tuna*) or possession by evil spirits (*bhut-preta*), or that it is the result of divine punishment.[6] Indeed the Gurus built hospitals and sanctuaries in which they themselves worked to heal the sick, particularly those afflicted by leprosy and smallpox. The theory and practice of the Sikh Gurus is particularly evident in contemporary trends in Sikh philanthropy, and as an example of a different kind of philanthropy, Sikh attitudes towards organ donation. Thus Sikhs, both rich and poor, regularly donate money to build hospitals and schools in South Asia. Organ donation is also a common trend among Sikhs and considered to be a good example of selfless giving as taught by the Sikh Gurus. According to Sikh belief the body is considered perishable and not needed in the cycle of rebirth. The real essence is the accumulation of memory traces that comprises one's soul: 'The dead sustain their bond with the living through virtuous deeds'. The final act of giving and helping others through organ donation is both consistent with and in the spirit of Sikh teachings.[7]

While the medical and nursing professions are highly regarded within Sikh tradition, health practitioners should nevertheless be aware that attitudes among Sikhs may vary depending on the individual's level of education and social background (rural or urban, etc.). Also, many Sikhs are increasingly turning away from the industrial drug-based approach of modern medicine, towards a more holistic view of disease. This is partly the result of a resurgence of interest in alternative modes of therapy. Reliance on homeopathic doctors is becoming increasingly common as patients become more aware of the side-effects of modern chemical treatments. This resurgence has been aided by South Asian TV programs which routinely teach yoga, Ayurvedic medicine and other techniques to combat a large variety of ailments.

Mental illness in the Sikh community poses a different kind of challenge to health professionals from somatic illnesses. For one thing, mental illness as it exists today in the Sikh and Punjabi communities is a relatively modern phenomenon. It is now recognized that prior to its extended period of contact with the Western world

in the nineteenth century, South Asian communities did not stig-
matize many of the symptoms that we commonly associate with
mental illness with the label of abnormality or disorder. In preco-
lonial South Asian culture signs of madness or eccentricity were
commonly connected to the spiritual quest and specifically to the
attainment of ecstatic, erotic and emotional mysticism and related
meditative states of mind. As the Indian psychologist Sudhir Kakar
argues, 'the mystic undergoes a creative immersion in the deepest
layers of his or her psyche, with its potential risk of chaos and
lack of integration. The mystical regression is akin to that of the
analysand, an absorbing and at times painful process at the service
of psychic transformation. . . . the potential mystic may be better
placed than the analysand to connect with – and perhaps correct –
the depressive core at the base of human life which lies beyond
language'.[8] Listen, for example, to Guru Nanak who describes his
struggle with his own family on this issue. After he had shown
physical and other signs of depression for several months, his family sent for a physician in order to remedy his apparent illness.
When the physician arrived and took Nanak's arm to check his
pulse, Nanak withdrew his arm saying:

> *The physician was sent to prescribe a remedy; he takes my hand
>   and feels my pulse,*
> *But the ignorant fool knows not that the pain is my mind.*
> *Physician, go home; take not my curse with you.*
> *What use is this medicine when my sickness is my state of
>   love?*
> *When there's pain, the physician stands ready with his store of
>   pills.*
> *My body weeps, the soul cries out, 'give me none of this
>   medicine'.*
> *Go home, physician, few understand the source of my pain.*
> *The One who gave me this pain, will remove it.*
>
>   (AG, p. 1156)

At the heart of this broadly South Asian perspective was a theory
and practice of transforming the ego which was seen as a means of
achieving a well-balanced and healthy state of being. With the rise
of secularized Western ego-centred psychology in the twentieth
century – a process that re-centres the person's psychic framework

within, and in reference to, a strong normative ego, the Indic perspective came to be thoroughly marginalized. This has had profound affects for South Asians, Sikhs included, as they have been more or less deprived of an outlet for dealing with psychological problems of all sorts. The problem is particularly acute for those people who migrated to and settled in Western countries but even more so for second generation Sikhs and South Asians who are caught between two or more cultures and languages and often have to work their way through the proverbial 'identity crisis'. More often than not such psychological crises can be triggered by any number of events including most commonly for first-generation migrants: economic failures, or marital problems due to changing roles of Sikh men and women trying to balance a culturally conservative 'home' culture with a more 'liberal' culture outside, or the problems associated with children who demand a greater cross-over between the two cultures. More common these days are the problems stemming from racial and religious non-acceptance, addictions of various kinds or failure to live up to the social ideals of one culture which often express themselves in the early years of marriage or inability to find appropriate partners, or simply being torn between conflicting cultural requirements, experienced by second-generation Sikhs.

These problems may be compounded by the fact that there is often no social, spiritual or other support mechanism for second-generation Sikhs. So when Sikh and South Asian patients suffering from a psychological crisis are given counselling along Western models – usually in the form of a 'talking therapy' – these patients normally terminate the counselling after one or two sessions.[9] This may be because Western-trained psychologists and counsellors may not understand the complexities of the patient's world-view. Very often this results in South Asians being stereotyped as inappropriate patients for talking therapy. At the very least health practitioners need to be aware of their own biases and value assumptions when treating Sikh and South Asian patients for mental 'disorders'. By understanding the Sikh world view, for example, it may be possible to develop very different intervention techniques and strategies which recognize that different cultures can offer equally valid and often more appropriate cures even though their theory and practice may be diametrically opposed to Western-based methods and therapies.

In recent years, more and more Sikh MD's, psychologists and counsellors have begun to develop and incorporate therapies based on Sikh spirituality. Many of these models adapt traditional Sikh teachings about spiritual liberation to modern Western models. Central to these models is learning how to make the transition from a *manmukh* (self- or ego-centred personality) to a *gurmukh* (personality that incorporates ego-loss into his or her every thought, word and deed).[10] The passage from *manmukh* to *gurmukh* goes through several steps: (i) learning to identify the work of the ego in one's psyche; (ii) to understand the nature of ego; (iii) to undertake a path of self-realization through theory and devoted practice or meditation based on *nam simaran* (remembrance of the Name); (iv) to understand the 'five vices' (basic weaknesses of human nature manifest as: concupiscence, covetousness, delusion/attachment, anger, pride) and to identify the psychological charge associated with each 'vice' that specifically affects the personality concerned; (v) to supplant the 'vices' with the opposing virtues (strengths or qualities): wisdom, truthful existence, temperance, justice, courage and humility; (vi) ending with the achievement of a state of psychological and social balance (*sahaj*).

Genetic engineering, stem cell research and the environment

Basic questions: Is genetic engineering permissible? Should stem cell research be allowed? Are enviromental concerns part of the Sikh ethos? Do animals have a moral standing in Sikhi?

Genetic engineering refers to technologies used to change the genetic makeup of cells and move genes across species boundaries to produce novel organisms. Genes are the chemical blueprints that determine an organism's traits. Moving genes from one organism to another transfers those traits. Through genetic engineering, organisms are given new combinations of genes – and therefore new combinations of traits – that do not occur in nature and, indeed, cannot be developed by natural means. Such artificial technology is radically different from traditional forms of plant and animal breeding. As far as a Sikh position is concerned, there is as yet no clear consensus on genetic engineering. The natural evolution of organisms is understood as encompassed by the principle of *hukam* (life is ever changing by its very nature). So as long as it is therapeutic in intent and motive, there seems to be no clear reason for a Sikh position against it. On the other hand, its use for eugenic purposes, the creation of chimera, human clones or for cosmetic purposes is much more problematic. For example, while gene therapy to prevent or cure illness is acceptable, tampering with the design of human (or animal) species to increase certain abilities, to select a child's characteristics, might be regarded as going against the principle of *hukam*.

Stem cell research (SCR) is a new technology that can extract primitive human cells and develop them into 220 different cell types found in the human body. Some scientists have argued that SCR may hold the key to uncover treatments and cures for some of the worst diseases such as diabetes, neurodegenerative diseases such as Alzheimer's and Parkinson's. Stem cells can be extracted from three sources: adult tissue, the umbilical cord and embryos. The first two sources present difficulties for extraction. While embryonic stem cells are much easier to extract and have greater uses than their adult counterparts, much of the ethical controversy surrounding SCR is also centred around the use of embryos because of questions about when life begins. The actual debate involves two key ethical concerns: (i) the potential of SCR for human cloning and (ii) whether these embryos actually constitute human life. The pro-life lobby, which is particularly strong in the United States and in Catholic countries like Poland and Italy, argues that since the extraction process requires the destruction of the blastocyst, it is tantamount to murder. Against this, advocates of SCR argue first, that the embryo at the blastocyst stage has no human features, and secondly, that the process involving removal and implantation of nuclear material, has already existed for several decades in the common practice of *in vitro* fertilization which has helped many childless couples to conceive. From a Sikh standpoint, religious arguments that assume some certainty as to exactly when human life begins, or arguments regarding the sanctity of life, might not seem too convincing. From a Sikh standpoint, the very question 'when does life begin?' is itself problematic since we are confusing our role and ability to begin life with the fact that life is simply ongoing. It was there before us and will be there after us. In their writings the Gurus ask: Who can know when life will end or when it begins? Or

how many myriads of streams of life there may be? Life is life. The
force that propels life is outside our comprehension. It is arrogant to
think of ourselves as guardians of life. We should simply live it. It is
neither sacred nor profane, neither good nor evil.

As far as the environment is concerned, there are many compositions by the Sikh Gurus which suggest that the spiritual quest
and the attainment of equipoise for the mind cannot be separated
from a concern for the natural environment. The two processes
are intrinsically linked. There are frequent references to the basic
elements of the environment (air, water, earth) in the Guru Granth
Sahib. The earth is referred to as our mother (*mata dharat mahat*)
and great care needs to be taken to ensure that the delicate balance of natural elements is not upset. Accordingly the Sikh way
of life needs to be attuned to the natural process as any pollution
of the natural elements is against the principles laid down by the
Gurus. The Guru says: *Air, water, earth and sky – in these Lord
makes his home and temple* (GGS, p. 723). Following the example
of the Gurus, many Sikh and Punjabi poets have long eulogized
the natural environment by attuning their feelings and emotions
with the rhythms of nature. In the last two centuries, however,
an environmental crisis has been caused by an unhealthy belief
in some key principles of the modern (Western) outlook, such as
the need to separate humanity from nature in order to achieve
progress. Modern humanity's exploitation of nature has led to the
depletion of renewable resources, destruction of forests and overuse of land for agriculture and habitation. Today pollution con-
taminates the air, land and water. Carbon dioxide, industrial waste
and consumer trash poisons streams and rivers, ponds and lakes.
Much of the waste is a product of modern technology. It is not
biodegradable and not reusable, and its long-term consequences
are unknown. The continuity of many animal and plant species,
and possibly that of the human species itself, is threatened. Punjab
has not been immune to this environmental crisis as seen in the
large-scale deforestation and overuse of fertilizers.

On the question of animals and their standing, the simple answer
is yes! Animals are sentient beings and part of an inter-connected
web of existence (*sargun*) and non-existence (*nirgun*) in which any
particular being has as much right to exist as any other. In other
words, in as much as every being (elemental, plant, mineral, animal and human) is imbued with *nam*, then each being is sovereign,

not in its own right (as though beings exist independently), but only in their expression of *nam*, here envisioned as the interdependent being-with others that is the natural organic intelligence of life itself. *Sikhi* envisions *nirgun* and *sargun* as aspects of one process that Guru Nanak calls *hukam* which equally encompasses the timeless infinite (or transcendent) and temporally finite (immanent) as absolutely inseparable. Thus the term moral here cannot originate from human comprehension and calculation (see above). Moral here is tied to *hukam* – the organic law of intelligence that supports life's ever-freshness, its perpetual renewal. That which supports all life forms in their increasing diversity is in tune with *hukam* – this is moral standing. And for life forms to sustain themselves may mean that they eat each other but in balance. Although they eat each other, animals do not take this to extinction as they live within *hukam*. Killing is therefore not against sovereignty or this kind of *hukam*-tied-morality. Human killing is a different matter – its net effect is the destruction of all life forms and putting an increasing number out of existence. The loss of species and the rate of that loss is telling of a being's mode of existing that has become self-addicted, dislocated from *hukam*. It is a reverse economy that many mystics speak of. Hence *gurbani*'s emphasis on constantly losing oneself (to know *hukam* let not the ego say 'I am' – *hukamai je bujhai ta haumai kahe na koi* as Guru Nanak says in his Japji). Moral standing is thus related to this ability to live by negating the 'I am', to live beyond the 'I am'. It could be argued that animals live life in a similar state – and hence (whether they do or not) – they have become part of the mystic's grammar across cultures – as exemplars of beings that can live beyond ego, 'I', etc., that is without fear, without hate, in *sahaj*, spontaneity.

In short, the being of beings has moral standing in whomever and wherever it flows without I, without fear of death and hope for life, that is, when life is lived in or with the Name, in tune with Guru-Shabad.[11]

CHAPTER SEVEN

Sikhs and the Public Sphere

The first three chapters of this book explored the evolution of the Sikh Panth through very different political climates from the period of the Sikh Gurus to the late twentieth century. During the time of the Sikh Gurus and in the early decades of the eighteenth century Sikhs witnessed the different faces of Islamic rule, both benign and intolerant. The principle of sovereign experience bequeathed by Guru Nanak and developed by the later Gurus – based on the reality of a liberating experience that is open to and achievable by all, an experience that becomes actualized as *shabad-guru* and then further concretized as the twin institutions of Guru Granth and Guru Panth (Adi Granth and Khalsa) – these principles constituted a model of sovereignty that might be regarded as heteronomic. A heteronomic sovereignty can be envisaged as one whose fundamental rule is the self's relationship to the other; the notion that the self exists in the world only on the basis of its tangible relation to its other (ego-loss). The consequence of this heteronomic model of sovereignty, was a Sikh lived-experience that derived its conceptual vitality from the consonance between the institutions of *shabad-guru* and *miri–piri*. It refers to a lived-experience that: (i) allowed an internal diversity to flourish within the Panth, even as the Panth continued to evolve concrete forms of social identity such as the Khalsa; (ii) did not admit any metaphysical distinction between the spiritual and the worldly, the religious and the political.

Following the encounter with secularizing forces of Western modernity, and especially since the annexation of the Sikh kingdom in 1849, however, the earlier heteronomic model was forced to compete with a very different model of sovereignty imposed by the European colonial machine and the successive nationalization of Sikh traditions by Sikh modernists drawn from the Singh Sabha movement and later on the Akali–SGPC network. In order to compete against the vast political forces arraigned against them, modernist Sikhs reformulated *Sikhī* as a 'world religion' and 'nation' along Western lines by emphasizing the term *qaum* as a translation of nation in the late nineteenth and early twentieth centuries. In the process of projecting themselves as a legitimate body in the public sphere governed by British law, the earlier principle of heteronomic sovereignty was overlain, and to some extent displaced, by a distinctly modernist principle of autonomic sovereignty characterized by the notion of a people with its proper religion (Sikh*ism*), their own language (Punjabi) and a geographical territory or homeland they could call their own (Punjab). Under the hegemonic influence of this modernist form of sovereignty, whose primary marker is the enunciation of an autonomous Sikh self that disavows its relationship to the other, the Sikh lived-experience is forced to express itself through the dichotomy of the private versus the public. The most virulent form of this autonomic sovereignty was the Sikh ethno-nationalist movement of the late 1980s and early 1990s. Despite the modernization process, however, the earlier form of heteronomic sovereignty never really disappeared. As I suggested in Chapter Three, it was present even in statements such as Kahn Singh Nabha's 1898 *Hum Hindu Nahin*. By the early twentieth century, however, it was relegated to the private sphere especially following the birth of the Indian nation and has continued its existence surfacing alongside the modern version mostly in traditionalist discourses that are kept privatized.

This brings us to the third model of sovereignty, signs of which begin to emerge in the 1990s as the model of the modern nation state started to come under scrutiny. As we noted earlier, today the vast majority of the world's Sikhs reside in secular democracies such as India (18 million), United Kingdom and Europe (0.6 million) and North America (0.6 million). Throughout much of the twentieth century these secular democracies maintained a political normalcy based on the Westphalian model that has legally enforced a separation between the secular state which retains control of the public sphere and religion(s) which was relegated to the private sphere in the belief that it would eventually disappear under the weight of progressive modernization/secularization. The Westphalian order was based on the model of the nation state whose claim to sovereignty was tied to its territorial boundaries. Since the late nineteenth century, Sikhs like others, had to adjust their lived-experience, which encompassed social and intellectual frameworks, to conform with this modernizing–secularizing trend by constructing *Sikhi* as a religion (which is forced into the private sphere) and as nation/*qaum* (which desires to exist and express itself in the public sphere but consistently fails to achieve recognition and so is forced into the private sphere).

By the 1990s however, this Westphalian political order was rocked by two seismic events: (i) the world-wide return of religion into the public sphere and an equally global crisis of belief in secularism and the secularization thesis; (ii) an accelerated phase of globalization and transnational migration of people, prompting speculation about the rise of a future post-Westphalian, hence post-secular, international order.[1] Together these two events have disrupted the previously normalized opposition between public and private, and created conditions for a very different political climate that provides not only difficult challenges but also possible rewards for visible and vulnerable minorities like the Sikhs. Although the disruptions in the political order have differently affected Sikhs in India and Sikhs in the diaspora (even though both groups nominally live in secular democracies), nevertheless, both groups of Sikhs have used the disruptions to help revive earlier principles of sovereign existence that continue to motivate the Panth, to reassess novel and different ways of articulating their lived-experience within the public sphere and emerging from the shadow of secular modernity. For diaspora and Indian Sikhs alike, this revitalizing movement involves strategies that on the one hand *contest* public space within existing secular democracies, and on the other hand, *persuade* fellow Sikhs within the private sphere to see things differently. And it is this contestation that provides conditions for a new understanding of Sikh sovereignty to emerge that might be termed heteronomy II which evokes the memory and feeling of heteronomy I even as it exists within the ambit of the modernist autonomic sovereignty. The purpose of this chapter is to examine some of the ways in which Sikhs are beginning to use their lived-experience to renegotiate the boundaries between the private and public space in the twenty-first century. To do this my discussion will be focused on four key areas in which this renegotiation has occurred: (i) **Politics**, (ii) **Education**, (iii) **Media** and (iv) **Music**.

(i) Politics

Sikhs in Punjab

The early 1990s witnessed major changes to the Indian political landscape such as the liberalization of the Indian economy by the finance minister Dr Manmohan Singh, and the unexpected electoral success of the Hindu nationalist BJP. Although Punjab had returned to some semblance of normality after the defeat of the main Sikh militant groups, the Akalis remained out of power until they forged an alliance with the BJP. Having spent almost four decades pursuing an ostensibly 'secular' political stance, the alliance with the BJP, if anything, complicated the position of the Akali Dal. While it provided a level of political security for the Akali leader Prakash Singh Badal, their credibility continued to wane within the Sikh electorate in Punjab and even more so with Sikhs in the diaspora, partly due to corruption within the Akali ranks and partly due to the right wing Hindu ideology of the BJP. In one sense both the BJP and the Akalis continue to represent 'religious' interests and oppose the Western style secularism of the Congress. Whereas the Akali Dal has traditionally promoted the interests of rural Sikh farmers and landowners, the BJP represents the interests of mainly upper caste Hindus and urban traders. These two constituencies have never been comfortable allies in the past, but there are changes underway that may alter this relationship. These include the increasing expansion of Punjab's cities to absorb villages, as Sikh farmers continue to sell their land at high prices, thereby migrating to the cities or abroad in search of meaningful employment that has eluded them.

But the thornier issue is that of Sikh sovereignty which had long been championed by the Akali Dal. Although the Akali leadership under Badal tried to bury the issue by adjusting Sikh political aspirations to conform to present realities, the issue of sovereignty has continued to surface again and again, both in Punjab and the

Sikh diaspora, prompted in no small way by the BJP's fundamental belief that Sikhs are part of the broader Hindu fold. Although the Akali–BJP alliance has continued at the provincial level, at the national level the BJP suffered a major defeat at the polls in the 2004 general election. Indian voters rejected the legacy of religious violence perpetrated by Hindu organizations aligned with the BJP, exemplified by their systematic targeting of Muslims and Christians. An unexpected outcome of the 2004 general election was the selection of Dr Manmohan Singh and his elevation to the position of Prime Minister – the first time that a Sikh had held this high post. Manmohan Singh's selection and subsequent re-election on a popular mandate in 2009, was a cause for much celebration on the part of Sikhs all over the world. At the very least it forced the Indian media to portray a more positive image of the Sikhs in the public sphere, a trend that was followed by the Indian film industry (see below). Although, as one might expect, Manmohan Singh remained a staunch Congress loyalist, in an effort to woo Sikh opinion he offered a formal apology on behalf of the Congress Party in the Lok Sabha, for Congress's misdeeds such as Operation Blue Star and the 1984 anti-Sikh pogroms across India.[2] While this formal apology satisfied some Sikhs, many others remained sceptical.[3]

Sikhs in the Diaspora

If we turn to the Sikh diaspora, especially countries such as the United Kingdom, Canada and the United States, what seems evident is that the ebb and flow of Sikhs politics can be usefully divided into three more or less distinct stages: (i) the pre-1984 stage, (ii) the Khalistani phase 1984–92 and (iii) the post-Khalistani and post 9/11 phase. In all three phases, while the objective of Sikh political activity has been to attain some form of recognition from the state of their difference from other groups in the diaspora, there has also been a progressive reconfiguration of the 'homeland' in each of these phases.[4]

In Britain, for example, many of the early debates on immigration and integration of migrants such as the Sikhs, were framed by a perceived difference between 'British public culture' and the 'culture of immigrants in the private sphere'.[5] Thus, since the 1960s the British model of managing immigration racialized cultural difference in keeping with the colonial model of managing cultural diversity. According to this racialized sense of diversity, Sikhs could be 'in Britain' but not 'of Britain'.[6] Even though the early Sikh contestations of the public sphere from the 1960s to the early 1980s were attempts to preserve external symbols of the faith, these struggles were cast within the desire to achieve social recognition. One such case was that of G. S. Sagar who was refused employment as a bus conductor with Manchester Transport because he refused to remove his turban and wear the uniform cap. This was followed by similar cases such as that of Tarsem S. Sandhu who was dismissed by Wolverhampton Transport Authority for wearing a turban in violation of the dress code. In the 1970s Sikhs in Britain were exempted from wearing crash helmets when riding motorcycles after the passage of the Motorcycle Crash Helmets (Religious Exemption) Act of 1976. The act was seen as a 'public affirmation' of Sikhs' separate identity from other South Asian minorities. However, the landmark case was that of Mandla vs Dowell Lee in 1983.[7] Gurinder Singh Mandla, a *keshdhari* Sikh was excluded from an English public school for wearing a turban. The case was initially dismissed by the Court of Appeals on grounds that the Sikhs did not constitute a racial group. But after a period of agitation by British Sikh communities spearheaded by various chapters of the Akali Dal, the case was overturned by the House of Lords. The Law Lords recognized the Sikhs as a distinct 'ethnic group' with a 'long shared history' and cultural tradition of their own. Mandla eventually won the case against the headmaster Dowell Lee and the court's ruling made it possible for Sikhs to enter educational institutions without discarding the external markers of their cultural identity. The problem with the Mandla case, however, was that it racialized or ethnicized Sikh identity but it did not change the basic paradigm of diversity management in Britain which continued to relegate non-Christian religious identity to the private sphere in a manner not dissimilar to the colonial period.

Cases such as Mandla and Dowell Lee were followed by others in the late 1980s and 1990s that sought exemption for Sikhs from wearing safety helmets in the construction industry (Dhanjal vs British Steel, 1993)[8], and for the right to wear *kirpan* while on public duty (Kuldip Singh vs British Rail, 1985). Because of their singular mode of engagement with the public sphere Sikhs came to be regarded as 'the paradigm case of a special interest group that can negotiate an opt-out from general rule making',[9] but nevertheless were instrumental in helping to redefine the shift towards multiculturalism as official public policy beginning in the late 1980s and early 1990s. The Sikh dress code raised dilemmas for public policy makers allowing proponents of multiculturalism to argue for a broader vision of liberal democracy better capable of accommodating religious and cultural diversity.[10] Although Sikhs can indeed be regarded as 'pioneers of British multiculturalism', achieving this has required various strategies of public reasoning, transnational lobbying, and occasionally, when all other means failed, a resort to physical resistance to the hegemony of liberal democracy, especially when the latter curtailed the inherent principles of Sikh sovereignty.[11]

Sikhs in Canada have charted a similar trajectory to British Sikhs in their engagements with public space, partly because of the similarities between the Canadian and British political systems. These engagements took the form, once again, of legal battles fought in the Canadian courts with the aim of allowing Sikhs to maintain external identity markers. In the mid-1980s, as Canada experimented with a form of multiculturalism that was in some senses ahead of the British version, the Toronto police allowed Sikh officers to wear turbans as part of their uniform. A landmark case involved Baltej Singh Dhillon, a Sikh officer in the Royal Canadian Mounted Police (RCMP). The debate around this case was highly charged with conservative Canadians adamant that religious rights should not be allowed to supersede established Canadian traditions as upheld by the RCMP. In 1991 Baltej Singh became the first turbaned Sikh to serve in the blue and red colours of the RCMP.

Many other legal cases have gained public attention in Canada. These have involved the right of Sikhs to wear the *kirpan* in public spaces such as schools. One such case arose in December 1984 in a provincial Winnipeg court. Five Sikh men who had protested the Indian army's attack on the Golden Temple were charged for assaulting the Indian Acting High Commissioner to Canada. The Winnipeg court ruled that the *kirpan* could not be allowed into the courtroom thereby excluding the *kirpan*-wearing Sikhs to a position of regulated inclusion, inside and outside the law. In 1991 Harbhajan Singh Pandori filed a complaint against the Peel Board of Education following the prohibition of the *kirpan* in an Ontario school. A Board of

Inquiry found that the school policy contravened the 1981 Ontario Human Rights Code and discriminated against the Sikhs. The 1996 case of Nijjar vs Canada 3000 highlighted the problem for Sikhs wearing *kirpans* on Canadian Airlines. More recently, in January 2011, the Quebec National Assembly denied entry to a group of Sikhs scheduled to make a presentation at the legislative assembly because they refused to remove their *kirpans*. Such cases illustrate how Sikh external signifiers have functioned as sites of contestation of the public sphere but within the politics of recognition.

In the United States, Sikh engagement with the public sphere has followed a somewhat different trajectory. In the early decades of the twentieth century Sikhs were barred from even becoming American citizens as exemplified by the 1923 case of US Supreme Court vs Bhagat Singh Thind. The decision of this famous case ended immigration from so-called Asiatic zones, including India, Burma and Thailand making it impossible for Sikhs to sponsor family members and allowing the United States to revoke citizenship of those who did not conform to the Caucasian racial type, which was made the marker of American citizenship. The civil rights movement of the 1960s succeeded in drawing public attention to the racialized nature of American democracy but its beneficiaries were mainly African–Americans. Despite several waves of immigration between the 1960s and 1990s Sikhs continued to be marginalized and discriminated against.

The centrality of religion and race to the fabric of the American public sphere and its dangerous implications for highly visible minorities such as the Sikhs, became evident in the wake of the 9/11 attacks on the World Trade Center in New York. The attacks of 11 September 2001 on the United States by radical Islamists linked to Osama bin Laden, brought a superficial connection between religion and violence into the forefront of public debate by the global media. Within hours of the 9/11 attacks, a frenzied US media was awash with images and posters of a bearded and turbaned Osama bin Laden creating an unexpected and deadly problem of 'mistaken identity' for many Sikhs and South Asians living in the United States and Europe. Mistaken for Muslims, turbaned Sikhs were targeted in a wave of hate-crimes that resulted in several murders. In an atmosphere heightened by the dangerous religious and racial rhetoric deployed by the US political establishment (which indirectly implicated all minorities who looked like Muslims), male Sikhs very quickly became substitute embodiments for 'bin Laden' and 'Islamic terror' and as such represented a socially and politically sanctioned hate-crime target. Once sanctioned in this way, Sikhs were a legitimate target for the 'socially appropriate emotion' of revenge and retributive justice that was expressed in 'socially inappropriate ways'.[12] As one scholar notes, 'these hate crimes became normalized within a refashioned post 9/11 racial landscape, but more significantly, they became immanent to the counter terrorism objectives of the state, operating as an extended arm of the nation, encouraging the surveillance and strike capacities of the patriotic populace'.[13]

Just as important as the heteronormative nature of the American public sphere, which designated the turbaned man with a terrorist masculinity, was its religious underpinning which motivated liberal and conservative sentiments alike. Within this religio-heteronormativity, the turbaned man represented more than just 'a resistant anti-assimilationalist stance'. He became a deviant figure of monstrosity, a barbaric evil that refused to become civilized/Americanized and so had to be outlawed. Not surprisingly, the turban, in its capacity to invade the visual public space of an American citizenry of both religious and secular persuasions, became a source of constant public anxiety.[14]

Since 9/11 there have been more than 700 recorded hate-crime attacks on turbaned Sikhs in the United States, including at least 15 deaths. Ironically, the frequency of attacks rose during the last two years of the Obama administration. This is largely due to the hate-rhetoric against immigrants in general and Muslims in particular inspired by the ultra-right-wing 'Tea Party' activists who had more or less hijacked the Republican Party agenda. Pumped out on a regular basis by right wing American radio-stations, conservative TV channels such as Fox News and internet sites, this hate-rhetoric seeped into the consciousness of a post-9/11 generation of young white Americans. A direct result of this were the tragic shootings of Sikhs in Wisconsin. On the morning of 5 August 2012, a heavily armed gunman walked into the Oak Creek Gurdwara and opened fire on a *sangat* that had gathered for the morning service. The gunman, a confirmed white supremacist sporting a 9/11 tattoo, shot dead six Sikhs including the President of the gurdwara and critically injured a number of people. The death toll could have been much higher had the gurdwara been more full.

Since 9/11, Sikh Americans have responded to such racial and religious profiling in a number of ways. Large numbers of Sikh males, particularly the children of new immigrants, chose to disrobe their turbans in order to conform to the public perception of American-ness. Other Sikhs who refused to disrobe their turbans adopted different types of self-preservationist but ultimately assimilative tactics. Candlelight vigils accompanied by group-singing of the US national anthem became common. This was a way in which Sikhs could mark themselves as patriotic but victimized citizens. Sikhs increasingly began to hang American flags outside their homes, on their cars, or outside gurdwara premises. Public relations firms were hired and Sikh advocacy groups sprang up to try and educate fellow Americans about Sikhs and to alleviate their anxieties about the turban. The real irony here is that many of these same Sikh organizations had been petitioning the US government about human rights abuses committed by the Indian state against Sikhs and that the Sikhs were a separate religious identity to Hindus.

Another common response among Sikh communities throughout the United States was to engage in interfaith dialogues with neighbouring Christian and Jewish communities. This was clearly driven by a desire to correct the 'mistaken identity' and to inhabit the normative religious space that is part and parcel of American patriotism. A key component of these dialogues was the emphatic enunciations that: (i) Sikhs were not terrorists, (ii) that Sikhs were not Muslims, (iii) that Sikhism was a 'world religion'. Identification as a world religion ensured two coveted prizes. On the one hand an admittance into the moral space governed by Christianity, and, as a result of this, a safe passage and proper placement within secular public space. The idea here is that being seen to be like Christianity accrued both religious and secular benefits.

However, in 2004, such attempts to negotiate the artificial opposition between religion and secularism caused a different kind of dilemma for Sikhs living in France in the wake of the French government's widely publicized ban on the wearing of 'religious symbols' in public – a ban that included the turban. For French Sikhs the problem was exacerbated by the fact that the American and British Sikh groups advocating on their behalf were divided about how to actually contest the French government's ban. While the London-based Sikh Human Rights Group opted for a more pragmatic argument (that Sikhism was not necessarily a religion but a culture, and that it had become a religion through its entry into the colonial frame), the New York-based United Sikhs continued to argue that Sikhism was a religion, that the turban was a mandatory religious item and that the French government was in violation of their fundamental religious rights. The ostensibly secular nature of the British group's argument may have favourably impacted the French government had it not been for a well-publicized legal battle that was going on in New York at roughly the same time. Shortly after September 2001, a Sikh traffic enforcement officer, Jasjit Singh Jaggi, employed by the New York Police Department (NYPD) filed a law suit against his employer alleging that the NYPD had denied him numerous requests for a 'religious' accommodation, that is, the right to wear a turban while on duty. In April 2004 the presiding judge ruled that traffic agent Jaggi was discriminated against on the basis of religious beliefs when the NYPD ordered him to remove his turban and beard or face dismissal.[15]

What seems to be noteworthy about the French and American cases respectively, is that in order to argue their case for wearing turbans in public space, and thus to be integrated into secular liberal society, Sikhs found it necessary to formulate two different kinds of language that in turn recognized and negotiated between two different kinds of public space – the *religious* space of American secularism and the *seemingly non-religious* space of French *laïcité*. Despite the apparent differences between Indian, American and French forms of secularism, Sikh identity ended up being framed as a violator of the public space. Yet this 'violation' was due to nothing more than the desire of many Sikhs to assert a sovereign existence, the ability not only to be within the world but also to make and remake this world in ways that allows them to escape imprisonment within the limits of a private religious sphere.

(ii) Education

Academic Sikh studies

As Sikhs migrated and settled in different parts of the world, their traditions and way of life attracted the interest of scholars, journalists and other educators from the host countries. Initially very little information was available to the general public in the host countries. Today, not only is there a respectable body of knowledge about Sikhs in many world-religion textbooks and religious studies programs, there is a distinct and flourishing scholarly field of Sikh studies within the university sector, a growing number of scholars who wish to study Sikhs and Sikhism, and an increasing number of university chairs devoted to Sikh studies. At the precollege level in Britain there are at least two established state-funded Sikh schools that combine the teaching of the national curriculum with the Sikh ethos. In addition, Punjabi language teaching is a common feature both within the gurdwaras and also within the school and college curriculum particularly in the United Kingdom, and also in Canada and the United States where there are sizeable Sikh populations. Much has therefore changed since the early days of Sikh settlement, but the journey towards attaining recognition for academic Sikh studies and precollege Sikh schools, was by no means an easy one. Given that education and scholarship constitute a key aspect of public policy, it required a political negotiation and contestation with the public sphere similar to the struggle for recognition of Sikh identity. A brief look at the evolution of academic Sikh studies illustrates the nature of this struggle.

The emergence of Sikh studies within the humanities and social sciences can be usefully seen in terms of several phases of development. The first phase can be traced to the confluence of two disciplines: area studies and religious studies. Both these disciplines coincided with Western interests in the Cold War era and became central to organizing the study of non-Western cultures in the university system. The first generation of scholars were attracted to the study of Sikhs and the Punjab region for various reasons. They included W. H. McLeod, N. G. Barrier, Mark Jurgensmeyer and Christopher Shackle, all of whom can be regarded as pioneers of modern Western Sikh studies. An important early event was the 1976 international conference on Sikhism organized by Jurgensmeyer at the University of California, Berkeley, which laid the basis for future university–community collaborations.

During the second major phase of Sikh studies the intellectual growth of the field was matched by an impressive expansion of funding resources from the community. But this fortuitous combination of funding and new scholarship was overshadowed by the political crisis in Punjab during the 1980s when communal tensions were heightened and Western governments became concerned with Sikhs from a security standpoint. Some Sikh community leaders and intellectuals responded to this crisis by turning towards the university as forum which they believed would help balance the negative media imagery about Sikhs at the time. Collectively there was a flurry of conferences throughout North America which ultimately led to the creation of the first chairs and programs in Sikh studies.[16] Programs were initiated at prestigious centres such as the University of Toronto, University of British Columbia, University of Michigan and Columbia University. Very soon all of these programs came under sustained attack from influential sectors of the Sikh community. The Columbia and Toronto programs were closed but the ones at Michigan and UBC survived. Much of the community's opposition was focused on the work of W. H. McLeod, regarded by his peers as the pre-eminent scholar of Sikh history of his generation, and that of his students who came to occupy key positions at Michigan, UBC and Columbia.

The decade spanning the late 1980s to the late 1990s was a bewildering one for scholars in Sikh studies. Despite the fact that many of them were breaking new ground by questioning received canons of scripture and history, or opening up Sikh studies to new avenues of inquiry such as feminism, political ethnography, etc., they found themselves trapped within the competing rhetoric of Sikh ethno-nationalism and anti-Sikh sentiment generated by the Indian and secular Western media. As the scholar N. G. Barrier has noted:

> Just as American politics and public discourse were altered by the attacks of September 11th 2001, so the growing militancy and turmoil of this period reshaped the relationship between religion and politics among Sikhs. Academic research and authors quickly became enmeshed in the ensuing debates over controversial elements in Sikh public life – debates turned into polemics and polemics turned into wars of scholarship.[17]

By the year 2000, as the political landscape of Punjab and the Sikh diaspora calmed down, there was a renewed optimism about the future of Sikh studies and major American universities once again began attracting funds from Sikh donors. As the situation stands,

in 2013 there are now nine functional chairs of Sikh studies in
North America with the possibility of two more in the near future.[18]
Moreover there is a large and growing network of Sikh studies
scholars and an academic journal devoted solely to Sikh studies
(*Sikh Formations*, published three times a year by Routledge).

But perhaps more importantly, since 2000 there has been a tangible shift in the *nature* of Sikh studies discourse. In the 1980s to
1990s scholars of the so-called 'McLeod group' banded together
in defence of academic freedom, objectivity and the centrality of
secular critical methodologies to Sikh studies, which they believed
was under threat from what they perceived as 'fundamentalist elements' of the Sikh community who did not understand the rules of
the public sphere. The shift came when a new generation of scholars began to expose the deeply problematic nature of the opposition
between University and Community, and show that the conventional dominant methodologies used by the generation of scholars
groomed by W. H. Mcleod, were simply reflections of the secular
ideology of public versus private spheres, politics versus religion,
critical versus devotional scholarship, etc., that demanded the privatization of the Sikh subjective position or lived-experience, on
the grounds that it was 'religious' and therefore inherently sectarian.[19] Thus the shift in Sikh studies was centred around the adoption of a paradoxical standpoint that was able, on the one hand, to
harness the potential of post-secular critical theory to articulate a
subjective Sikh position and Sikh modes of reasoning, while on the
other hand it contested the cultural bias inherent within Western
theory. In this new phase Sikhs are able to become active agents of
knowing as opposed to being mere objects of knowledge. This is
an important breakthrough as it gives Sikhs the ability to contest
the intellectual framework of the public sphere, and therefore the
political systems of the host country, by claiming it as their own
rather than being positioned as foreigners within it.

Sikh Schools

Complimenting the growth of Sikh studies is the emergence of
state-funded Sikh schools, particularly in the United Kingdom.
The first such school was the Guru Nanak Sikh School in Hayes,
Middlesex, which was granted state funding in 1999 following a

two-year campaign by local Sikh parents who felt that their cultural and spiritual needs were not served by other schools in neighbouring districts. Now with over 700 pupils, the Guru Nanak
Sikh School has established an enviable reputation for academic
excellence as attested to by the long waiting list that includes many
non-Sikhs. Boys proudly don the Sikh turban while girls wear traditional Punjabi *salvaar kameez*. Although pupils are taught Punjabi
language and are made aware of Sikh principles, they still follow
the National Curriculum. In a similar development, the Nishkam
Primary School was opened in Handsworth, Birmingham, in 2012.
The Nishkam School is linked to the Nishkam Sevak Jatha, a leading Sikh organization that prides itself on its dedication to the
principle of self-less service (*nishkam*: service without the desire
for reward). This school also follows the National Curriculum but
makes provision for transmission of Sikh values and principles to
its pupils.

(iii) Media

Just like Christians, Buddhists, Hindus, Jews and Muslims, Sikhs
have made use of the various forms of modern mass media. Through
booklets, radio broadcasts, cassette tapes, CDs, TV, cinema, docu-
mentary films and more recently the internet, Sikhs have become
more than objects of representation (particularly in movies) but at
the same time have found the means to address multiple publics
and offer alternative forms of belonging as a way of contesting
the hegemony of the secular nation-state. As the examples given
below suggest, new technological practices have begun to blur the
boundaries between private and public spheres, enabling Sikhs
to simultaneously consolidate and transform their traditions and
practices. The adoption of new media is also transforming Sikh
understandings of the way they have been represented as well as
notions of religious authority, community and lived-experience.

Cinema

Since the late 1960s Sikhs have been represented in various roles
in Indian and to a much lesser extent Western cinema and TV. An

intriguing early reference to Sikhs can be found in the cult sci-fi series *Star Trek: The Original Series* (Episode: Space Seed, 1967). The central character in this episode is Khan Noonien Singh, a genetically engineered superhuman with long hair whose ancestry can be traced to the 'Sikh race'. The character appears again as an Indian/Sikh in the 1982 Star Trek movie *The Wrath of Khan* where Khan Noonien Singh is at once reviled and admired by the crew of the Enterprise. Clearly the executive editors, Gene Roddenberry and Harve Bennet were drawing (if somewhat inaccurately) on the British colonial construction of Sikhs as a legendary martial race.

The first reasonably extended and accurate portrayal of the Sikhs in Western film occurs in the children's series *The Devil's Children*. On the basis of the novel by Peter Dickenson, *The Devil's Children*, was adapted by the BBC in 1975. The central characters are an English girl, Nicky Gore and two Sikh children Ajeet and Gopal. Nicky Gore finds herself alone in London at a time when ordinary British people are compelled by some strange madness to revolt against technology and machines. Only a group of Sikhs are left unaffected by the madness. The Sikhs allow Nicky to join their group as a 'canary', able to warn the Sikhs against attacks by crazed Britons as they search for open land and clean water. Dickenson's novel portrays the Sikhs sympathetically as a dignified and hospitable people ready to come to the aid of British villagers. After *The Devil's Children*, Sikhs rarely appeared in Western TV or film except as comic characters in comedy series such as *It Ain't Half Hot Mum* (1977–9) or *Mind Your Language* (1983). One exception is the 1981 James Bond movie *Octopussy*, co-starring the Punjabi Sikh actor Kabir Bedi as the tall turbaned villain's aide, Gobinda, who battles Roger Moore from start to finish.

In the Indian film industry of the 1960s and 1970s the representation of Sikhs was restricted to very minor roles but was relatively benign. Only in Punjabi films such as *Nanak Nam Jahaz Hai* or *Dukh Bhanjan Tera Nam* did Sikh characters play leading roles. These films depicted Sikhs as moral in character and the sword-arm of India with the leading characters as military heroes or honest landowners. During the 1980s and early 1990s, Bollywood script-writing followed the trends in Indian politics by typecasting Sikhs as fearsome terrorists colluding with arch-rival Pakistan to undermine Indian unity. With the defeat of Sikh militancy in the 1990s, Bollywood trends began to change once again, with films such as *Maachis* and *Hawaieen* which complicated the representation of the Sikhs through three types of character: a pro-Indian type ready to sacrifice for the Indian nation; a conflicted, confused militant type who could be reintegrated into the national mainstream; and thirdly the Sikh as a comic village-idiot type. By the late 1990s the Sikh character had been typecast almost completely as the comic buffoon, although a few films by Punjabi Bollywood actors Sunny and Bobby Deol, did cast Sikhs in leading heroic roles (*Soldier*, 1996, *Gadar – Ek Prem Katha* (2007) and *Jo Bole So Nihal* (2008)). By the middle of the first decade of the new century, and with a Sikh as the Prime Minister of India, it suddenly became fashionable for leading Bollywood stars such as Amitabh Bachan, Akshay Kumar, Ajay Devghan, Saif Ali Khan, Ranbir Kapoor and actress Rani Mukherji to don turbans and beards and play the main roles as Sikhs (*Singh is King* 2010, *Love Aaj Kal* 2012, *Rocket Singh* 2012, *The Legend of Bhagat Singh* 2006). On a slightly different note, a spate of Punjabi films starring popular singers Gurdas Mann, Harbhajan Mann and the comedian Gurpreet Ghuggi tried to instil a new sense of Punjabi chauvinism by enforcing the culture of the homeland through the depiction of the diaspora as a mere extension of the Punjabi homeland. In films such as *Jee Ayaan Nu* (2002) or *Asa Nu Maan Vatan Du* (2004), the Punjabi identity, even within the diaspora is shown as insulated from host communities in Canada, the United Kingdom and United States in order to preserve the original heritage of the homeland.

In recent years a few Hollywood films also began to depict the Sikh character in a more favourable light. The Oscar-winning film *The English Patient* (1996), a screen adaptation of Michael Ondatjee's book of the same name, portrays a Sikh as one of the main characters. Kip, or Kirpal Singh (played by Naveen Andrews) is a bomb disposal officer in the British Indian army stationed in wartime France. The film shows a particularly beautiful scene with Kirpal Singh washing and combing his long hair. In another blockbuster film *The League of Extraordinary Gentlemen*, with an all star cast led by Sean Connery, the Sikh character is an Indian pirate and techno genius Captain Nemo, played by Indian actor Naseerudin Shah. More recently British born actor Art Malik played a supporting role in the film *Wolfman* (2011) which shows Malik as the Sikh manservant

(Singh) of the anti-hero Sir John Talbot (Anthony Hopkins). Perhaps the most sustained representation of Sikhs in the British film industry can be credited to the Kenyan born Sikh film maker Gurinder Chadha whose films *Bend it Like Beckham* (2002), *Bhaji on the Beach* (1999) and *Bride and Prejudice* (2004), were all box-office successes. *Bend it Like Beckham* was the highest grossing British-financed, British-distributed film ever in the United Kingdom (prior to the Oscar winning *Slumdog Millionaire*). The film was a critical and commercial success internationally, topping the box-office charts in the United States, Australia, New Zealand, Switzerland and South Africa, and winning film awards at the Locarno, Sydney and Toronto film festivals. The film plot is centred around young Sikh girl (Jes) who wants to attain success as a female footballer, but falls in love with her white coach (played by Jonathon Rhys Meyers). Primarily a comedy, *Bend It Like Beckham* provides an entertaining if skewed introduction to Punjabi Sikh family life.

Although the overall representation of Sikhs within Western and Indian cinema has been marginal and highly selective at best, Sikh communities all over the world quickly realized its very real potential to damage the perception of Sikhs in the secular public sphere, in most instances reducing them to comic objects of entertainment. Even more sobering was the lesson that Sikhs had little leverage to change the process due to their extremely marginal status. They were effectively slaves of a public sphere that could be manipulated by dominant political forces. As noted earlier, this was amply highlighted after 9/11 when Sikhs were confused with Muslims or Arabs in North America and Europe and became targets of hate crimes perpetrated by the host communities misguided by an all-pervasive news media. For this reason Sikhs in North America began to invest in small-scale film-making projects with the idea of presenting a more positive image of Sikhs to their own communities. This resulted in the growth of Sikh Film Festivals which are now held annually in Toronto, New York and Los Angeles. The film festivals in turn encouraged amateur film makers, many of them Sikhs, to produce short films that highlighted the predicament faced by their community. These included documentaries such as *Mistaken Identity: Discovering Sikh Americans (*by Vinanti Sarkar, 2001), *Divided We Fall* (by Valerie Kaur Brar, 2004), *American Made* (by Sharat Raju, 2004) and many others. Other documentaries

Continuous Journey (Ali Kazami, 2003) and *Roots in the Sand* focused on the settlement of Sikhs in North America, while films such as *Ocean of Pearls* (Sarab Neelam, 2010) highlighted the problems of wearing a turban in the diaspora.

A promising recent development has been the emergence of Sikh TV channels in the diaspora. While South Asian channels such as ZEE TV or SONY had been transmitting for almost two decades, many Sikhs had felt that their heritage was being diluted and often misrepresented by the predominantly Hindi and Bollywood programming in these channels. There are now two competing Sikh channels in the United Kingdom alone: Sikh Channel and Sangat TV. At the moment these channels cater mainly for a first-generation Sikh audience. Programs are conducted mainly in Punjabi and tend to have either a predominantly Punjab-centric or Khalsa-centric focus that does not appear to interest second- and third-generation Sikhs whose language is primarily English. The website for the Sikh Channel, which operates from a studio in the Aston area of Birmingham, suggests that it focuses primarily on education and religious programming for the Sikh community. But important features of this channel also include its regular campaigns to combat the misrepresentation of Sikhs by other UK media, its portrayal of a specific, though narrow, conception of Sikh identity, and its championing of political causes linked to Sikh nationalism. The Sikh Channel can be considered an example of the complex blurring of public and private sphere: the public sphere is contested but primarily in a manner that relies on the maintenance and regulation of the private sphere (i.e. its paid subscribers are almost exclusively Sikhs who adhere to a particular form of Sikh nationalism). However the Sikh Channel is also streamed through the internet making it available to a much wider viewing public and providing the possibility of further disrupting the public/private boundary. Its effect has been to popularize a very specific mode of reasoning, ethical speech and lived-experience that is meant to inculcate in its audiences certain shared dispositions meant for regulating Sikh identity and embracing what are considered to be 'correct' modes of enunciation and conduct. A good example of this is the effort by Sikh channel presenters to stop using the word 'Sikhism', which is increasingly recognized as a colonial construction, and revert to indigenous terms such as *Sikhi* (see Introduction). In ways that are only now being realized, these Sikh TV channels are slowly but surely creating a Sikh counter-public that can claim its own public space (even as its subscription base keeps it effectively privatized) by contesting liberal notions of public space and locating itself outside the dichotomy of tradition and modernity.

Internet

Sikh organizations have not been slow to utilize the democratizing potential of online media since it first became available in the early 1990s. In contrast to the restrictive potential of other forms of media (print, cinema, etc.) the internet has provided Sikhs with the possibility of transitioning from media consumers to media producers. This became very obvious as Sikh organizations in the diaspora were able to give the impression of an ongoing Khalistan movement long after the actual insurgency had been defeated in Punjab. Sikh discussion forums debating the viability of Khalistan remained active well into the first decade of the twentieth century and enabled the Anglophone articulation of a Sikh nationalist discourse to a new generation of Sikhs in the diaspora. The aim of this discourse was to instil a sense of global unity among all Sikhs by involving them in the 'politics of the homeland'. This was not possible in the mainly Punjabi news media such as *Des Pardes*, *Awaze Qaum* and *Punjab Times* which were effectively propaganda organs for different Sikh separatist groups. The internet, on the other hand, enabled the otherwise popularly discredited idea of Khalistan to continue to be revived as a deterritorialized imagined community, described on the homepage of Khalistan.net as a 'new global reality' that anyone could visit.[20] Thus in cyberspace, the global Sikh *qaum* could be seen as a new 'imagined political community' whose membership was restricted to *keshadhari* Punjabi-speaking Sikhs irrespective of their place of origin.[21] The internet therefore allowed a certain expression of sovereignty wherein all political and spiritual power is located in the Khalsa Panth. It was a form of sovereignty that resisted the Westphalian political order based on the international order of territorialized nation states.

Immediately after the 9/11 attacks several Sikh American advocacy groups were formed in response to the targeting of Sikhs and South Asians across the United States. These included groups such as the Sikh American Legal Defense and Education Fund (SALDEF), Sikh Coalition and United Sikhs. Prior to 9/11, members of these groups had no trouble balancing their identity as Americans with their Sikh identity. Almost all of them were part of Sikh activist fraternities and many had strong sympathies with Sikh nationalist movements. But after 9/11 the significance of the term 'Sikh American' changed for them. Whereas before it served to differentiate Sikhs from other Indians in the American consciousness, after 9/11 it became loaded with an anxiety to reaffirm their presence in America as 'proper' American citizens by playing down their connection to Punjabi culture. The internet became the modus operandi of these groups providing them with a presence that belied their very small numbers in the community. These advocacy groups have been active in building relations with local and federal organizations and have successfully targeted college students through their web presence. But what is less well known, however, is that in order to achieve these objectives they have also been instrumental in popularizing an image of the Sikhs and Sikhism essentially freed from the rural Punjabi culture, replacing this with an urbanite diasporic Sikh identity more palatable to white mainstream Americans.

Aside from the use of the internet by advocacy groups, the number of Sikh websites has grown almost exponentially since the mid-1990s making this medium an invaluable educational resource and learning tool for heritage transmission. It is now possible to find a variety of online versions of the Guru Granth Sahib, and access individual hymns and verses. Even the Apple ipad now has applications for downloading and accessing the Guru Granth Sahib. One can learn about Sikh history and music online. There are cyber courses that offer tools for learning the Punjabi language and for healing and meditation. Many Sikhs now make extensive use of video sites such as YouTube where they can access recordings of *gurbani kirtan*, share techniques and styles for turban-tying and post maps of their ancestral villages online. Also evident is the rise in the number of blogs by Sikh writers.

In the diaspora more and more cyber-*sangats* have arisen as young Sikhs have become alienated from traditional gurdwara *sangats* either as a result of generational differences, or because they cannot understand Punjabi, or simply because of the cynical politics that still affects many gurdwaras. In cyberspace young

Sikhs can find online forums where they can talk anonymously to like-minded Sikhs on topics that are still considered taboo, including homosexuality, abortion, identity and domestic abuse. The internet is fast becoming the go-to place for dating and arrangement of marriages. The versatility of cyberspace over classified columns in conventional newsprint has helped couples to meet and develop relationships free from the oversight of parents and third parties like *vicholas*.

As indicated above, there is certainly no guarantee that the internet will function neutrally in transmitting culture. Because anyone can build a website and set themselves up as an 'expert' or spokesperson for Sikhs and *Sikh*ism, there is a strong possibility that the version of *Sikh*ism being presented to potential audiences will not reflect the actual diversity of views and practices within the community.[22] As Doris Jakobsch has argued, the current representations of *Sikh*ism on the web suggest that certain homogenizing trends are at work. One such trend is the reinforcement of *Sikh*ism as a religion in the Western sense. Another is the disproportionately high number of images of turbaned men and women, which is also not entirely reflected in practice. More problematic is that many images of Sikh women show white American or European converts as authentic representatives of Sikh femininity, even though their numbers are extremely small.[23]

Nevertheless it is clear that the internet has facilitated a certain resistance to the homogenizing forces of mainstream secular public space fostered by nation-states in the diaspora. More importantly as shown by the Rajoana case in the spring of 2012, the internet, specifically in the form of the new social media such as Facebook and Twitter, in combination with Sikh TV channels, has provided an immensely useful tool for bringing Sikh public opinion together across the diaspora/homeland divide. Balwant Singh Rajoana was convicted by an Indian court of complicity in the assassination of Punjab Chief Minister, Beant Singh, in 1996. Rajoana openly confessed his involvement but strongly expressed his lack of faith in the Indian judiciary. He refused to defend himself by taking legal representation, instead accusing the Indian judicial system of applying dual standards and shielding the culprits of the 1984 anti-Sikh pogroms. Rajoana was sentenced to death by a special CBI court and his execution was scheduled for 31 March 2012. During the three weeks leading up to this execution date, Sikh communities all over the world conducted a vigorous campaign on Facebook and Twitter with the support of Sikh TV channels to commute the death sentence, even though Rajoana himself was opposed to this. The combined effect of the social media and TV campaign was to put the ruling Akali Dal in a difficult position forcing the Chief Minister Prakash Singh Badal to plead with the Indian Home Minister for a stay of execution. As a result of the campaign, on 28 March 2012 India's Home Ministry stayed the execution following clemency appeals filed by the SGPC. It was a clear demonstration of how Sikhs can now effectively contest the public space for political causes.

(iv) Music

The inclusion of music in a discussion of public space might seem a little odd. But as I shall argue below, by cultivating the quite different genres of music such as *bhangra* (a folk dance) and *kirtan* (both classical and popular), Sikhs have managed to perforate the boundaries between public and private spheres in novel and interesting ways.

Bhangra

This is a genre of beat-oriented folk music and dance associated with the male peasant dance performed to drums (*dhol*) in joyful celebration of the grain harvest festival of Baisakhi in the greater Punjab region. After the division of Punjab, *bhangra* became an iconic symbol of *Punjabiyat* (Punjabi identity) with the dance itself being transformed through the inclusion of new singing styles and movements from other traditions. *Bhangra* was brought to the United Kingdom in the late 1960s by the brothers Balbir and Dalbir Singh Khanpuri who effectively pioneered British bhangra music through the *Bhujangi* group. Other groups such as Alaap, Heera and Golden Star UK followed in the late 1970s and early 1980s. By the 1980s *bhangra* had become routinely associated with British Asian youth culture, spearheaded largely by the children of first-generation Sikhs. It became a key element in the second generation's backlash against racism and marginalization by the mainstream white British culture. In the late 1980s many *bhangra* artists responded to the traumatic conflict between Sikhs and the Indian state that was taking place in Punjab. By that time *bhangra* had evolved even further by fusing with other cultural forms, such as rock, but especially with different varieties of Afro-Carribean music such as Hip–Hop, Rap and Reggae. Notable figures in this early fusion scene were Apache Indian and Bally Sagoo, both from Sikh backgrounds. With these fusions, instigated not only by *bhangra* artists but just as much by innovative D. J.'s, *bhangra* was able to translate itself into and infect mainstream popular culture, reach new and much larger audiences, and tackle a variety of cultural issues such as internal prejudices, gender inequality and caste. In this way a certain aspect of a Punjabi identity, however diluted in form and typically inflected through Sikhs, was projected to mainstream British culture. Ironically, by the late 1990s *bhangra's* influence had also spread back to India where it was quickly incorporated into the enormously influential Bollywood Hindi-music scene, infusing its otherwise stale dance routines with a more energetic rhythm and pulse. *Bhangra* also flourishes in North America where it is an essential component of the South Asian youth culture scene. Any doubts about *bhangra's* acceptance by mainstream popular culture, and therefore in public space, were dispelled by the inclusion of a colourful *bhangra* routine at the closing ceremony of the London 2012 Olympic Games which was viewed by a global audience of well over a billion people.

In the mid 1980s and early 1990s, the South Asian and Punjabi university and college scene in the United Kingdom and North America was strongly influenced by the *bhangra* scene as South Asian societies tended to be dominated by Punjabis. Since the mid-1990s, however, there has been something of a moral backlash against the influence of *bhangra* as witnessed by the increasing numbers of Sikh student associations being formed at the expense of Punjabi and South Asian associations. Backed by major Sikh political bodies, some Sikh student bodies began to show concern with the morality of folk dance, arguing that *bhangra* was essentially a component of Punjabi identity and had minimal connections with *Sikhi*. Particularly worrying for their parents was the potential of *bhangra* to recast gender relationships and heighten sensuality in the youth, as well as its connection to the nightclub scene. At its height this argument raged on the internet for almost

a decade casting the difference between Punjabi and Sikh identity in terms of the secularism versus religion debate. These days
the argument has largely subsided as Sikh students associations
have grown in membership and vastly outnumber Punjabi or South
Asian associations in Britain and North America. Furthermore
their activity has shifted towards more reflective and serious concerns as seen by the prevalence of *kirtan* performances by students
themselves and emphasis on debating current issues. This shift has
changed the self-representation of Sikhs particularly in the student
community.

However, the interest in *bhangra* among Sikh students and Sikhs
in general has far from subsided. Most Sikhs have recognized the
absurdity of the opposition between Punjabi culture and *Sikhi*, and
have settled on a compromise which easily retains the two identities together. A telling indication of this common sense approach
is that most young Sikh students see no real problem in participat-
ing equally in Sikh students' associations which promote *Sikhi*, and
being involved in Punjabi folk activities of which *bhangra* is one
component. Thus it is not uncommon in North America to have
a student serving as President of a Sikh student's association, promoting *kirtan* performances and perhaps even performing *kirtan* on
the one hand, and on a different stage representing one's college of
University in national *bhangra* competitions. And this is not just the
case with students. There are many Sikhs who serve faithfully in
Gurdwara committees and, on different occasions, teach aspects of
Punjabi folk culture including *bhangra* to students. There is no ten
sion felt between religious and secular culture here. Indeed this is
how the majority of Sikhs live. A somewhat frivolous example which
demonstrates that the supposed tension between *Punjabiat* and *Sikhi*
is not really a tension for Sikhs themselves, is the hilarious figure of
'Bhangra Man' in the British comedy series *Goodness Gracious Me!*
During the day Balwant Singh Jaggi is just an ordinary turbaned
Sikh man going about his everyday duties. But when danger calls he
transforms into a comic super-hero 'Bhangra-Man' who fights and
defeats the evil doers with his gyrating *bhangra* dance.

Kirtan

Just as pertinent to the public sphere issue, is the example of Sikh *kirtan* and the current debates in the field of Sikh musicology. One such debate centres around the effects of colonial modernization of traditional Sikh *kirtan* which is grounded in the aesthetic reception of its primary source, the Guru Granth Sahib. As we have seen in Chapters Two, Three and Four, the traditional reception of Sikh scripture reinforces the unity of language and music as equal constituents of *shabad* (Word). That is to say, *shabad* could be experienced both musically and linguistically, and the unity that emanated from this experience was in some way synonymous with the attainment of a sovereign consciousness. Consequently the traditional vehicles for experiencing the philosophical and theological teaching of the Guru (*gurmat*) either through a mode of reflection (*gurmat vichar*) or through music (*gurmat sangeet*) were intrinsically connected. Musical practitioners were thinkers and devotees, and vice versa, thinkers and devotees were practitioners of music. Indeed both strands (language and music) were necessary to the imparting of *gurmat*.

During the period of colonial modernization, however, something important happened. In their desire to unify modern Sikh identity the Sikh reformist scholars, and later the SGPC, standardized the way in which Sikh teachings (*gurmat*) came to be *experienced*. In short, the experiential aspect of *gurmat* was refashioned by driving a wedge between the literary (*shabad*) and the musical (*raga*) aspects of the central Sikh text, the Guru Granth Sahib. From the time of its composition the main body of hymns in the Granth had been strictly organized under specific melodies and (rhythms) *ragas* and *taals* that could not be changed. During the late nineteenth and early twentieth centuries there was a progressive rationalization and eventual separation of the literary and musical aspects of the Guru Granth Sahib. This rationalization gave rise on the one hand to a systematic theology and a belief system based around a new relationship to the text as primarily a literary and 'religious' object to be understood through a proper grasp of grammar and a correct concept of the divine (monotheism). And on the other hand, it re-codified the Indian system of musical notation based on *raag/taal*, according to Western staff notation. Music in general, but particularly Indian classical music, was implicitly associated with weaker, non-representable forms of consciousness that correspond to improper, that is sensuous, concepts of the divine.

Partly through the agency of the SGPC, modernization exacerbated the distinction between performers of Sikh music (*ragis*) and theologians of Sikh scripture (*gianis* or *parcharaks*) – a division that was directly based on the idea that music, as a performative art, appealed to the non-rational, sensuous faculties, whereas scriptural interpretation is based on the deployment of rationality. The dichotomization was implemented by the SGPC in two ways thereby affecting the key modes of receiving Sikh 'scripture' (*gurbani kirtan* and *viakhia*). First, once the SGPC had approved the use of a new instrument, the harmonium, to replace the traditional string instruments associated with *gurbani kirtan*, they were able to mass produce *ragis* who could be easily trained to use the harmonium and quickly deployed to gurdwaras in villages and towns. The downside of the harmonium was that it could not reproduce the exact range of *ragas* that was possible with string instruments, which in turn meant that over several decades these *ragis* started to produce a more popular form of *kirtan* style whose aesthetic component had been dulled to the point of becoming a mode of popular entertainment in the guise of religious performance. The newer harmonium-based forms of *kirtan* were convenient for the sake of performance but substantially deviated from the established traditions of singing and *raga* notation, whose proponents eventually started to lose patronage and die out. Secondly, this modernized form of *kirtan* was brought into line with the literalist message of *gianis* and *pracharaks* (theologians, preachers and missionaries) whose task was to convey a standardized understanding of scripture in line with the political message of the SGPC and the Akali Dal. By making effective use of cassette culture and other media, the SGPC helped to privatize the realm of *kirtan* which was used to keep the masses in check, leaving the public realm relatively free for their political agenda.

Thirdly, while all this was taking effect in the gurdwaras, a similar institutionalization took place for the academic study of *kirtan*. In other words the scholarly study of *kirtan* was institutionalized under two opposing categories – the performative (secular) and the textual (religious/theological), within different departments within the modern Punjabi universities such that, one could study text history and meaning in a department of religion, history, literature, etc., but *gurbani kirtan* could only be studied in a department of music. The modernist emphasis on separating the musical and the literary could hardly be more different from the premodern forms of experiencing *gurmat*. Surprisingly, though, this dichotomy is not only operative in 'public' institutions such as the modern university (both in Punjab and in the West). It has also become, at least implicitly and particularly in regard to pedagogy, part of the (private) experience of reception and transmission of the Guru Granth in the modern gurdwara. The result of these rationalizing trends was to reinforce the standardization of Sikh identity as a specifically religious identity and of Sikhism as a 'world religion'.

In the last two decades there has been something of a renaissance in the traditional styles of *gurbani kirtan*, driven by proponents such as the thirteenth-generation exponent and master, Bhai Baldeep Singh, scholars of Sikh musicology such as Dr Gurnam Singh at Punjabi University Patiala, and teacher-entrepreneurs such as Surinder Singh Matharu in the United Kingdom and North America. Today, through the efforts of such 'revivalists', traditional styles can be heard once again ironically through the very media technologies (audio, visual, print, internet) that helped to marginalize them between the 1950s and 1980s. Moreover these revived traditional styles are once again being performed in local gurdwaras, and promoted as the musical standard within the Harimandir Sahib.[24] Spurred by a similar revival of the production of traditional string instruments, the performance of *gurbani kirtan* in its original classical form has also achieved a high level of popularity within Sikh diaspora communities. It has been promoted as a unique musical genre and has begun to be institutionalized as an academic discipline within Western universities. Although the primary interest of the revivalists was simply to reconnect Sikh communities to older styles of *kirtan*, the effect of this classical resurgence goes beyond the sphere of music alone. In fact the musical revival, if properly realized, has the potential to reconnect the sundered aspects of *raga* and *shabad* that is so central to the reception of Sikh scripture, thereby bringing together musical praxis with literature, and the conceptual with the non-conceptual. Indeed, although the 'revivalists' may not see it in these terms, it has the potential to challenge the public/private split that has been internalized by Sikh communities through the agency of bodies such as the SGPC.

GLOSSARY OF INDIC TERMS

Adi Granth lit. the first or original text, that is the sacred scripture of the Sikhs; also known as the Guru Granth Sahib.

akal member of the Akali Dal, a Sikh political party.

Akali Dal political party represented Sikh and Punjabi interests in Punjab

akal purakh 'The Timeless Being'; God.

Akal Takht the principal center of Sikh temporal authority, this institution is located immediately adjacent to the Harimander Sahib or Golden Temple.

amrit lit. nectar of immortality; sweetened water used in Sikh initiation ceremony.

amritdhari a Sikh who has undergone initiation and become a member of the Khalsa.

anhad (anahat) shabad 'unstruck' sound or word; poetic language in which ego-traces are erased.

artha the meaning of a word or sentence.

Arya Samaj a Hindu reformist movement founded by Dayananda Saraswati in the late nineteenth century.

avatar a 'descent' or incarnation of deity, usually Visnu.

bhagat (*bhakta*) exponent of bhakti.

bhakti form of loving devotion directed towards a personal or impersonal divine.

bhai 'brother'; honorific applied to Sikhs of learning or piety.

brahman the absolute as described in the Upanishads; self-appointed highest caste in Hindu caste hierarchy.

Chief Khalsa Diwan (CKD) a Sikh institution formed in 1902 to conduct the affairs of the Lahore and Amritsar Singh Sabhas.

darshan the act of seeing or having an audience with the divine.

Dasam Granth a Sikh scripture parts of which are attributed to the authorship of the tenth Sikh Guru, Gobind Singh.

dharam (Skt. *dharma*) duty, righteousness, law, sacred duty.

fakir (*faqir*) a Muslim ascetic loosely used to designate Sufis.

gian (*Skt. jñāna*) wisdom or knowledge.

Granth lit. text, referring to the Guru Granth Sahib or central Sikh scripture.

guṇa attribute or quality.

gurbani 'utterance of the Guru'; compositions of the Sikh Gurus.

Gurbilas 'Praise of the Guru'; hagiographical literature about the lives of the sixth and tenth Gurus.

gurdwara a Sikh temple.

gurmat teachings of the Sikh Gurus.

gurmat sangeet Sikh musicology; sacred music of the Sikhs.

gurmukh one who lives according to the guru's teaching; one who has overcome ego.

gurmukhi 'From the Guru's mouth'; the Punjabi script.

guru a spiritual master; either a person or a mystical inner principle which aids emancipation of the disciple.

Guru Granth Sahib the Ādi Granth in its role as Guru.

Guru Granth the Granth or text in its role as Guru.

Guru Panth the community or Panth in its role as Guru.

gurumata 'Intention of the Guru'; a resolution passed by the Sarbat Khalsa (wider community of Khalsa Sikhs) in the presence of the Guru Granth Sahib.

Harimandar Sahib the Golden Temple.

hatha-yoga yoga of physical exercises practiced by adherents of the Nath tradition.

haumai 'I am myself'; self-centredness.

hukam order.

ik oankar the one being manifest as Word; the opening words of Sikh scripture.

janamsakhi hagiographical narratives based on the life of Guru Nanak.

jap the act of repeating the divine name, mantras or sacred texts.

kal time or death.

katha homily.

Khalistan 'land of the Pure', a name adopted by supporters of an independent Sikh state.

Khalsa a spiritual-cum-military order of Sikhs established by Guru Gobind Singh in 1699.

kirtan singing of hymns (see *gurmat sangeet*).

Krishna Hindu god; narrator of the *Bhagvada Gita*.

man (pronounced 'mun') mind; a common Indian term for the complex of heart, mind and soul.

manmukh one who acts according to egotistical desires; trapped within the structure of the ego.

mantar (Skt. *mantra*) a verse, phrase or syllable invested with spiritual efficacy that is repeated by sounding.

mat intellect.

maya the illusory status of reality.

miri–piri doctrine of combined temporal (*mīrī*) and spiritual (*pīrī*) authority attributed initially to the living Sikh Guru but later adopted by the Khalsā.

mukti (Skt. *mokṣha*) ultimate freedom; liberation from the cycle of transmigration.

murti form or image of a deity in Hinduism.

nam the Name; a term expressing the central attribute of a paradoxical divine that is existent and non-existent at the same time.

nada sound.

nadar sight; divine grace.

Namdhari member of the Sikh sect called Namdharis (also known as Kuka Sikhs).

nam japana repetition of the divine Name.

nam simara ṇ devotional practice of meditating on the Name initially through vocalized repetition and eventually through interiorized repetition.

Nath tradition practitioners of hatha yoga; yogic sect influential in Punjab prior to and during the time of the Sikh Gurus.

nirban (*nirvana*) extinction of suffering; without form.

nirgun (Skt. *nirguṇa*) without qualities or attributes, not incarnated.

Nirmala a sect of celibate Sikhs influential in the nineteenth century.

nit-nem daily rituals; Sikh liturgy.

om (*aum*) the primal syllable said to contain the entire Sanskrit alphabet in seed form.

Panth lit. the way; the Sikh community.

path recitations or readings from Sikh scriptures.

prana life force, breath.

puja Hindu worship.

Purana early Hindu literatures containing mythologies and detailing sectarian rites.

Puratan janamsakhi one of the oldest extant collections of biographies of Guru Nanak.

raga a traditional melodic type in Hindustani music, consisting of a theme that expresses an aspect of spiritual feeling and sets forth a tonal system on which variations are improvised within a prescribed framework of typical progressions, melodic formulas and rhythmic patterns.

shabad word, language; verse or hymn of the Guru Granth Sahib.

shabad-guru the word-as-guru; guru-as-word.

sabha society or association.

sadhan method or technique of spiritual achievement.

sadhu a renunciate, mendicant or ascetic.

sargun (Skt. *saguṇa*) 'with qualities', possessing form or attributes.

Saiva (*Saivism/Śaivite*) worshipper of the god Śiva.

sahaj naturally achieved condition of equipoise or bliss resulting especially from the practice of nam simaran.

Sahajdhari a non-Khalsa Sikh.

samadhi state of deep absorption and concentration, especially in yoga.

sampradaya sect holding certain beliefs; traditional doctrine; a school of thought.

sansara the material world; cycle of rebirth.

sanskara trace; sacrament.

sanatan without origins; eternal; that which does not cease to be.

sanatan dharma eternal tradition referring also to Vedic dharma and tradition.

Sanatan Sikhs those who (mistakenly) considered Guru Nanak to be an incarnation or avatar of the Hindu deity Visnu and thereby aligned Sikh traditions with the Hindu traditionalist (i.e. Brahmanical) social structure based on *varnāśramadharma* or caste ideology.

Sant person who has discovered the truth of existence and non-existence; teacher of gurmat.

Sant tradition a spiritual tradition of North India which stressed the need for interiorized devotion.

sat (Skt. *satya*) truth, existence.

sati practice of burning widows or concubines on the husband's funeral pyre.

satnam truth is (your) Name.

satsang gathering of seekers after truth; Sikh congregation.

seva service.

SGPC Shiromani Gurdawara Prabandhak Committee – a committee that controls the Sikh places of worship.

Shiva one of the great gods of Hinduism.

siddha men highly adept in yogic practice and believed to have attained immortality through it.

Siddh Gosht composition in Guru Granth Sahib representing a dialogue between Guru Nanak and adepts of yoga named Siddhas.

Singh Sabha Sikh reform movement initiated in 1873 which split into two factions in response to stigmatization from Hindu reformist and traditionalist groups.

sruti 'that which is heard'; the Vedas and Upanishads.

Sufi member of a Muslim mystical order.

Sutra concise text expounding a teaching.

Udasi member of Udasis, an order of ascetics claiming Sri Chand (elder son of Guru Nanak) as their progenitor.

Upanishads fourth division of Hindu literatures; wisdom texts.

Vaisnava follower of the god Viṣṇu.

vak 'saying', randomly chosen passage from the Guru Granth Sahib; in Hinduism early Vedic term for the divine Word and the goddess of speech.

varna 'color'; caste hierarchy comprising Brahman, Kshatriya, Vaishya and Sudra; individual letter in the Sanskrit language.

Veda knowledge; earliest texts of the Hindus.

Vedanta the last part of the Veda; Upanishads.

Viraha (or biraha) pining or longing for the beloved from whom one is separated.

vismad wonder; awe.

yoga 'yoke'; system of Indian philosophy and practice in which the mind is brought under control.

NOTES

Introduction

1 See Richard King, Orientalism and Religion, London: Routledge, 2004, and Arvind-Pal S. Mandair, Religion and the Specter of the West, New York: Columbia University Press, 2009.

2 There is a large and growing set of texts that address this issue going back to the early 1960s, including: W. C. Smith, The Meaning and End of Religion, New York: Macmillan, 1962; J. Z. Smith, Imagining Religion: From Babylon to Jonestown, Chicago: University of Chicago Press, 1982; Asad, Genealogies of Religion, Baltimore: Johns Hopkins University Press (1992), S. N. Balagangadhara, The Heathen in His Blindness: Asia, the West and the Dynamic of Religion, Leiden: E.J. Brill Publishers, 1994; Daniel Dubuisson, The Western Construction of Religion: Myths, Knowledge and Ideology, Baltimore: Johns Hopkins University Press, 2003; Timothy Fitzgerald, The Ideology of Religious Studies, Oxford: Oxford University Press, 1998; Richard King, Orienatalism and Religion, London: Routledge, 1999, Tomoko Masuzawa, The Invention of World Religions, Chicago: Chicago University Press, 2005; William Cavanaugh, The Myth of Religious Violence, New York: Oxford University Press, 2008; Hurd, Arvind-Pal S. Mandair, Religion and the Specter of the West: Sikhism, India, Postcoloniality and the Politics of Translation, New York: Columbia University press, 2009.

3 See Timothy Fitzgerald, Discourse on Civility and Barbarity, New York: Oxford University Press, 2008.

4 See Elizabeth Shakman Hurd, The Politics of Secularism in International Relations, Princeton: Princeton University Press, 2008, Tomoko Masuzwa, etc.

5 Timothy Fitzgerald, Discourse on Civility and Barbarity, New York: Oxford University Press, 2008.

6 Talal See Asad, Wendy Brown, Judith Butler, Saba Mahmood, Is Critique Secular? Blasphemy, Injury and Free Speech, Berkeley: University of California Press, 2009.

7 An indication of what I mean by 'sovereignty' can be found scattered throughout the chapters of my Religion *and the Specter of the West*, Columbia University Press, 2009. However a more rigorous examination of this term will be carried out in the monograph I am currently working on called 'Mourning Sovereignty'.

Chapter 1

1 The *janamsakhi* quotations referenced in this chapter are based on two main sources: (i) The B40 Janamsakhi, compiled in 1733, edited by W. H. McLeod and published in 1980; (ii) the Puratan Janamsakhi (ed.) Bhai Vir Singh in 1948. This is a compendium of other janamsakhis and was first published in the *Khalsa Samachar* in 1948, reprinted as *Janamsakhi Guru Nanak Dev ji*, by Bhai Vir Singh Sahit Sadan, 1996.

2 For detailed discussion on this, see W. H. Mcleod, *Early Sikh Tradition*, Oxford: Clarendon Press, 1980.

3 This episode is also recorded in the Guru Granth Sahib, *Raga Asa*.

4 B40 Janam-Sakhi, p. 11.

5 Ibid., p. 16.

6 Guru Granth Sahib, p. 1279 (translation mine).

7 B40 Janam-Sakhi, pp. 20–1.

8 Bhai Gurdas, 'Tikki Di Var', *Varan Bhai Gurdas*.

9 'Tikki di Var', from the Vars of Satta and Balwand.

10 Puratan Janamsakhi, p. 129.

11 Also known as the Sants – see W. H. McLeod and Karine Schomer (eds), *The Sants: Studies in a Devotional Tradition of India*, New Delhi: Motilal Banarsidas, 1987.

12 See W. H. McLeod and Karine Schomer, *The Sants: A Study of a Devotional Tradition of North India*, New Delhi: Motilal Banarsidas, 1987. Others such as Mark Jurgensmeyer and John Stratton Hawley also follow this interpretation.

13 According to the *janamsakhi* a soldier named Malu Shah asked Guru Angad whether the use of force could be morally justified. The Guru advised him that if people needed protection it was the soldiers' duty to fight regardless of the odds against him.

14 According to one source, the langar motto was: pehle pangat piche sangat – 'First be seated together in a row, then seek the company of the Guru'. Suraj Parkash, i, p. 30.

15 The Muslim chronicler Mohsin Fani, a contemporary of fifth Guru, states that 'In short, during the time of each Mahal or Guru, the Sikhs increased in number till in the reign of Guru Arjan Mal, they became numerous and there were not many cities in the inhabited countries where some Sikhs were not to be found', *Dabistan-i-Mazahib*, Lucknow: Naval Kishore Press, p. 234.

16 See, for example, Sujan Rai's late seventeenth-century text, 'Khulasat ut-Tawarikh', in *Makhiz-i-Tawarikh-i-Sikhan*, ed. Ganda Singh, p. 59.

17 An important source for this is the diary of *Akbar: Akbar Namah* (Persian), Vol. III, p. 801.

18 There is a reference to this in the Guru Granth Sahib, pp. 1137–8.

19 Persian text of Jahangir's Memoirs printed in *Makhiz-i-Tawarikh-i-Sikhan*, ed. Ganda Singh, Sikh History, Amritsar, 1949, pp. 20–2.

20 *Tuzuk-i-Jahangiri*, translated by Rogers and Beveridge. In his diary (tuzuk) Jahangir writes: 'At last, when Khusrau (his son) passed along this road this insignificant fellow [Arjan] proposed to wait upon him. Khusrau happened to halt at the place where he was, and he came out and did homage to him. He behaved to Khusrau in certain special ways and made on his forehead a finger mark in saffron, which the Indians call qasqa and is considered to be propitious. So many of the simple-minded Hindus, and even foolish Muslims too, had been fascinated by his ways and teachings. He was noised about as a religious and worldly leader. They call him Guru, and from all directions crowds of fools would come to him and express great devotion to him. This busy traffic had been going on for three or four generations. For years the thought had been preventing itself to my mind that either I should put an end to this false traffic, or he should be brought into the fold of Islam.'

21 This was in the form of a letter *Muktubate Alif Sani* addressed to Jahangir.

22 There is mention of this in Mohsin Fani's *Dabistan*, II, p. 272.

23 Jahangir writes in his Memoirs: 'I fully knew his heresies, and I ordered that he should be brought into my presence, that his houses and children be made over to Murtaza Khan, that his property be confiscated, and that he should be put to death' – *Tuzuk-i-Jahangiri*, I, pp. 72–3.

24 See Pashaura Singh, *Life and Work of Guru Arjan*, New Delhi: Oxford University Press, 2006.

25 See also the account by the Jesuit priest Jerome Xavier in E. R. Hambye, 'A Contemporary Jesuit Document on Guru Arjan Dev's Martyrdom', *Punjab Past and present: Essays in Honour of Dr.*

Ganda Singh (eds. Harbans Singh and N. Gerald Barrier, Patiala: Punjabi University, 1976, pp. 113–18. In this paper, Hambye gives a well documented and and exhaustive account of the contents of Father Jerome Xavier's private letter (dated 25 September 1606) addressed to the Jesuit Provincial Superior of Goa, father Gaspar Fernandes. The Jesuit missionaries had had a church in Lahore since 1597.

Chapter 2

1 Some events in the life of Guru Hargobind are depicted by the Muslim chronicler, Mohsin Fani, but there is some disagreement with Sikh sources. See his *Dabistan-i-Mazahib*, translated by Dr Ganda Singh and D. Shea and A. Troyer, Calcutta, 1809.

2 Bhai Gurdas also indicates that different measures were adopted by the sixth Guru. See *Varan Bhai Gurdas*, ed. Giani Hazara Singh, Amritsar: Wazir-i-Hind Press, 1962.

3 *Dabistan-i-Mazahib, Makhiz-i-Tawarikh-i-Sikhan*, p. 38.

4 Bhai Gurdas, var. 26, pauri p. 24.

5 See also J. S. Grewal, *Sikhs of the Punjab*, New Delhi: Cambridge University Press, 1990, p. 65.

6 *Dabistan-i-Mazahib, Makhiz-i-Tawarikh-i-Sikhan*, p. 39.

7 The late nineteenth century Sikh historian Giani Gian Singh suggests that Guru Har Rai cured Dara Shikoh of the effects of poison. When asked why he saved the life of a Mughal prince whose forefathers had tormented the Guru's own father and grandfather, he replied: 'A man breaks flowers with one hand and offers them with the other, but the flower perfumes both hands alike', *Panth Prakash*, Amritsar, 1880, pp. 121–2.

8 Makhan Shah Lobana, etc.

9 J. S. Grewal, *Sikhs of the Punjab*, New Delhi: Cambridge University Press, 1990, pp. 69–70.

10 For details of Aurangzeb's policies, see Sir Jadu Nath Sarkar, *History of Aurangzeb*, III, p. 267ff, who quotes the Muslim chronicler Khafi Khan.

11 Kesar Singh Chhibbar makes mention of the dust storm in his *Bansavali Nama Dasan Padhshahian da* (1836). He states: *Samvat sataran patti maghar sudi panjami aahei, Sri Guru Tegh Bahadur ji uth gei daragahei, tis din andheri, gardh gubari rahi.*

12 Guru Gobind Singh, *Bachittar Natak*.

13 The Guru was attracting increasingly larger numbers of peasants from the lower castes who threatened insubordination to the high caste make up of the hill rajas' armies.

14 Guru Gobind writes about the battle of Bhangani in his autobiographical work, *Bachittra Natak* included in *Shabadarth Dasam Granth Sahib*, pp. 77–9.

15 This battle is also narrated in Bachittra Natak included in Shabadarth Dasam Granth Sahib, pp. 182–9.

16 See for example, Ganda Singh (ed.), *Hukamnamey* (Punjabi) pp. 33–65.

17 The term Khalsa derives from the Arabic *khalis* (lit. pure or unsullied) and the Persian *khalisah* (a term used during Muslim rule to refer to lands belonging to the crown and administered directly by the king. The term 'Khalsa' had already been used by Guru Hargobind and Guru Tegh Bahadur to refer to the Sikhs initiated directly by the Gurus themselves, as opposed to intermediaries such as the masands, who by that time had become unreliable. It appears for the first time in one of the *hukamnamas* of Guru Hargobind addressed to and eastern sangat, and in a letter by Guru Tegh Bahadur addressing the sangat of Patna as his khalsa. Guru Gobind Singh formalized this connection and abolished the order of masands, thereby creating a direct link with the Sikh sangats and giving the term and gave 'Khalsa' a new signification of direct unmediated link with the Guru.

18 Most of the historical sources are sketchy in their details and often at variance over exactly what happened. One of the most important sources is Sainapat's *Sri Guru Sobha* which is dated at 1711. Sainapat was one of the poets in the court of the tenth Guru. But his narrative focuses mainly on the abolition of the masands and lacks the more colourful details of later works in the *Gurbilas* (or heroic) tradition such as Koer Singh's *Gurbilas Patshahi 10*. Koer Singh's version of the creation of the Khalsa is part of what might be regarded as traditionalist sources that include Ratan Singh Bhangu's *Prachin Panth Prakash* and Santokh Singh's *Suraj Prakash* and *Gurpratap Suray*, or Giani Gian Singh's *Tawarikh Guru Khalsa*. The version of events presented in this chapter is based mainly on these latter sources, and the traditions of oral exegesis which form part of the contemporary Sikh community's memory. Indeed this is the way that Sikhs are initiated into the Khalsa today and so can be regarded as authoritative.

19 The earliest Rahitnamas do not prescribe the five Ks, and mention no more than two or three of the Ks. For example, Sainapati's *Gur Sobha* definitely mentions the need for Khalsa initiates to wear long uncut hair (Kesh) and to bear arms (Kirpan). The full five Ks may be a later development probably in the early- to mid-eighteenth century.

20 See William Cavanaugh, *The Myth of Religious Violence*, New York: Oxford University Press, 2010.

21 See *Last Days of Guru Gobind Singh*, by Ganda Singh, and Bhagat Lakhsman Singh's *A Short Sketch of the Life and Works of Guru Gobind Singh*.

22 These battles are mentioned in Sainapati's *Gur Sobha*, ed. Ganda Singh, p. 63.

23 This episode, including the Sirsa crossing, the fight at Chamkaur, etc. are mentioned in Guru Gobind Singh's composition Zafarnama, the defiant letter of victory written to Aurangzeb when all seemed lost.

24 The accounts of the Guru's travels to and from Damdama, including the letter he wrote to Aurangzeb and his meeting with Bahadur Shah are all mentioned in Sainapat's *Gur Sobha*.

25 J. S. Grewal, 'Guru Gobind Singh and Bahadur Shah', *From Guru Nanak to Maharajah Ranjit Singh*, pp. 85–93.

26 J. S. Grewal, *The Sikhs of Punjab*, New Delhi: Cambridge University Press, 1990, pp. 82–4.

27 J. S. Grewal, *The Sikhs: Ideology, Institutions and Identity*, New Delhi: Oxford University Press, 2009, p. 80.

28 Ibid.

29 Two events in this period stand out in Sikh tradition. These are known as chhota ghallugara (the 'lesser carnage') where several thousands of the Khalsa troops were killed in a single relentless campaign carried out by the Lakhpat Rai, the diwan of Lahore; and the vaddha ghallugara (or 'greater carnage') where more than 5,000 Singhs were killed in a single day by Ahmad Sha Abdalli. See J. S. Grewal, 1990, pp. 90–1.

30 This coin bore the same inscription as the one struck by Banda Bahadur in 1711.

31 Grewal, Cambridge, pp. 92–3.

32 Surjit Singh Gandhi, *Sikhs in the Eighteenth Century*. New Delhi: Manohar Publications, 1993.

33 For details see Sita Ram Kohli, *Sunset of the Sikh Empire*, New Delhi, 1967.

Chapter 3

1 Elsewhere I have termed this process 'religion-making'. See, for example, the 'Introduction' to Markus Dressler and Arvind-Pal S.

Mandair (eds), *Secularism and Religion-Making*, New York: Oxford University Press, 2011; also very useful are Timothy Fitzgerald's *Discourse on Civility and Barbarity*, New York: Oxford University Press, 2007, and Richard King's *Orientalism and Religion*, London: Routledge, 1999.

2 The two terms can be broadly defined as follows. *Orientalist*: a representation of Oriental cultures by scholars and administrators and travel writers whose belief system was broadly deist (the idea that there is a God, and that all humans are born with reason; but since creating the world, this God has moved away from it leaving it (and mankind) to run itself through recourse to reason. Deism prepared the ground for secularism to emerge in the seventeenth and eighteenth centuries. Orientalists had sympathy for indigenous forms of knowledge and languages which they equated with European languages, and they wanted to help natives bring about renaissance of their cultures, etc. *Anglicists*: those whose belief system was drawn from a more Evangelical strain of Christianity. They argued that indigenous cultures and their learning needed to be completely replaced by English and the natives Anglicized to produce Indians in colour but English in customs and manners. For details of the difference between Anglicism and Orientalism, see chapter 2 of Arvind-Pal S. Mandair, *Religion and the Specter of the West*, New York: Columbia University Press, 2009.

3 Jeffrey Cox, *Imperial Fault Lines: Christianity and Colonial Power in India, 1818–1940*, Stanford: Stanford University Press, 2002.

4 Darshan Singh, *Western Perspectives on the Sikh Religion*, New Delhi: Singh Brothers, 1991.

5 Charles Wilkins, Seeks and their College', *Asiatic Researches* 2 (1788): 288.

6 John Malcolm, '*Sketch of the Sikhs: A Singular Nation Who Inhabit the Provinces of Peunjab*, 1st edn, London: Murray, 1812, p. 144.

7 J. D. Cunningham, *History of the Sikhs*, London: John Murray, 1849.

8 Peter van der Veer, *Imperial Encounters: Religion and Modernity in India and Britain*, Princeton: Princeton University Press, p. 21.

9 J. S. Grewal, *The Sikhs of the Punjab*, New Delhi: Cambridge University Press, 1990, pp. 128–40.

10 W. H. McLeod, 'Sikh Sects' in *Sikhism*, London: Penguin, 1998, pp. 188–92.

11 Khushwant Singh, *A History of the Sikhs, Vol. II* (1839–2004), New Delhi: Oxford University Press, 2009.

12 Peter van der Veer, 2000, pp. 20–2.

13 See William Cavanaugh, *The Myth of Religious Violence*, New York: Oxford University Press, pp. 87–92.

14 As the term Anglo-Vernacular implies, these schools taught a vernacular language (usually Hindi or Urdu) as well as English, which, naturally, was promoted as the language of Empire and moral progress. The teaching of vernaculars was structured in such a way as to conform these native languages to the grammatical structure of English. The end result of this was to make the native mind set more receptive to the effects of modernity and thus foreign concepts such as 'religion', secularism, the separation of state and religion, and to be comprehended in a manner conforming to Western understanding. The process of training the native mind set was thereby made more effective. See Harjot Oberoi, *The Construction of Religious Boundaries: Culture, Identity and Diversity in the Sikh Tradition*, New Delhi: Oxford University Press, 1994; and Arvind-Pal S. Mandair, *Religion and the Specter of the West: Sikhism, India, Postcoloniality and the Politics of Translation*, New York: Columbia University Press, 2009.

15 Arvind-Pal S. Mandair, 2009, pp. 66–77.

16 Kenneth Jones, *Arya Dharam: Hindu Consciousness in Nineteenth Century Punjab*, Berkeley: University of California Press, 1976.

17 See J. S. Grewal's 'Colonial Rule and Cultural Reorientation', in *The Sikhs: Ideology, Institutions and Identity*, New Delhi: Oxford University Press, pp. 270–78.

18 For details see chapter 4 of Harjot Oberoi, *The Construction of Religious Boundaries: Culture, Identity and Diversity in the Sikh Tradition*, New Delhi: Oxford University Press, 1994.

19 Christopher Shackle and Arvind-Pal S. Mandair, *Teachings of the Sikh Gurus: Selections from Sikh Scripture*, London: Routledge, 2005, p. xxxvii.

20 A detailed discussion of this can be found in chapter 4 of Arvind-Pal S. Mandair, *Religion and the Specter of the West: Sikhism, India, Postcoloniality and the Politics of Translation*, New York: Columbia University Press, 2009.

21 Ernest Trumpp, *The Adi Granth*, London, 1877.

22 See Mandair, *RSW*, 2009.

23 J. S. Grewal, *The Sikhs*, 2009, pp. 268–78.

24 Arvind-Pal S. Mandair, *RSW*, 2009, pp. 201–3.

25 J. S. Grewal, *Sikhs of the Punjab*, 1990, p. 150.

26 D. Petrie, 'Recent Developments in Sikh Politics', *The Punjab Past and Present*, Vol. 4, Part 2 (October 1970), pp. 302–79.

27 Based on Mohinder Singh's, *The Akali Movement*, Delhi: Macmillan, Delhi, 1978, which remains one of the most useful sources for understanding this episode in Sikh history.

28 Mohinder Singh, *The Akali Movement*, p. 21.

29 See J. S. Grewal, 'The Akalis and Khalistan', in *The Sikhs: Ideology, Institutions and Identity*, New Delhi: Oxford University Press, 2009, pp. 289–90.

30 Sadhu Singh Hamdard, *Azad Punjab* (Urdu), Amritsar: Ajit Book Agency, 1984.

31 See J. S. Grewal, *The Sikhs*, 2009, pp. 301–2; Khuswant Singh, *History of the Sikhs*, Vol. II, pp. 341–2.

32 A. S. Narang, *Storm Over the Sutlej: The Akali Politics*, New Delhi: Gitanjali Publishing House, 1983.

33 A good example of such bias is Rajiv A. Kapoor's, *Sikh Separatism: The Politics of faith*, London: Allen and Unwin, 1986. This book, like most others of that period, present the conflict as entirely 'communal', sparked and driven by religious fundamentalism, rather than taking a critical approach to the Indian state's central role in the entire affair.

Chapter 4

1   Christopher Shackle and Arvind-Pal S. Mandair, *Teachings of the Sikh Gurus: Selections From the Sikh Scripture*, London: Routledge, 2005, p. xvii.

2   Ibid., p. xviii.

3   Ibid.

4   Ibid.

5   Ibid., p. xxii.

6   Ibid., p. xxiv.

7   Ibid., pp. xxiv–xxv.

8   Ibid., p. xix.

9   Ibid., pp xix–xx.

10 See also W. H. McLeod, *Sikhism*, London: Penguin, 1998, p. 138.

11 For an excellent description of this process see W. H. McLeod, *Sikhism*, London: Penguin, 1998, pp. 138–40.

12 John Bowker (ed.), *Oxford Dictionary of World Religions*, Oxford: Oxford University Press, pp. 819–20.

Chapter 5

1 See for example, W. H. McLeod's 'A Sikh Theology For Modern Times', in *Sikh History and Religion in the Twentieth Century*, edited by W. H. McLeod, W. Oxtoby, M. Israel, J. S. Grewal and J. T. O'Connell, New Delhi: Manohar *Publications*, 1990; W. H. McLeod, 'Teachings of Guru Nanak', in *Guru Nanak and the Sikh Religion*, Oxford: Oxford University Press. 'Sikh theology' has also been favoured as a term designating the content of the teaching of the Sikh Gurus by Sikh scholars in the modern reformist tradition. The relationship between McLeod and the Singh Sabha scholars in regard to the adoption of 'Sikh theology' is closely scrutinized in my *Religion and the Spectre of the West: Sikhism, India, Postcoloniality and the Politics of Translation*, New York: Columbia, 2009.

2 The main limitation of categories such as 'philosophy' and 'theology' stems from the fact that they function only by first transplanting the indigenous concepts into a very different conceptual soil. They are therefore totally dependent on the function of representation.

3 Ontotheology is a hugely misunderstood term especially in conventional Sikh and South Asian studies. It consists of three terms: *ontos, theos* and *logos* refers to three historical discourses: (i) the Greek philosophy of being (*ontos*); (ii) the Christian discourse on the nature of God (*theos*); (iii) the humanistic/atheistic discourse of reason (*logos*). These three terms combine in the medieval period giving rise to the tradition of ontotheology which outwardly claims that the foundation of human reason is apparently a transcendent God, but in reality, God's transcendence becomes subservient to human reason, and the secret mechanism behind secularism. Ontotheology is therefore a key mechanism in the rise of modern secularism and in the privatizing of religion.

4 Incidentally this theological self-definition of *Sikhi*(sm) has never been challenged by modern Western Sikh studies which in fact accepted it in order, ironically, to more firmly establish the historico-anthropological, that is secular, domain of Sikh studies.

5 It should not be forgotten that the lives of some of the greatest exponents of Hindu and Buddhist philosophy (e.g. Sankara, Ramanuja, Nagarjuna, Candrakirti, Shinran, etc.) were grounded in devotional practices of different kinds. It is therefore mistaken, certainly within the Indian context, to think of philosophy and devotion as totally

different practices. Unlike the Western notion of philosophy (which succumbed to the religion-secular distinction following the separation between Church and State), in the Indic context philosophy and devotion are completely intertwined.

6 In the gurdwaras, for example Darshan Singh, Maskin, Taksaali, Sant deras, etc.

7 But the experience is NOT 'ineffable' unless ineffability is connected to a spontaneous outpouring of language.

8 This has been the central problem with certain scholars who have tried to outline a Sikh philosophy. They have ended up simply replicating 'epistemology' or 'ontology' in the Western sense as if these categories could be transparently translated. Good examples are Sher Singh's *Philosophy of Sikhism* (1942), Nirbhai Singh's similarly entitled *Philosophy of Sikhism* (1990) and Gurnam Kaur's *Reason and Revelation in the Sikh Tradition* (1991). For a more detailed readings of these three works see my *Thinking Between Cultures: Revisioning the Encounter Between Sikh and Western Thought* (forthcoming, 2014).

9 *Ad sach, jugadh sach, hai bhi sach, Nanak hosi bhi sach.* Adi Granth, p. 1.

10 See for example the following verses in the Adi Granth:

   Oan gurmukhi kio akara
   Ekahi suti parovanhara,
   Bhin bhin traigun bisathāran,
   Nirgun te sargun dhistaran. AG, p. 250.

   Or the following:

   Eka surati jete hai jia,
   Surati vihunā koi na kia,
   Jehti surati teha tin rahu. AG, pp. 24–5.

11 See the following verses:

   Eko eku ravia sabh thai, tisu binu duja koi nahi,
   Adi madhi anti prabhu ravia trisan bujhi bharamangna. AG, p. 1080.
   Traigun sabha dhatu hai duja bhau vikaru. AG, p. 33.
   Nirankāru akaru hai ape, bharami bhulae,
   Kari kari karata ape vekhai, jitu bhavai titu lae. AG, p. 1257.

12 The following verses in the Adi Granth describe the notion of delusion in relation to duality and the One:

   Hau hau kart nahī sacu paiai,
   Haumai jai param pad paiai (rahau-1). AG, p. 226.

Hau hau mai vicahu khovai,
Duja metai eko hovai, . . . AG, p. 943.
Haumai mera duja bhaia,. . . . AG, p. 1051.
13 *sochai soch na hovi je sochi lakh var.* AG, p. 1.
14 *chupai chup na hovi je lai raha liv tar.* AG, p. 1.
15 *bhukhian bhuk na uttari je baniaa purrin par.* AG, p. 1.
16 *kiv kurai turai pal.* AG, p. 1.
17 *kiv sachiara hoaia.* AG, p. 1.
18 *hukam rajai chalana, Nanak likhia nal.* AG, p. 1.
19 *haumai kahai na koi.* AG, p. 1.
20 *Haumai dirag rog hai, daru bi is mahe.* AG, p. 466.
21 *Haumai dirag rog hai, daru bi is mahe.* AG, p. 466.
22 *Mere man pardesi ve piare, ao milo, ji ao milo.* AG, p. 451.
23 *Baiar bollai mituli bhai sac kahai pir bhae,*
     Birhai bedi sac vasi bhai adhik rahi har nai. AG, p. 637.
     Birha birha akhiai birha tū sultan,
     Farida jit tan birhu na upjai so tan janu masanu. AG, p. 1378.
     Birha lajaia daras paia amio dristi sachinti,
     Binvant Nanak meri ich puni mile jis khojanti. AG, p. 460.
     Hor birha datu hai lagu sahib preet na hoi,
     Is man maya mohia vekhan sunan na hoi. AG, p. 83.
     Avau milau sahelio sacra nam laia,
     Rove birha tan ka apna sahib samaliha. AG, p. 579.
24 *nirgun ap sargun bi ohi, kala tar jin sagli mohi.* AG, p. 287.
25 *sargun nirgun nirankar sun samadhi ap,apan kia Nanaka ape hi phir jap.* AG, p. 280.
26 *sargun nirgun thape nao,doh mil ekai kinau tao.* AG, p. 387.

Chapter 6

1 www.bbc.co.uk/sikhism/euthanasia.
2 Avtar Singh, *Ethics of Sikhism*, Patiala, 1983, p. 31.
3 Harold Coward and Tejinder Sandhu, 'Bioethics For Clinicians: Hinduism and Sikhism', Canadian *Medical Association Journal*, October 31, 2000, 163(9): 1167.

4   www.bbc.co.uk/religion/contraception/contraception_abortion. shtml.

5   Kala Singh, 'The Sikh Spiritual Model of Counseling', *Spirituality and Health International*, 2008, 9: 32–43.

6   Kala Singh, 'The Sikh Spiritual Model of Counseling', p. 35.

7   See for example: www.bbc.co.uk/Sikhism/organ donation.

8   Sudhir Kakar, *The Indian Psyche*, New Delhi: Viking Penguin, vol. 1, p. 129

9   A. Ivey, 'Counseling Psychology: The Most Broadly Based Applied Psychology Speciality', *The Counselling Psychologist*, 1978, 8(3): 3–6.

10 A. S. Mandair and C. Shackle, *Teachings of the Sikh Gurus: Selections From the Sikh Scriptures*, Routledge, 2005, p. xxix.

11 For a recent discussion of the status of the animal see Balbinder Singh Bhogal's *The Animal Sublime, Journal of the American Academy of Religion*, 2012. I am grateful to Professor Bhogal for help with this section.

Chapter 7

1   See for example: Hent De Vries, 'In Media Res: Global Religion, Public Spheres, and the Task of Contemporary Comparative Religious Studies', *Religion and Media*, Stanford: Stanford University Press, 2001 and Arvind-Pal S. Mandair and Markus Dressler, 'Modernity, Religion-Making and the Postsecular', in *Secularism and Religion-Making*, Markus Dressler and Arvind-Pal S. Mandair (eds), New York: Oxford University Press, 2011.

2   www.thehindu.com/news/the-india-cables/article1715620.ece.

3   http://punjabnewsline.com/node/21598.

4   Giorgio Shani, *Sikh Nationalism and Identity in a Global Age*, London: Routledge, 2008, p. 155.

5   Giorgio Shani, p. 106.

6   Avtar Brah, *Cartographies of Diaspora*, London: Routledge, 1996, p. 32.

7   See Gurharpal Singh and Darshan Singh Tatla, *Sikhs in Britain: The Making of a Community*, London: Zed Books, pp. 130–3.

8   Ibid., p. 134.

9   Ibid., p. 126.

10 Ibid.

11 This is amply illustrated by the so-called Behezti Affair which highlighted the problem of religion in public life. See Singh and Tatla, pp. 138–41.

12 Jasbir Puar, '"The Turban is not a Hat": Queer Diaspora and Practices of Profiling', *Sikh Formations: Religion, Culture and Theory*, 4(1) (2008): 47–91.

13 Ibid., p. 47.

14 Ibid., p. 57.

15 *India Abroad*, 14 May 2004.

16 Christopher Shackle, 'Four Generations of Sikh Studies', *Sikh Formations: Religion, Culture and Theory*, 1(1), 2005.

17 N. G. Barrier, foreword to *Discovering the Sikhs: Autobiography of a Historian*, by Hew McLeod, New Delhi: Permanent Black, 2004, p. ix.

18 These include chairs at: University of Michigan, University of British Columbia, two at Hofstra University (New York), University of California: Santa Barbara, Riverside, Mercedes and Santa Cruz, and one in California State University.

19 These issues have been rigorously debated and argued in publications such as: Arvind-Pal S. Mandair, 'Thinking Differently About Religion and History: Issues For Sikh Studies', in *Sikh Religion, Culture and Ethnicity*, by C. Shackle, G. Singh and Arvind-Pal S. Mandair (eds), pp. 47–72; Arvind-Pal. S. Mandair, *Religion and the Specter of the West*, New York: Columbia University Press, 2009.

20 Shani, p. 142.

21 Ibid.

22 See For a useful discussion of this topic see Doris Jakobsch' *Sikhism*, University of Hawaiee Press, 2012, pp. 113–15.

23 Jakobsch, p. 115.

24 Historically the Harimandir Sahib has served as the standard bearer of musical excellence and authority. It has only recently begun to once again promote a standard of traditional musical proficiency. Since 2006 they have employed stringed instruments to accompany the Ragis and promote singing in raga.

INDEX